Charles Wentworth Dilke

Greater Britain

A record of travel in English-speaking countries during 1866-7

Charles Wentworth Dilke

Greater Britain
A record of travel in English-speaking countries during 1866-7

ISBN/EAN: 9783337205843

Printed in Europe, USA, Canada, Australia, Japan

Cover: Foto ©ninafisch / pixelio.de

More available books at **www.hansebooks.com**

GREATER BRITAIN:

A RECORD OF TRAVEL

IN

ENGLISH-SPEAKING COUNTRIES

DURING

1866 AND 1867.

BY

CHARLES WENTWORTH DILKE.

IN TWO VOLUMES.—VOL. II.

WITH MAPS AND ILLUSTRATIONS

London:
MACMILLAN AND CO.
1868.

LONDON:
R. CLAY, SONS, AND TAYLOR, PRINTERS,
BREAD STREET HILL.

CONTENTS

OF

THE SECOND VOLUME

PART III.

CHAP.		PAGE
I.	Sydney	1
II.	Rival Colonies	12
III.	Victoria	21
IV.	Squatter Aristocracy	39
V.	Colonial Democracy	46
VI.	Protection	59
VII.	Labour	71
VIII.	Woman	83
IX.	Victorian Ports	88
X.	Tasmania	93
XI.	Confederation	106
XII.	Adelaide	111
XIII.	Transportation	124
XIV.	Australia	140
XV.	Colonies	148

PART IV.

CHAP.		PAGE
I.—Maritime Ceylon		161
II.—Kandy		176
III.—Madras to Calcutta		185
IV.—Benares		197
V.—Caste		206
VI.—Mohamedan Cities		221
VII.—Simla		234
VIII.—Colonization		252
IX.—The "Gazette"		260
X.—Umritsur		272
XI.—Lahore		286
XII.—Our Indian Army		291
XIII.—Russia		299
XIV.—Native States		313
XV.—Scinde		328
XVI.—Overland Routes		338
XVII.—Bombay		349
XVIII.—The Mohurrum		357
XIX.—English Learning		365
XX.—India		374
XXI.—Dependencies		390
XXII.—France in the East		397
XXIII.—The English		405

LIST OF ILLUSTRATIONS.

	PAGE
A CINGHALESE GENTLEMAN . . . . *Frontispiece.*	
THE OLD AND THE NEW: BUSH SCENERY—COLLINS STREET EAST, MELBOURNE	22
GOVERNOR DAVEY'S PROCLAMATION	96

MAPS.

AUSTRALIA AND TASMANIA	12
OVERLAND ROUTES	340

PART III.

AUSTRALIA.

GREATER BRITAIN.

CHAPTER I.

SYDNEY.

AT early light on Christmas-day, I put off from shore in one of those squalls for which Port Nicholson, the harbour of Wellington, is famed. A boat which started from the ship at the same time as mine from the land was upset, but in such shallow water that the passengers were saved, though they lost a portion of their baggage. As we flew towards the mail steamer, the *Kaikoura*, the harbour was one vast sheet of foam, and columns of spray were being whirled in the air, and borne away far inland on the gale. We had placed at the helm a post-office clerk, who said that he could steer, but, as we reached the steamer's side, instead of luffing-up, he suddenly put the helm hard a-weather, and we shot astern of her, running violently before the wind, although our treble-reefed sail was by this time altogether down. A rope was thrown us from a coal-hulk, and, catching it, we were soon on board, and spent our Christmas walking up and down her deck on the slippery black dust, and watching the effects of the gale. After some hours, the wind moderated, and I reached the *Kaikoura* just before she sailed. While we were steaming out of the harbour through the boil of waters that marks the position of the submarine crater, I found that there was but one other passenger for Australia to share with me the services of ten officers and ninety men, and the accommodations of a ship of 1,500 tons. "Serious preparations and a large ship for a mere voyage from one Australasian colony to another," I felt inclined to say, but during the voyage and my first week in New South Wales I began to discover that in England we are given over to a singular delusion as to the connexion of New Zealand and Australia.

Australasia is a term much used at home to express the whole of our Antipodean possessions; in the colonies themselves, the name is almost unknown, or, if used, is meant to embrace Australia and Tasmania, not Australia and New Zealand. The only reference to New Zealand, except in the way of foreign news, that I ever found in an Australian paper, was a congratulatory paragraph on the amount of the New Zealand debt; the only allusion to Australia that I detected in the Wellington *Independent* was in a glance at the future of the colony, in which the editor predicted the advent of a time when New Zealand would be a naval nation, and her fleet engaged in bombarding Melbourne, or levying contributions upon Sydney.

New Zealand, though a change for the better is at hand, has hitherto been mainly an aristocratic country;

New South Wales and Victoria mainly democratic. Had Australia and New Zealand been close together, instead of as far apart as Africa and South America, there could have been no political connexion between them so long as the traditions of their first settlement endured. Not only is the name "Australasia" politically meaningless, however, but it is also geographically incorrect, for New Zealand and Australia are as completely separated from each other as Great Britain and Massachusetts. No promontory of Australia runs out to within 1,000 miles of any New Zealand cape; the distance between Sydney and Wellington is 1,400 miles; from Sydney to Auckland is as far. The distance from the nearest point of New Zealand of Tasman's peninsula, which itself projects somewhat from Tasmania, is greater than that of London from Algiers: from Wellington to Sydney, opposite ports, is as far as from Manchester to Iceland, or from Africa to Brazil.

The sea that lies between the two great countries of the South is not, like the Central or North Pacific, a sea bridged with islands, ruffled with trade winds, or overspread with a calm that permits the presence of light-draught paddle steamers. The seas which separate Australia from New Zealand are cold, bottomless, without islands, torn by Arctic currents, swept by polar gales, and traversed in all weathers by a mountainous swell. After the gale of Christmas-day, we were blessed with a continuance of light breezes on our way to Sydney, but never did we escape the long rolling hills of seas that seemed to surge up from the Antarctic pole: our screw was as often out of as in the water; and, in a fast new ship, we could scarcely average nine knots an hour throughout the day. The ship which had brought the last Australian mail to Wellington before we sailed was struck by a sea which swept her from stem to stern, and filled her cabins two feet deep, and this in December, which here is Midsummer, and answers to our July. Not only is the intervening ocean wide and cold, but New Zealand presents to Australia a rugged coast guarded by reefs and bars, and backed by a snowy range, while she turns towards Polynesia and America all her ports and bays.

No two countries in the world are so wholly distinct as Australia and New Zealand. The islands of New Zealand are inhabited by Polynesians, the Australian continent by negroes. New Zealand is ethnologically nearer to America, Australia to Africa, than New Zealand to Australia.

If we turn from ethnology to scenery and climate, the countries are still more distinct. New Zealand is one of the groups of volcanic islands that stud the Pacific throughout its whole extent; tremendous cliffs surround it on almost every side; a great mountain chain runs through both islands from north to south; hot springs abound, often close to glaciers and eternal snows; earthquakes are common, and active volcanoes not unknown. The New Zealand climate is damp and windy; the land is covered in most parts with a tangled jungle of tree-ferns, creepers, and parasitic plants; water never fails, and, though winter is unknown, the summer heat is never great; the islands are always green. Australia has for the most part flat, yellow, sun-burnt shores; the soil may be rich, the country good for wheat and sheep, but to the eye it is an arid plain; the winters are pleasant, but in the hot weather the thermometer rises higher than it does in India, and dust storms and hot winds sweep the land from end to end. It is impossible to conceive countries more unlike each other than are our two great dominions of the south. Their very fossils are as dissimilar as are their flora and fauna of our time.

At dawn of the first day of the new year, we sighted the rocks where the *Duncan Dunbar* was lost with all hands, and a few minutes afterwards we were boarded by the crew engaged by the Sydney *Morning Herald*, who had been lying at "The Heads" all night, to intercept our news and telegraph it to the city. The pilot and regular news-boat hailed us a little later, when we had fired a gun. The contrast between this Australian energy and the supineness of the New Zealanders was striking, but not more so than that between my first view of Australia and my last view of New Zealand. Six days earlier I had lost sight of the snowy peak of Mount Egmont, graceful as the Cretan Ida, while we ran before a strong breeze, in the bright English sunlight of the New Zealand afternoon, the albatrosses screaming around our stern: to-day, as we steamed up Port Jackson, towards Sydney Cove, in the dead stillness that follows a night of oven-like heat, the sun rose flaming in a lurid sky, and struck down upon brown earth, yellow grass, and the thin shadeless foliage of the Australian bush; while, as we anchored, the ceaseless chirping of the crickets in the grass and trees struck harshly on the ear.

The harbour, commercially the finest in the world, is not without a singular beauty if seen at the best time. By the "hot-wind sunrise," as I first saw it, the heat and glare destroy the feeling of repose which the endless succession of deep, sheltered coves would otherwise convey; but if it be seen from shore in the afternoon, when the sea-breeze has sprung up, turning the sky from red to blue, all is changed. From a neck of land that leads out to the Government House, you catch a glimpse of an arm of the bay on either side, rippled with the cool wind, intensely blue, and dotted with white sails: the brightness of the colours that the sea-breeze brings almost atones for the wind's unhealthiness.

In the upper portion of the town, the scene is less picturesque; the houses are of the commonplace English ugliness, worst of all possible forms of architectural imbecility, and are built, too, as though for English fogs, instead of semi-tropical heat and sun. Water is not to be had, and the streets are given up to clouds of dust, while not a single shade-tree breaks the rays of the almost vertical sun.

The afternoon of New Year's day I spent at the "Midsummer Meeting" of the Sydney Jockey Club, on the race-course near the city, where I found a vast crowd of holiday-makers assembled on the bare red earth that did duty for "turf," although there was a hot wind blowing, and the thermometer stood at 103° in the shade. For my conveyance to the race-course I trusted to one of the Australian hansom cabs, made with fixed Venetian blinds on either side, so as to allow a free draught of air.

The ladies in the grand stand were scarcely to be distinguished from Englishwomen in dress or countenance, but the crowd presented several curious types. The fitness of the term "corn-stalks" applied to the Australian-born boys was made evident by a glance at their height and slender build; they have plenty of activity and health, but are wanting in power and weight. The girls, too, are slight and thin; delicate, without being sickly. Grown men who have emigrated as lads and lived ten or fifteen years in New Zealand, eating much meat, spending their days in the open air, constantly in the saddle, are burly, bearded, strapping fellows, physically the perfection of the English race, but wanting in refinement and grace of mind, and this apparently by constitution; not through the accident of occupation or position. In Australia there is promise of a more intellectual nation: the young Australians ride as well, shoot as well, swim as well, as the New Zealanders; are as little given to book-learning, but there is more shrewd intelligence, more wit and quickness, in the sons of the larger continent. The Australians boast that they possess the Grecian climate, and every young face in the Sydney crowd showed me that their sky is not more like that of the Peloponnesus than they are like the old Athenians. The eager burning democracy that is springing up in the Australian great towns is as widely different from the republicanism of the older States of the American Union as it is from the good-natured conservatism of New Zealand, and their high capacity for personal enjoyment would of itself suffice to distinguish the Australians from both Americans and British. Large as must be the amount of convict blood in New South Wales, there was no trace of it in the features of those present upon the race-course. The inhabitants of colonies which have never received felon immigrants often cry out that Sydney is a convict city, but the prejudice is not borne out by the countenances of the inhabitants, nor by the records of local crime. The black stain has not yet wholly disappeared: the streets of Sydney are still a greater disgrace to civilization than are even those of London; but, putting the lighter immoralities aside, security for life and property is not more perfect in England than in New South Wales. The last of the bushrangers were taken while I was in Sydney.

The race-day was followed by a succession of hot winds, during which only the excellence of the fruit-market made Sydney endurable. Not only are all the English fruits to be found, but plantains, guavas, oranges, loquats, pomegranates, pine-apples from Brisbane, figs of every kind, and the delicious passion-fruit abound; and if the gum-tree forests yield no shady spots for picnics, they are not wanting among the rocks at Botany, or in the luxuriant orange-groves of Paramatta.

A Christmas week of heat such as Sydney has seldom known was brought to a close by one of the heaviest southerly storms on record. During the stifling morning, the telegraph had announced the approach of a gale from the far south, but in the early afternoon the heat was more terrible than before, when suddenly the sky was dark with whirling clouds, and a cold blast swept through the streets, carrying a fog of sand, breaking roofs and windows, and dashing to pieces many boats. When the gale ceased, some three hours later, the sand was so deep in houses that here and there men's feet left footprints on the stairs.

Storms of this kind, differing only one from another in violence, are common in the hot weather: they are known as "southerly bursters;" but the early settlers called them "brickfielders," in the belief that the dust they brought was whirled up from the kilns and brickfields to the south of Sydney. The fact is that the sand is carried along for one or two hundred miles, from the plains in Dampier and Auckland counties; for the Australian "burster" is one with the Punjaub dust-storm, and the "dirt-storm" of Colorado.

CHAPTER II.

RIVAL COLONIES.

NEW SOUTH WALES, born in 1788, and Queensland in 1859, the oldest and youngest of our Australian colonies, stand side by side upon the map, and have a common frontier of 700 miles.

The New South Welsh cast jealous glances towards the more recently founded States. Upon the brilliant prosperity of Victoria they look doubtingly, and, ascribing it merely to the gold-fields, talk of "shoddy;" but of Queensland—an agricultural country, with larger tracts of rich land than they themselves possess—the Sydney folks are not without reason envious.

A terrible depression is at present pervading trade and agriculture in New South Wales. Much land near Sydney has gone out of cultivation; hands are scarce, and the gold discoveries in the neighbouring colonies, by drawing off the surplus population, have made harvest labour unattainable. Many properties have fallen to one-third their former value, and the colony—a wheat-growing country—is now importing wheat and flour to the value of half-a-million sterling every year.

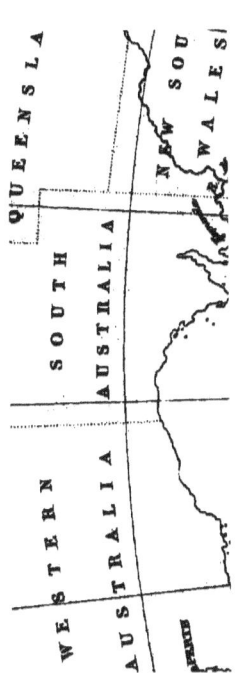

The depressed condition of affairs is the result, partly of commercial panics following a period of inflation, partly of bad seasons, now bringing floods, now drought and rust, and partly of the discouragement of immigration by the colonial democrats—a policy which, however beneficial to Australia it may in the long run prove, is for the moment ruinous to the sheep-farmers and to the merchants in the towns. On the other hand, the labourers for their part assert that the arrivals of strangers—at all events, of skilled artisans—are still excessive, and that all the ills of the colony are due to over-immigration and free trade.

To a stranger, the rush of population and outpour of capital from Sydney, first towards Victoria, but now to Queensland and New Zealand, appear to be the chief among the causes of the momentary decline of New South Wales. Of immigrants there is at once an insufficient and an over-great supply. Respectable servant-girls, carpenters, masons, blacksmiths, plasterers, and the like, do well in the colonies, and are always wanted; of clerks, governesses, iron-workers, and the skilled hands of manufacturers, there is almost always an over-supply. By a perverse fate, these latter are the immigrants of whom thousands seek the colonies every year, in spite of the daily publication in England of dissuading letters.

As the rivalry of the neighbour-colonies lessens in the lapse of time, the jealousy that exists between them will doubtless die away, but it seems as though it will be replaced by a political divergence, and consequent aversion, which will form a fruitful source of danger to the Australian confederation.

In Queensland the great tenants of Crown lands—"squatters" as they are called—sheep-farmers holding vast tracts of inland country, are in possession of the government, and administer the laws to their own advantage. In New South Wales, power is divided between the pastoral tenants on the one hand, and the democracy of the towns upon the other. In Victoria, the democrats have beaten down the squatters, and in the interests of the people put an end to their reign; but the sheep-farmers of Queensland and of the interior districts of New South Wales, ignoring wells, assert that the "up-country desert" or "unwatered tracts" can never be made available for agriculture, while the democracy of the coast point to the fact that the same statements were made only a few years back of lands now bearing a prosperous population of agricultural settlers.

The struggle between the great Crown tenants and the agricultural democracy in Victoria, already almost over, in New South Wales can be decided only in one way, but in Queensland the character of the country is not entirely the same: the coast and river tracts are tropical bush-lands, in which sheep-farming is impossible, and in which sugar, cotton, and spices alone can be made to pay. To the copper, gold, hides, tallow, wool, which have hitherto formed the stereotyped list of Australian exports, the Northern colony has already added ginger, arrowroot, tobacco, coffee, sugar, cotton, cinnamon, and quinine.

The Queenslanders have not yet solved the problem of the settlement of a tropical country by Englishmen, and of its cultivation by English hands. The future, not of Queensland merely, but of Mexico, of Ceylon, of every tropical country, of our race, of free government itself, are all at stake; but the success of the experiment that has been tried between Brisbane and Rockampton has not been great. The colony, indeed, has prospered much, quadrupling its population and trebling its exports and revenue in six years, but it is the Darling Downs, and other tableland sheep-countries, or, on the other hand, the Northern gold-fields, which are the main cause of the prosperity; and in the sugar and cotton culture of the coast, coloured labour is now almost exclusively employed, with the usual effect of degrading fieldwork in the eyes of European settlers, and of forcing upon the country a form of society of the aristocratic type.

It is possible that just as New England has of late forbidden to Louisiana the importation of Chinamen to work her sugar-fields, just as the Kansas radicals have declared that they will not recognise the Bombay Hammal as a brother, just as the Victorians have refused to allow the further reception of convicts by West Australia, separated from their territories by 1,000 miles of desert, so the New South Welsh and Victorians combined may at least protest against the introduction of a mixed multitude of Bengalees, Chinamen, South Sea Islanders, and Malays, to cultivate the Queensland coast plantations. If, however, the other colonies permit their Northern sister to continue in her course of importing dark-skinned labourers, to form a peon population, a few years will see her a wealthy cotton and sugar-growing country, with all the vices of a slave-holding government, though without the name of slavery. The planters of the coast and villages, united with the squatters of the table-lands or "Downs," will govern Queensland, and render union with the free colonies impossible, unless great gold discoveries take place, and save the country to Australia.

Were it not for the pride of race that everywhere shows itself in the acts of English settlers, there might be a bright side to the political future of the Queensland colony. The coloured labourers at present introduced—industrious Tongans, and active Hill-coolies from Hindostan, laborious, sober, and free from superstition—should not only be able to advance the commercial fortunes of Queensland as they have those of the Mauritius, but eventually to take an equal share in free government with their white employers. To avoid the gigantic evil of the degradation of hand labour, which has ruined morally as well as economically the Southern States of the American republic, the Indian, Malay, and Chinese labourers should be tempted to become members of land-holding associations. A large spice and sugar-growing population in Northern Queensland would require a vast agricultural population in the south to feed it; and the two colonies, hitherto rivals, might grow up as sister countries, each depending upon the other for the supply of half its needs. It is, however, worthy of notice that the agreements of the Queensland planters with the imported dark-skinned field-hands provide only for the payment of wages *in goods*, at the rates of 6s. to 10s. a month. The "goods" consist of pipes, tobacco, knives, and beads. Judging from the experience of California and Ceylon, there can be little hope of the general admission of coloured men to equal rights by English settlers, and the Pacific islands offer so tempting a field to kidnapping skippers that there is much fear that Queensland may come to show us not merely semi-slavery, but peonage of that worst of kinds, in which it is cheaper to work the labourer to death than to " breed " him.

Such is the present rapidity of the growth and rise to power of tropical Queensland, such the apparent poverty of New South Wales, that were the question merely one between the Sydney wheat-growers and the cotton-planters of Brisbane and Rockampton, the sub-tropical settlers would be as certain of the foremost position in any future confederation, as they were in America when the struggle lay only between the Carolinas and New England. As it is, just as America was first saved by the coal of Pennsylvania and Ohio, Australia will be saved by the coal of New South Wales. Queensland possesses some small stores of coal, but the vast preponderance of acreage of the great power of the future lies in New South Wales.

On my return from a short voyage to the north, I visited the coal-field of New South Wales at Newcastle, on the Hunter. The beds are of vast extent; they lie upon the banks of a navigable river, and so near to the surface that the best qualities are raised, in a country of dear labour, at 8s. or 9s. the ton, and delivered on board ship for 12s. For manufacturing purposes the coal is perfect; for steam-ship use it is, though somewhat "dirty," a serviceable fuel; and copper and iron are found in close proximity to the beds. The Newcastle and Port Jackson fields open a singularly brilliant future to Sydney in these times, when coal is king in a far higher degree than was ever cotton. To her black beds the colony will owe not only manufactures, bringing wealth and population, but that leisure which is begotten of riches — leisure that brings culture, and love of harmony and truth.

Manufactories are already springing up in the neighbourhood of Sydney, adding to the whirl and the bustle of the town, and adding, too, to its enormous population, already disproportionate to that of the colony in which it stands. As the depôt for much of the trade of Queensland and New Zealand, and as the metropolis of pleasure to which the wealthy squatters pour from all parts of Australia, to spend, rapidly enough, their hard-won money, Sydney would in any case have been a populous city; but the barrenness of the country in which it stands has, until the recent opening of the railroads, tended still further to increase its size, by failing to tempt into the country the European immigrants. The Irish in Sydney form a third of the population, yet hardly one of these men but meant to settle upon land when he left his native island.

In France there is a tendency to migrate to Paris, in Austria a continual drain towards Vienna, in England towards London. A corresponding tendency is observable throughout Australia and America. Immigrants hang about New York, Philadelphia, Boston, Sydney, Melbourne; and, finding that they can scrape a living in these large cities with toil somewhat less severe than that which would be needed to procure them a decent livelihood in the bush, the unthrifty as well as the dissipated throng together in densely-populated "rookeries" in these cities, and render the first quarter of New York and the so-called "Chinese" quarter of Melbourne an insult to the civilization of the world.

In the case of Australia this concentration of population is becoming more remarkable day by day. Even under the system of free selection, by which the Legislature has attempted to encourage agricultural settlement, the moment a free selector can make a little money he comes to one of the capitals to spend it. Sydney is the city of pleasure, to which the wealthy Queensland squatters resort to spend their money, returning to the north for fresh supplies only when they cannot afford another day of dissipation, while Melbourne receives the outpour of Tasmania.

The rushing to great cities the moment there is money to be spent, characteristic of the settlers in all these colonies, is much to be regretted, and presents a sad contrast to the quiet stay-at-home habits of American farmers. Everything here is fever and excitement;—as in some systems of geometry, motion is the primary, rest the derived idea. New South Welshmen tell you that this unquiet is peculiar to Victoria; to a new-comer, it seems as rife in Sydney as in Melbourne.

Judging from the Colonial Government reports, which immigrants are conjured by the inspectors to procure and read, and which are printed in a cheap form for the purpose, the New South Welsh can hardly wish to lure settlers into "the bush;" for in one of these documents, published while I was in Sydney, the curator of the Museum reported that in his explorations he never went more than twelve miles from the city, but that within that circuit he found seventeen distinct species of land-snakes, two of sea-snakes, thirty of lizards, and sixteen of frogs —seventy-eight species of reptiles rewarded him in all. The seventeen species of land-snakes found by him within the suburbs were named by the curator in a printed list; it commenced with the pale-headed snake, and ended with the death-adder.

CHAPTER III.

VICTORIA.

THE smallest of our southern colonies except Tasmania,—one-fourth the size of New South Wales, one-eighth of Queensland, one-twelfth of West Australia, one-fifteenth of South Australia,—Victoria is the wealthiest of the Australian nations, and, India alone excepted, has the largest trade of any of the dependencies of Great Britain.

When Mr. Fawkner's party landed in 1835 upon the Yarra banks, mooring their boat to the forest trees, they formed a settlement upon a grassy hill behind a marsh, and began to pasture sheep where Melbourne, the capital, now stands. In twenty years, Melbourne became the largest city but one in the southern hemisphere, having 150,000 people within her limits or those of the suburban towns. Victoria has grander public buildings in her capital, larger and more costly railroads, a greater income, and a heavier debt than any other colony, and she pays to her Governor 10,000*l.* a year, or one-fourth more than even New South Wales.

When looked into, all this success means gold. There is industry, there is energy, there is talent, there is generosity and public spirit, but they are the abilities and virtues that gold will bring, in bringing a rush from all the world of dashing fellows in the prime of life. The progress of Melbourne is that of San Francisco; it is the success of Hokitika on a larger scale, and refined and steadied by having lasted through some years—the triumph of a population which has hitherto consisted chiefly of adult males.

Sydney people, in their jealousy of the Victorians, refuse to admit even that the superior energy of the Melbourne men is a necessary consequence of their having been the pick of the spirited youths of all the world, brought together by the rush for gold. At the time of the first "find" in 1851, all the resolute, able, physically strong do-noughts of Europe and America flocked into Port Phillip, as Victoria was then called; and such timid and weak men as came along with them being soon crowded out, the men of energy and tough vital force alone remained.

Some of the New South Welsh, shutting their eyes to the facts connected with the gold-rush, assert so loudly that the Victorians are the refuse of California, or "Yankee scum," that when I first landed in Melbourne I expected to find street-cars, revolvers, big hotels, and fire-clubs, euchre, caucusses, and mixed drinks. I could discover nothing American about Melbourne except the grandeur of the public buildings and the width of the streets, and its people are far more thoroughly British than are the citizens

THE OLD AND THE NEW

BUSH SCENERY.

COLLIN'S STREET-EAST; MELBOURNE.

of the rival capital. In many senses, Melbourne is the London, Sydney the Paris, of Australia.

Of the surpassing vigour of the Victorians there can be no doubt; a glance at the map shows the Victorian railways stretching to the Murray, while those of New South Wales are still boggling at the Green Hills, fifty miles from Sydney. Melbourne, the more distant port, has carried off the Australian trade with the New Zealand gold-fields from Sydney, the nearer port. Melbourne imports Sydney shale, and makes from it mineral oil, before the Sydney people have found out its value; and gas in Melbourne is cheaper than in Sydney, though the Victorians are bringing their coal five hundred miles, from a spot only fifty miles from Sydney.

It is possible that the secret of the superior energy of the Victorians may lie, not in the fact that they are more American, but more English, than the New South Welsh. The leading Sydney people are mainly the sons or grandsons of original settlers—"cornstalks" reared in the semi-tropical climate of the coast; the Victorians are full-blooded English immigrants, bred in the more rugged climes of Tasmania, Canada, or Great Britain, and brought only in their maturity to live in the exhilarating air of Melbourne, the finest climate in the world for healthy men: Melbourne is hotter than Sydney, but its climate is never tropical. The squatters on the Queensland downs, mostly immigrants from England, show the same strong vitality that the Melbourne men possess; but their brother immigrants in Brisbane—the

Queensland capital, where the languid breeze resembles that of Sydney—are as incapable of prolonged exertion as are the "cornstalks."

Whatever may be the causes of the present triumph of Melbourne over Sydney, the inhabitants of the latter city are far from accepting it as likely to be permanent. They cannot but admit the present glory of what they call the "Mushroom City." The magnificent pile of the new Post-office, the gigantic Treasury (which, when finished, will be larger than our own in London), the University, the Parliament House, the Union and Melbourne Clubs, the City Hall, the Wool Exchange, the viaducts upon the Government railroad lines,—all are Cyclopean in their architecture, all seem built as if to last for ever; still, they say that there is a certain want of permanence about the prosperity of Victoria. When the gold discovery took place, in 1851, such a trade sprang up that the imports of the colony jumped from one million to twenty-five millions sterling in three years; but, although she is now commencing to ship bread-stuffs to Great Britain, exports and imports alike show a steady decrease. Considerably more than half of the hand-workers of the colony are still engaged in gold-mining, and nearly half the population is resident upon the gold-fields; yet the yield shows, year by year, a continual decline. Had it not been for the discoveries in New Zealand, which have carried off the floating digger population, and for the wise discouragement by the democrats of the monopolization of the land, there would have been distress upon the gold-fields during the last few years. The Victorian population is already nearly stationary, and the squatters call loudly for assisted immigration and free trade, but the stranger sees nothing to astonish him in the temporary stagnation that attends a decreasing gold production.

The exact economical position that Victoria occupies is easily ascertained, for her statistics are the most perfect in the world; the arrangement is a piece of exquisite mosaic. The brilliant statistician who fills the post of Registrar-General to the colony, had the immense advantage of starting clear of all tradition, unhampered and unclogged; and, as the Governments of the other colonies have the last few years taken Victoria for model, a gradual approach is being made to uniformity of system. It was not too soon, for British colonial statistics are apt to be confusing. I have seen a list of imports in which one class consisted of ale, aniseed, arsenic, asafœtida, and astronomical instruments; boots, bullion, and salt butter; capers, cards, caraway seed; gauze, gin, glue, and gloves; maps and manure; philosophical instruments and salt pork; sandal-wood, sarsaparilla, and smoked sausages. Alphabetical arrangement has charms for the official mind.

Statistics are generally considered dull enough, but the statistics of these young countries are figure-poems. Tables that in England contrast jute with hemp, or this man with that man, here compare the profits of manufactures with those of agriculture, or pit against each other the powers of race and race.

Victoria is the only country in existence which possesses a statistical history from its earliest birth; but, after all, even Victoria falls short of Minnesota, where the settlers founded the "State Historical Society" a week before the foundation of the State.

Gold, wheat, and sheep are the three great staples of Victoria, and have each its party, political and commercial—diggers, agricultural settlers, and squatters—though of late the diggers and the landed democracy have made common cause against the squatters. Gold can now be studied best at Ballarat, and wheat at Clunes, or upon the Barrabool hills behind Geelong; but I started first for Echuca, the head-quarters of the squatter interest, and metropolis of sheep, taking upon my way Kyneton, one of the richest agricultural districts of the colony, and also the once famous gold-diggings of Bendigo Creek.

Between Melbourne and Kyneton, where I made my first halt, the railway runs through undulating lightly-timbered tracts, free from underwood, and well grassed. By letting my eyes persuade me that the burnt-up herbage was a ripening crop of wheat or oats, I found a likeness to the views in the weald of Sussex, though the foliage of the gums, or eucalypti, is thinner than that of the English oaks.

Riding from Kyneton to Carlsruhe, Pastoria, and the foot-hills of the "Dividing Range," I found the agricultural community busily engaged on the harvest, and much excited upon the great thistle question. Women and tiny children were working in the fields, while the men were at Kyneton, trying in vain to hire harvest hands from Melbourne at less than 2*l*. 10*s*. or 3*l*. a week and board. The thistle question was not less serious: the "thistle inspectors," elected under the "Thistle Prevention Act," had commenced their labours; and although each man agreed with his friend that his neighbour's thistles were a nuisance, still he did not like being fined for not weeding out his own. The fault, they say, lies in the climate; it is too good, and the English weeds have thriven. Great as was the talk of thistles, the fields in the fertile Kyneton district were as clean as in a well-kept English farm, and showed the clearest signs of the small farmer's personal care.

Every one of the agricultural villages that I visited was a full-grown municipality. The colonial English, freed from the checks which are put by interested landlords to local government in Britain, have passed, in all the settlements, laws under which any village must be raised into a municipality on fifty of the villagers (the number varies in the different colonies) signing a requisition, unless within a given time a larger number sign a petition to the contrary effect.

After a short visit to the bustling digging town of Castlemaine, I pushed on by train to Sandhurst, a borough of great pretensions, which occupies the site of the former digging camp at Bendigo. On a level part of the line between the two great towns, my train dashed through some closed gates, happily without hurt. The *Melbourne Argus* of the next day said that the crash had been the result of the signalman taking the fancy that the trains should wait on him, not he upon the trains, so he had "closed the gates, hoisted the danger signal, and adjourned to a neighbouring store to drink." On my return from Echuca, I could not find that he had been dismissed.

When hands are scarce, and lives valuable not to the possessor only, but to the whole community, care to avoid accidents might be expected; but there is a certain recklessness in all young countries, and not even in Kansas is it more observable than in Victoria and New South Wales.

Sandhurst, like Castlemaine, straggles over hill and dale for many miles, the diggers preferring to follow the gold-leads, and build a suburb by each alluvial mine, rather than draw their supplies from the central spot. The extent of the worked-out gold-field struck me as greater than in the fields round Placerville, but then in California many of the old diggings are hidden by the vines.

In Sandhurst, I could find none of the magnificent restaurants of Virginia city; none of the gambling saloons of Hokitika; and the only approach to gaiety among the diggers was made in a drinking-hall, where some dozen red-shirted, bearded men were dancing by turns with four well-behaved and quiet-looking German girls, who were paid, the constable at the gate informed me, by the proprietor of the booth. My hotel—"The Shamrock"—kept by New York Irish, was a thoroughly American house; but then, digger civilization is everywhere American—a fact owing, no doubt, to the

American element having been predominant in the first-discovered diggings—those of California.

Digger revolts must have been feared when the Sandhurst Government Reserve was surrounded with a ditch strangely like a moat, and palings that bear an ominous resemblance to a Maori pah. In the morning I found my way through the obstructions, and discovered the police-station, and in it the resident magistrate, to whom I had a letter. He knew nothing of "Gumption Dick," Hank Monk's friend, but he introduced me to his intelligent Chinese clerk, and told me many things about the yellow diggers. The bad feeling between the English diggers and the Chinese has not in the least died away. Upon the worked-out fields of Castlemaine and Sandhurst, the latter do what they please, and I saw hundreds of them washing quietly and quickly in the old Bendigo creek, finding an ample living in the leavings of the whites. So successful have they been that a few Europeans have lately been taking to their plan, and an old Frenchman who died here lately, and who, from his working persistently in worn-out fields, had always been thought to be a harmless idiot, left behind him twenty thousand pounds, obtained by washing in company with the Chinese.

The spirit that called into existence the Ballarat anti-Chinese mobs is not extinct in Queensland, as I found during my stay at Sydney. At the Crocodile Creek diggings in Northern Queensland, whither many of the Chinese from New South Wales have lately gone, terrible riots occurred the week after I landed in Australia. The English diggers announced their intention of "rolling up" the Chinese, and proceeded to "jump their claims"—that is, trespass on the mining plots, for in Queensland the Chinese have felt themselves strong enough to purchase claims. The Chinese bore the robbery for some days, but at last a digger who had sold them a claim for 50*l*. one morning, hammered the pegs into the soft ground the same day, and then "jumped the claim" on the pretence that it was not "pegged out." This was too much for the Chinese owner, who tomahawked the digger on the spot. The English at once fired the Chinese town, and even attacked the English driver of a coach for conveying Chinamen on his vehicle. Some diggers in North Queensland are said to have kept bloodhounds for the purpose of hunting Chinamen for sport, as the rowdies of the old country hunt cats with terriers.

On the older gold-fields, such as those of Sandhurst and Castlemaine, the hatred of the English for the Chinese lies dormant, but it is not the less strong for being free from physical violence. The woman in a baker's shop near Sandhurst, into which I went to buy a roll for lunch, shuddered when she told me of one or two recent marriages between Irish "Biddies" and some of the wealthiest Chinese.

The man against whom all this hatred and suspicion is directed is no ill-conducted rogue or villain. The chief of the police at Sandhurst said that the Chinese were "the best of citizens;" a member of the Victorian Parliament, resident on the very edge of their quarter at Geelong, spoke of the yellow men to me as "well-behaved and frugal;" the Registrar-General told me that there is less crime, great or small, among the Chinese, than among any equal number of English in the colony.

The Chinese are not denied civil rights in Victoria, as they have been in California. Their testimony is accepted in the courts against that of whites; they may become naturalized, and then can vote. Some twenty or thirty of them, out of 30,000, have been naturalized in Victoria up to the present time.

That the Chinese in Australia look upon their stay in the gold-fields as merely temporary is clear from the character of their restaurants, which are singularly inferior to those of San Francisco. The best in the colonies is one near Castlemaine, but even this is small and poor. Shark's fin is an unheard-of luxury, and even puppy you would have to order. "Silk-worms fried in castor-oil" is the colonial idea of a Chinese delicacy; yet the famous sea-slug is an inhabitant of Queensland waters, and the Gulf of Carpentaria.

From Sandhurst northwards, the country, known as Elysium Flats, becomes level, and is wooded in patches, like the "oak-opening" prairies of Wisconsin and Illinois. Within fifty miles of Echuca, the line comes out of the forest on to a vast prairie, on which was a marvellous mirage of water and trees at various step-like levels. From the other window of the compartment carriage (sadly hot and airless after the American cars), I saw the thin dry yellow grass on fire for a dozen miles. The smoke from these "bush-fires" sometimes extends for hundreds of miles to sea. In steaming down from Sydney to Wilson's Promontory on my way to Melbourne, we passed through a column of smoke about a mile in width when off Wolongong, near Botany Bay, and never lost sight of it, as it lay in a dense brown mass upon the sea, until we rounded Cape Howe, two hundred miles farther to the southward.

The fires on these great plains are caused by the dropping of fusees by travellers as they ride along smoking their pipes, Australian fashion, or else by the spreading of the fires from their camps. The most ingenious stories are invented by the colonists to prevent us from throwing doubt upon their carefulness, and I was told at Echuca that the late fires had been caused by the concentration of the sun's rays upon spots of grass owing to the accidental conversion into burning-glasses of beer-bottles that had been suffered to lie about. Whatever their cause, the fires, in conjunction with the heat, have made agricultural settlement upon the Murray a lottery. The week before my visit, some ripe oats at Echuca had been cut down to stubble by the hot wind, and farmers are said to count upon the success of only one harvest in every three seasons. On the other hand, the Victorian apricots, shrivelled by the hot wind, are so many lumps of crystallized nectar when you pierce their thick outer coats.

Defying the sun, I started off to the banks of the

Murray river, not without some regret at the absence of the continuous street verandahs which in Melbourne form a first step towards the Italian piazza. One may be deceived by trifles when the character of an unknown region is at stake. Before reaching the country, I had read, "Steam-packet Hotel, Esplanade, Echuca;" and, though experiences on the Ohio had taught me to put no trust in "packets and hotels," yet I had somehow come to the belief that the Murray must be a second Missouri at least, if not a Mississippi. The "esplanade" I found to be a myth, and the "fleet" of "steam-packets" was drawn up in a long line upon the mud, there being in this summer weather no water in which it could float. The Murray in February is a streamless ditch, which in America, if known and named at all, would rank as a tenth-rate river.

The St. Lawrence is 2,200 miles in length, and its tributary, the Ottawa, 1,000 miles in length, itself receives a tributary stream, the Gatineau, with a course of 420 miles. At 217 miles from its confluence with the Ottawa, the Gatineau is still 1,000 feet in width. At Albury, which even in winter is the head of navigation on the Murray, you are only some 600 or 700 miles by river from the open sea, or about the same distance as from Memphis in Tennessee to the mouth of the Mississippi.

During six months of the year, however, the Murray is for wool-carrying purposes an important river. The railway to Echuca has tapped the river system in the Victorians' favour, and Melbourne has become the port of the back country of New South Wales, and even Queensland. "The Riverina is commercially annexed" to Victoria, said the premier of New South Wales while I was in that colony, and the "Riverina" means that portion of New South Wales which lies between the Lachlan, the Murrumbidgee, and the Murray, to the northward of Echuca.

Returning to the inn to escape the sun, I took up the *Riverina Herald*, published at Echuca; of its twenty-four columns, nineteen and a half are occupied by the eternal sheep in one shape or another. A representation of Jason's fleece stands at the head of the title; "wool" is the first word in the first line of the body of the paper. More than half of the advertisements are those of wool-brokers, or else of the fortunate possessors of specifics that will cure the scab. One disinfectant compound is certified to by no less than seventeen inspectors; another is puffed by a notice informing flock-masters that, in cases of foot-rot, the advertiser goes upon the principle of "no cure, no pay." One firm makes "liberal advances on the ensuing clip;" another is prepared to do the like upon "pastoral securities." Ship-chandlers, regardless of associations, advertise in one line their bread and foot-rot ointment, their biscuit and sheep-wash solution; and the last of the advertisements upon the front page is that of an "agent for the sale of fat." The body of the paper contains complaints against the judges at a recent show of wool, and an account of the raising of a sawyer "120 feet in length and 23 feet in girth" by the new "snagboat" working to clear out the river for the floating down of the next wool-clip. Whole columns of small type are filled with "impounding" lists, containing brief descriptions of all the strayed cattle of each district. The technicalities of the distinctive marks are surprising. Who not to the manner born can make much of this: " Blue and white cow, cock horns, 22 off-rump, IL off-ribs?" or of this: " Strawberry stag, top off off-ear, J. C. over 4 off-rump, like H. G. conjoined near loin and rump?" This, again, is difficult: " Swallow tail, off-ear, D reversed and illegible over F off-ribs, PT off-rump." What is a "blue strawberry bull?" is a question which occurred to me. Again, what a phenomenon is this: " White cow, writing capital A off-shoulder?" A paragraph relates the burning of " 10,000*l.* worth of country near Gambier," and advertisements of Colt's revolvers and quack medicines complete the sheet. The paper shows that for the most part the colonists here, as in New Zealand, have had the wisdom to adopt the poetic native names of places, and even to use them for towns, streets, and ships. Of the Panama liners, the *Rakaia* and *Maitoura* bear the names of rivers, the *Ruahiné* and the *Kaikoura*, names of mountain ranges; and the colonial boats have for the most part familiar Maori or Australian names; for instance, *Rangitoto*, "hill of hills," and *Rangitiria*, "great and good." The New Zealand colonists are better off than the Australian in this respect: Wongawonga, Yarrayarra, and Wooloomooloo are not inviting; and some of the Australian villages have still stranger names. Nindooinbah is a station in Southern Queensland; Yallack-a-yallack, Borongorong, Bunduramongee, Jabbarabbara, Thuroroolong, Yalla-y-poora, Yanac-a-Yanac, Wuid Kerruick, Woolonguwoong-wrinan, Woori Yalloak, and Borhoneyghurk, are stations in Victoria. The only leader in the *Herald* is on the meat question, but there is in a letter an account of the Christmas festivities at Melbourne, which contains much merry-making at the expense of " unacclimatised new chums," as fresh comers to the colonies are called. The writer speaks rapturously of the rush on Christmas-day from the hot, dry, dusty streets to the " golden fields of waving corn." The " exposed nature of the Royal Park" prevented many excursionists from picnicking there, as they had intended; but we read on, and find that the exposure dreaded was not to cold, but to the terrible hot wind which swept from the plains of the north-west, and scorched up every blade of grass in the open spots. We hear of Christmas dinners eaten upon the grass at Richmond in the sheltered shade of the gum-forest, but in the Botanical Gardens the " plants had been much affected by the trying heat." However, " the weather on Boxing-day was more favourable for open-air enjoyment," as the thermometer was only 98° in the shade.

Will ever New Zealand or Australian bards spring up to write of the pale primroses that in September commence to peep out from under the melting snows, and to make men look forward to the blazing heat and the long December days? Strangely enough, the only English poem which an Australian lad can read without laughing at the old country conceit that connects frost with January, and hot weather with July, is Thomson's "Seasons," for in its long descriptions of the changes in England from spring to summer, from autumn to winter, a month is only once named: "rosy-footed May" cannot be said to "steal blushing on" in Australia, where May answers to our November.

In the afternoon, I ventured out again, and strolled into the gum-forest on the banks of the Campaspe river, not believing the reports of the ferocity of the Victorian bunyips and alligators which have lately scared the squatters who dwell on creeks. The black trees, relieved upon a ground of white dust and yellow grass, were not inviting, and the scorching heat soon taught me to hate the shadeless boughs and ragged bark of the inevitable gum. It had not rained for nine weeks at the time of my visit, and the thermometer stood at 116° in the shade, but there was nothing oppressive in the heat; it seemed only to dry up the juices of the frame, and dazzle you with intense brightness. I soon came to agree with a newly-landed Irish gardener, who told a friend of mine that Australia was a strange country, for he could not see that the thermometer had "the slightest effect upon the heat." The blaze is healthy, and fevers are unknown in the Riverina, decay of noxious matter, animal or vegetable, being arrested during summer by the drought. This is a hot year, for on the 12th of January the thermometer, even at the Melbourne Observatory, registered 108° in the shade, and 123° in the shade was registered at Wentworth, near the confluence of the Murray and the Darling.

As the afternoon drew on, and, if not the heat, at least the sun declined, the bell-birds ceased their tuneful chiming, and the forest was vocal only with the ceaseless chirp of the tree-cricket, whose note recalled the goatsucker of our English woods. The Australian landscapes show best by the red light of the hot-weather sunsets, when the dark feathery foliage of the gum-trees comes out in exquisite relief upon the fiery fogs that form the sky, and the yellow earth, gaining a tawny hue in the lurid glare, throws off a light resembling that which in winter is reflected from our English snows. At sunset there was a calm, but, as I turned to walk homeward, the hot wind sprang up, and died again, while the trees sighed themselves uneasily to sleep, as though fearful of the morrow's blast.

A night of heavy heat was followed by a breathless dawn, and the scorching sun returned in all its redness to burn up once more the earth, not cooled from the glare of yesterday. Englishmen must be bribed by enormous gains before they will work with continuous toil in such a climate, however healthy.

CHAPTER IV.

SQUATTER ARISTOCRACY.

"WHAT is a Colonial Conservative?" is a question that used to be daily put to a Victorian friend of mine when he was in London. His answer, he told me, was always, "A statesman who has got four of the 'points' of the People's Charter, and wants to conserve them;" but as used in Victoria, the term "Conservative" expresses the feeling less of a political party than of the whole of the people who have anything whatever to lose. Those who have something object to giving a share in the Government to those who have nothing; those who have much, object to political equality with those who have less; and, not content with having won a tremendous victory in basing the Upper House upon a 5,000*l.* qualification and 100*l.* freehold or 300*l.* leasehold franchise, the plutocracy are meditating attacks upon the Legislative Assembly.

The democracy hold out undauntedly, refusing all monetary tests, though an intelligence basis for the franchise is by no means out of favour, except with the few who cannot read or write. One day, when I was driving from Melbourne to Sandridge, in company with a colonial merchant, he asked our car-driver: "Now, tell me fairly: do you think these rogues of fellows that hang about the shore here ought to have votes?" "No, I don't." "Ah, you'd like to see a 5s. fee on registration, wouldn't you?" The answer was sharp enough in its tone. "Five shillings would be nothing to you; it would be something to me, and it would be more than my brother could pay. What I'd do would be to say that those who couldn't read shouldn't vote—that's all. That would keep out the loafers."

The plutocratic party is losing, not gaining, ground in Victoria; it is far more likely that the present generation will see the Upper House abolished than that it will witness the introduction of restrictions upon the manhood suffrage which exists for the Lower; but there is one branch of the plutocracy which actively carries on the fight in all the colonies, and which claims to control society—the pastoral tenants of Crown lands, or Squatter Aristocracy.

The word "squatter" has undergone a remarkable change of meaning since the time when it denoted those who stole Government land, and built their dwellings on it. As late as 1837, squatters were defined by the Chief Justice of New South Wales as people occupying lands without legal title, and subject to a fine on discovery. They were described as living by bartering rum with convicts for stolen goods, and as being themselves invariably convicts or "expirees." Escaping suddenly from these low associations, the word came to be applied to graziers who drove their flocks into the unsettled interior, and thence to those of them who received leases from the Crown of pastoral lands.

The squatter is the nabob of Melbourne and Sydney, the inexhaustible mine of wealth. He patronises balls, promenade concerts, flower-shows; he is the mainstay of the great clubs, the joy of the shopkeepers, the good angel of the hotels; without him the opera could not be kept up, and the jockey-club would die a natural death.

Neither squatters nor townsfolk will admit that this view of the former's position is correct. The Victorian squatters tell you that they have been ruined by confiscation, but that their neighbours in New South Wales, who have leases, are more prosperous; in New South Wales, they tell you of the destruction of the squatters by "free selection," of which there is none in Queensland, "the squatter's paradise;" but in Queensland the squatters protest that they have never made wages for their personal work, far less interest upon their capital. "Not one of us in ten is solvent," is their cry.

As sweeping assertions are made by the townsfolk upon the other side. The squatters, they sometimes say, may well set up to be a great landed aristocracy, for they have every fault of a dominant caste except its generous vices. They are accused of piling up vast hoards of wealth while living a most penurious life, and contributing less than would so many mechanics to the revenue of the country, in order that they may return in later life to England, there to spend what they have wrung from the soil of Victoria or New South Wales.

The occupation of the whole of the Crown lands by squatters has prevented the making of railways to be paid for in land, on the American system; but the chief of all the evils connected with squatting is the tendency to the accumulation in a few hands of all the land and all the pastoral wealth of the country, an extreme danger in the face of democratic institutions, such as those of Victoria and New South Wales. Remembering that manufactures are few, the swelling of the cities shows how the people have been kept from the land; considerably more than half of the population of Victoria lives within the corporate towns.

A few years back, a thousand men held between them, on nominal rents, forty million acres out of the forty-three and a half million—mountain and swamp excluded—of which Victoria consists. It is true that the amount so held has now decreased to thirty million, but on the other hand the squatters have bought vast tracts which were formerly within their "runs," with the capital acquired in squatting, and, knowing the country better than others could know it, have selected the most valuable land.

The colonial democracy in 1860 and the succeeding years rose to a sense of its danger from the land monopoly, and began to search about for means to put it down, and to destroy at the same time the system of holding from the Crown; for it is singular that while in England there seems to be springing up a popular movement in favour of the nationalisation of the land, in the most democratic of the Australian colonies the tendency is from Crown-land tenure towards individual freehold ownership of the soil. Yet, here in Victoria there was a fair field to start upon, for the land already belonged to the State—the first of the principles included under the phrase, nationalised land. In America, again, we see that, with the similar advantage of State possession of territories which are still fourteen times the size of the French Empire, there is little or no tendency towards agitation for the continuance of State ownership. In short, freehold ownership seems dear to the Anglo-Saxon race; while the national land plan would commend itself rather to the Celtic races: to the Highlander, who remembers clanship, to the Irishman, who regrets the Sept.

Since the Radicals have been in power, both here and in New South Wales, they have carried Act after Act to encourage agricultural settlers on freehold tenure, at the expense of the pastoral squatters. The "free selection" plan, now in operation in New South Wales, allows the agricultural settler to buy, but at a fixed price, the freehold of a patch of land, provided it be over forty acres and less than 320, anywhere he pleases—even in the middle of a squatter's "run," if he enters at once, and commences to cultivate; and the Land Act of 1862 provides that the squatting licence system shall entirely end with the year 1869. Forgetting that in every lease the Government reserved the power of terminating the agreement for the purpose of the sale of land, the squatters complain that free selection is but confiscation, and that they are at the mercy of a pack of cattle-stealers and horse-thieves, who roam through the country haunting their runs like "ghosts," taking up the best land on their runs, "picking the eyes out of the land," and turning to graze anywhere, on the richest grass, the sheep and cattle they have stolen on their way. The best of them, they say, are but "cockatoo farmers," living from hand to mouth on what they manage to grub and grow. On the other hand, the "free selection" principle "up country" is tempered by the power of the wealthy squatter to impound the cattle of the poor little freeholder whenever he pleases to say that they stray on to his "run ;" indeed, "Pound them off, or if you can't, buy them off," has become a much-used phrase. The squatter, too, is protected in Victoria by such provisions as that "improvements" by him, if over 40$l.$ on forty acres, cover an acre of land for each 1$l.$ The squatters are themselves buying largely of land, and thus profiting by the free selection. To a stranger it seems as though the interests of the squatter have been at least sufficiently cared for, remembering the vital necessity for immediate action. In 1865, Victoria, small as she is, had not sold a tenth of her land.

In her free selectors, Victoria will gain a class of citizens whose political views will contrast sharply with the strong anti-popular sentiments of the squatters, and who, instead of spending their lives as absentees, will stay, they and their children, upon the land, and spend all they make within the colony, while their sons add to its labouring arms.

Since land has been, even to a limited extent, thrown open, Victoria has suddenly ceased to be a wheat-importing, and become a wheat-exporting country; and flourishing agricultural communities, such as those of Ceres, Clunes, Kyneton, are springing up on every side, growing wheat instead of wool, while the wide extension which has in Victoria been given to the principle of local self-government in the shape of shire-councils, road-boards, and village-municipalities, allows of the union of the whole of the advantages of small and great farming, under the unequalled system of small holdings, and co-operation for improvements among the holders.

CHAPTER V.

COLONIAL DEMOCRACY.

PAYMENT of members by the State was the great question under debate in the Lower House during much of the time I spent in Melbourne, and, in spite of all the efforts of the Victorian democracy, the bill was lost. The objection taken at home, that payment degrades the House in the eyes of the people, could never arise in a new country, where a practical nation looks at the salaries as payment for work done, and obstinately refuses to believe in the work being done without payment in some shape or other. In these colonies, the reasons in favour of payment are far stronger than they are in Canada or America, for while there country or town share equally the difficulties of finding representatives who will consent to travel hundreds and thousands of miles to Ottawa or Washington; in the Australias, Parliament sits in towns which contain from one-sixth to one-fourth of the whole population, and under a non-payment system power is thrown entirely into the hands of Melbourne, Sydney, Perth, Brisbane, Adelaide, and Hobarton. Not only do these cities return none but their own citizens, but the country districts, often unable to find within their limits men who have sufficient time and money to be able to attend throughout the sessions at the capital, elect the city traders to represent them.

Payment of members was met by a proposition on the part of the leader of the squatter party in the Upper House to carry it through that assembly if the Lower House would introduce the principle of personal representation; but it was objected that under such a system the Catholics, who form a fifth of the population, might, if they chose, return a fifth of the members. That they ought to be able to do so never seemed to strike friend or foe. The Catholics, who had a long turn of power under the O'Shaughnessey Government, were finally driven out for appointing none but Irishmen to the police. "I always said this Ministry would go out on the back of a policeman," was the comment of the Opposition wit. The present Ministry, which is Scotch in tone, was hoisted into office by a great coalition against the Irish Catholics, of whom there are only a handful in the House.

The subject of national education, which was before the colony during my visit, also brought the Catholics prominently forward; for an episcopal pastoral was read in all their churches threatening to visit ecclesiastical censure upon Catholic teachers in the common schools, and upon the parents of the children who attend them. "Godless education" is as little popular here as it used to be at home, and the Anglican and Catholic clergymen insist that it is proposed to make their people pay heavily for an education in which it would be contrary to their conscience to share; but the laymen seem less distressed than their pastors. It has been said that the reason why the Catholic bishop declined to be examined before the Education Commission was that he was afraid of this question : " Are you aware that half the Catholic children in the country are attending schools which you condemn ? "

The most singular, perhaps, of the spectacles presented by colonial politics during my visit was that of the Victorian Upper House going deliberately into committee to consider its own constitution, with the view of introducing a bill for its own reform, or to meditate, its enemies said, upon self-destruction. Whether the blow comes from within or without, there is every probability that the Upper House will shortly disappear, and the advice of Milton and Franklin be followed in having but a single chamber. It is not unlikely that this step will be followed by the demand of the Victorians to be allowed to choose their own Governor, subject to his approval by the Queen, with a view to making it impossible that needy men should be sent out to suck the colony, as they sometimes have been in the past. The Australians look upon the liberal expenditure of a Governor as their own liberality, but upon meanness on his part as a robbery from themselves.

The Victorian have a singular advantage over the American democrats in being unhampered by a constitution of antiquity and renown. Constitution-tinkering is here continual; the new society is ever re-shaping its political institutions to keep pace with the latest developments of the national mind ; in America, the party of liberty, at this moment engaged in remoulding in favour of freedom the worn-out constitution, dares not even yet declare that the national good is its aim, but keeps to the old watchwords, and professes to be treading in the footsteps of George Washington.

The tone of Victorian democracy is not American. There is the defiant way of taking care of themselves and ignoring their neighbours, characteristic of the founders of English plantations in all parts of the world—the spirit which prompted the passing, in 1852, of the Act prohibiting the admission to the colony of convicts for three years after they had received their pardons; but the English race here is not Latinised as it is in America. If it were, Australian democracy would not be so "shocking" to the squatters. Democracy, like Mormonism, would be nothing if found among Frenchmen or people with black faces, but it is at first sight very terrible, when it smiles on you from between a pair of rosy Yorkshire cheeks.

The political are not greater than the social differences between Australia and America. Australian society resembles English middle-class society; the people have, in matters of literature and religion, tastes and feelings similar to those which pervade such communities as Birmingham or Manchester. On the other hand, the vices of America are those of aristocracies; her virtues, those of a landed republic. Shop and factory are still in the second rank; wheat and corn still the prevailing powers. In all the Australian colonies, land is coming to the front for the second time under a system of small holdings; but it is doubtful whether, looking to the size of Melbourne, the landed democracy will ever outvote the town-folk in Victoria.

That men of ability and character are proscribed has been one of the charges brought against colonial democracy. For my part, I found gathered in Melbourne, at the University, at the Observatory, at the Botanical Garden, and at the Government offices, men of the highest scientific attainments, drawn from all parts of the world, and tempted to Australia by large salaries voted by the democracy. The statesmen of all the colonies are well worthy of the posts they hold. Mr. Macalister, in Queensland, and Mr. Martin, at Sydney, are excellent debaters. Mr. Parkes, whose biography would be the typical history of a successful colonist, and who has fought his way up from the position of a Birmingham artisan free-emigrant to that of Colonial Secretary of New South Wales, is an able writer. The business powers of the present Colonial Treasurer of New South Wales are remarkable; and Mr. Higinbotham, the Attorney-General of Victoria, possesses a fund of experience and a power of foresight which it would be hard to equal at home. Many of the ministers in all the colonies are men who have worked themselves up from the ranks, and it is amusing to notice the affected horror with which their antecedents are recalled by those who have brought out a pedigree from the old country. A Government clerk in one of the colonies told me, that the three last ministers at the head of his department had been "so low in the social scale, that my wife could not visit theirs."

Class animosity runs much higher, and drives its roots far deeper into private life in Victoria than in any other English-speaking country I have seen. Political men of distinction are shunned by their opponents in the streets and clubs; and, instead of its being possible to differ on politics and yet continue friends, as in the old country, I have seen men in Victoria refuse to sit down to dinner with a statesman from whose views on land questions they happened to dissent. A man once warned me solemnly against dining with a quiet grave old gentleman, on the ground that he was " a most dangerous radical—a perfect firebrand."

Treated in this way, it is not strange that the democratic ministers and members stand much upon their dignity, and Colonial Parliaments are not only as haughty as the parent assembly at Westminster, but often inclined to assert their privileges by the most arbitrary of means. A few weeks before I arrived in Melbourne, a member of the staff of the *Argus* newspaper was given up by the proprietors to soothe the infuriated assembly. Having got him, the great question of what to do with him arose, and he was placed in a vault with a grated window, originally built for prisoners of the House, but which had been temporarily made use of as a coal-hole. Such a disturbance was provoked by the alleged barbarity of this proceeding, that the prisoner was taken to a capital room up stairs, where he gave dinner-parties every day. His opponents said the great difficulty was to get rid of him, for he seemed to be permanently located in the Parliament House, and that, when they ordered his liberation, his friends insisted that it should not take place until he had been carried down to the coal-hole cell which he had occupied the first day, and there photographed "through the dungeon bars" as the "martyr of the Assembly."

Though both Victoria and New South Wales are democratic, there is a great difference between the two democracies. In New South Wales, I found not a democratic so much as a mixed country, containing a large and wealthy class with aristocratic prejudices, but governed by an intensely democratic majority—a country not unlike the State of Maryland. On the other hand, the interest which attaches to the political condition of Victoria is extreme, since it probably presents an accurate view, "in little," of the state of society which will exist in England, after many steps towards social democracy have been taken, but before the nation as a whole has become completely democratic.

One of the best features of the colonial democracy is its earnestness in the cause of education. In England it is one of our worst national peculiarities that, whatever our station, we either are content with giving children an "education" which is absolutely wanting in any real training for the mind, or aid to the brain in its development, or else we give them a schooling which is a mere preparation for the Bar or Church, for it has always been considered with us that it is a far greater matter to be a solicitor or a curate than to be wise or happy. This is, of course, a consequence partly of the energy of the race, and partly of our aristocratic form of society, which leads every member of a class to be continually trying to get into the class immediately above it in wealth or standing. In the colonies, as in the United States, the democratic form which society has taken, has carried with it the continental habit of thought upon educational matters, so that it would seem as though the form of society influenced this question much more than the energy of the race, which is rather heightened than depressed in these new countries. The English Englishman says, " If I send Dick to a good school, and scrape up money enough to put him into a profession, even if he don't make much, at least he'll be a gentleman." The Australian or democratic Englishman says, " Tom must have good schooling, and must make the most of it ; but I'll not have him knocking about in broadcloth, and earning nothing ; so no profession for him ; but let him make money like me, and mayhap get a few acres more land."

Making allowance for the thinness of population in the bush, education in Victoria is extremely general among the children, and is directed by local committees with success, although the members of the boards are often themselves destitute of all knowledge except that which tells them that education will do their children good. Mr. Geary, an inspector of schools, told the Commissioners that he had examined one school where not a single member of the local committee could write; but these immigrant fathers do their duty honestly towards the children for all their ignorance, and there is every chance that the schools will grow and grow until their influence on behalf of freedom becomes as marked in Victoria as it ever has been in Massachusetts. Education has a great advantage in countries where political rights are widely extended: in the colonies, as in America, there is a spirit of political life astir throughout the country, and newspapers and public meetings continue an education throughout life which in England ceases at twelve, and gives place to driving sheep to paddocks, and shouting at rooks in a wheatfield.

There is nothing in the state of the Victorian schools to show what will be the type of the next generation, but there are many reasons for believing that the present disorganization of colonial society will only cease with the attainment of complete democracy or absolute equality of conditions, which must be produced by the already democratic institutions in little more than a generation. The squatter class will disappear as agriculture drives sheep-farming from the field, and, on the other hand, the town democracy will adopt a tone of manly independence instead of one of brag and bluster, when education makes them that which at present they are not—the equals of the wealthy farmers.

It has been justly pointed out that one of the worst dangers of democracy is the crushing influence of public opinion upon individuality, and many who have written upon America have assumed that the tendency has already shown itself there. I had during my stay in the United States arrived at the contrary opinion, and come to believe that in no country in the world is eccentricity, moral and religious, so ripe as in America, in no country individuality more strong; but, ascribing to intermixture of foreign blood this apparently abnormal departure from the assumed democratic shape of society, I looked forward to the prospect of seeing the overwhelming force of the opinion of the majority exhibited in all its hideousness in the democratic colonies. I was as far from discovering the monster as I had been in America, for I soon found that, although there may be little intellectual unrest in Australia, there is marvellous variety of manners.

There is in our colonies no trace of that multiplication of creeds which characterises America, and which is said to be everywhere the result of the abolition of Establishments. In Victoria, eighty per cent. of the whites belong to either Episcopalians, Catholics, or Presbyterians, and almost all of the remainder to the well-known English Churches; nothing is heard of such sects as the hundreds that have sprung up in New England—Hopkinsians, Universalists, Osgoodites, Rogerenes, Come-Outers, Non-Resistants, and the like. The Australian democrat likes to pray as his father prayed before him, and is strongly conservative in his ecclesiastic affairs. It may be the absence in Australia of enthusiastic religion which accounts for the want among the country folk of the peculiar gentleness of manner which distinguishes the farmer in America. Climate may have its effect upon the voice; the influence of the Puritan and Quaker in the early history of the thirteen States, when manners were moulded and the national life shaped for good or harm, may have permanently affected the descendants of the early settlers; but everywhere in America I noticed that the most perfect dignity and repose of manner was found in districts where the passionate religious systems had their strongest hold.

There is no trace in the colonies at present of that love for general ideas which takes America away from England in philosophy, and sets her with the Latin and Celtic races on the side of France. The tendency is said to follow on democracy, but it would be better said that democracy is itself one of these general ideas. Democracy in the colonies is at present an accident, and nothing more; it rests upon no basis of reasoning, but upon a fact. The first settlers were active, bustling men of fairly even rank or wealth, none of whom could brook the leadership of any other. The only way out of the difficulty was the adoption of the rule "All of us to be equal, and the majority to govern;" but there is no conception of the nature of democracy, as the unfortunate Chinese have long since discovered. The colonial democrats understand "democracy" as little as the party which takes the name in the United States; but there is at present no such party in the colonies as the great republican party of America.

Democracy cannot always remain an accident in Australia: where once planted, it never fails to fix its roots; but even in America its growth has been extremely slow. There is at present in Victoria and New South Wales a general admission among the men of the existence of equality of conditions, together with a perpetual rebellion on the part of their wives to defeat democracy, and to re-introduce the old "colonial court" society, and resulting class divisions. The consequence of this distinction is that the women are mostly engaged in elbowing their way; while among their husbands there is no such thing as the pretending to a style, a culture, or a wealth that the pretender does not possess, for the reason that no male colonist admits the possibility of the existence of a social superior. Like the American "democrat," the Australian will admit that there may be any number of grades below him, so long as you allow that he is at the top; but no republican can be stauncher in the matter of his own equality with the best.

There is no sign that in Australia any more than in America there will spring up a centre of opposition to the dominant majority; but there is as little evidence that the majority will even unwittingly abuse its power. It is the fashion to say that for a State to be intellectually great and noble, there must be within it a nucleus of opposition to the dominant principles of the time and place, and that the best and noblest minds, the intellects the most seminal, have invariably belonged to men who formed part of such a group.

It may be doubted whether this assumed necessity for opposition to the public will is not characteristic of a terribly imperfect state of society and government. It is chiefly because the world has never had experience of a national life at once throbbing with the pulse of the whole people, and completely tolerant not only in law but in opinion of sentiments the most divergent from the views of the majority—firm in the pursuit of truths already grasped, but ready to seize with avidity upon new; gifted with a love of order, yet prepared to fit itself to shifting circumstances—that men continue to look with complacency upon the enormous waste of intellectual power that occurs when a germ of truth such as that contained in the doctrines of the Puritans finds development and acceptance only after centuries have passed.

Australia will start unclogged by slavery to try this experiment for the world.

CHAPTER VI.

PROTECTION.

THE greatest of all democratic stumbling-blocks is said to be Protection.

"Encourage native industry!" the colonial shopkeepers write up; "Show your patriotism, and buy colonial goods!" is painted in huge letters on a shop-front at Castlemaine. In England, some unscrupulous traders, we are told, write "From Paris" over their English goods, but such dishonesty in Victoria takes another shape; there we have "Warranted colonial made" placed over imported wares, for many will pay a higher price for a colonial product confessedly not more than equal to the foreign, such is the rage for Native Industry, and the hatred of the "Antipodean doctrine of Free Trade."

Many former colonists who live at home persuade themselves, and unfortunately persuade also the public in England, that the Protectionists are weak in the colonies. So far is this from being the case in either Victoria or New South Wales, that in the former colony I found that in the Lower House the Free Traders formed but three-elevenths of the Assembly, and in New South Wales the pastoral tenants of the Crown may be said to stand alone in their support of

Free Trade. Some of the squatters go so far as to declare that none of the public men of the colonies really believe in the advantages of Protection, but that they dishonestly accept the principle, and undertake to act upon it when in office, in order to secure the votes of an ignorant majority of labourers, who are themselves convinced that Protection means high wages.

It would seem as though we Free Traders had become nearly as bigoted in favour of Free Trade as our former opponents were in favour of Protection. Just as they used to say "We are right; why argue the question?" so now, in face of the support of Protection by all the greatest minds in America, all the first statesmen of the Australias, we tell the New England and the Australian politicians that we will not discuss Protection with them, because there can be no two minds about it among men of intelligence and education. We will hear no defence of "national lunacy," we say.

If, putting aside our prejudices, we consent to argue with an Australian or American Protectionist, we find ourselves in difficulties. All the ordinary arguments against the compelling people by Act of Parliament to consume a dearer or inferior article are admitted as soon as they are urged. If you attempt to prove that Protection is bolstered up by those whose private interests it subserves, you are shown the shrewd Australian diggers and the calculating Western farmers in America—men whose pocket interest is wholly opposed to Protection, and who yet, almost to a man, support it. A digger at Ballarat defended Protection to me in this way: he said he knew that under a protective tariff he had to pay dearer than would otherwise be the case for his jacket and his moleskin trousers, but that he preferred to do this, as by so doing he aided in building up in the colony such trades as the making-up of clothes, in which his brother and other men physically too weak to be diggers could gain an honest living. In short, the self-denying Protection of the Australian diggers is of the character of that which would be accorded to the glaziers of a town by the citizens, if they broke their windows to find their fellow-townsmen work: "We know we lose, but men must live," they say. At the same time they deny that the loss will be enduring. The digger tells you that he should not mind a continuing pocket loss, but that, as a matter of fact, this, which in an old country would be pocket loss, in a new country such as his only comes to this—that it forms a check on immigration. Wages being 5s. a day in Victoria and 3s. a day in England, workmen would naturally flock into Victoria from England until wages in Melbourne fell to 3s. 6d. or 4s. Here comes in prohibition, and by increasing the cost of living in Victoria, and cutting into the Australian handicraftsman's margin of luxuries, diminishes the temptation to immigration, and consequently the influx itself.

The Western farmers in America, I have heard, defend Protection upon far wider grounds: they admit that Free Trade would conduce to the most rapid possible peopling of their country with foreign immigrants; but this, they say, is an eminently undesirable conclusion. They prefer to pay a heavy tax in the increased price of everything they consume, and in the greater cost of labour, rather than see their country denationalized by a rush of Irish or Germans, or their political institutions endangered by a still further increase in the size and power of New York. One old fellow said to me: "I don't want the Americans in 1900 to be 200 millions, but I want them to be happy."

The American Protectionists point to the danger that their countrymen would run unless town kept pace with country population. Settlers would pour off to the west, and drain the juices of the fertile land by cropping it year after year, without fallow, without manure, and then, as the land became in a few years exhausted, would have nowhere whither to turn to find the fertilizers which the soil would need. Were they to depend upon agriculture alone, they would sweep in a wave across the land, leaving behind them a worn out, depopulated, jungle-covered soil, open to future settlement, when its lands should have recovered their fertility, by some other and more provident race. The coastlands of most ancient countries are exhausted, densely bushed, and uninhabited. In this fact lies the power of our sailor race: crossing the seas, we occupy the coasts, and step by step work our way into the upper country, where we should not have attempted to show ourselves had the ancient population resisted us upon the shores. In India, in Ceylon, we met the hardy race of the highlands and interior only after we had already fixed ourselves upon the coast, with a safe basis for our supply. The fate that these countries have met is that which colonists expect to be their own, unless the protective system be carried out in its entirety. In like manner the Americans point to the ruin of Virginia, and if you urge "Slavery," answer, "Slavery is but agriculture."

Those who speak of the selfishness of the Protectionists as a whole can never have taken the trouble to examine into the arguments by which Protection is supported in Australia and America. In these countries, Protection is no mere national delusion; it is a system deliberately adopted with open eyes as one conducive to the country's welfare, in spite of objections known to all, in spite of pocket losses that come home to all. If it be, as we in England believe, a folly, it is at all events a sublime one, full of self-sacrifice, illustrative of a certain nobility in the national heart. The Australian diggers and Western farmers in America are setting a grand example to the world of self-sacrifice for a national object; hundreds and thousands of rough men are content to live—they and their families—upon less than they might otherwise enjoy, in order that the condition of the mass of their countrymen may continue raised above that of their brother toilers in Old England. Their manufactures are beginning now to stand alone, but hitherto, without Protection, the Americans would have had no cities but seaports. By picturing to ourselves England dependent upon the city of London, upon Liverpool, and Hull, and Bristol, we shall see the necessity the Western men are now under of setting off Pittsburg against New York and Philadelphia. In short, the tendency, according to the Western farmers, of Free Trade, in the early stages of a country's existence, is to promote universal centralization, to destroy local centres and the commerce they create, to so tax the farmer with the cost of transport to distant markets, that he must grow wheat and corn continuously, and cannot but exhaust his soil. With markets so distant, the richest forest lands are not worth clearing, and settlement sweeps over the country, occupying the poorer lands, and then abandoning them once more.

Protection in the colonies and America is to a great degree a revolt against steam. Steam is making the world all one; steam "corrects" differences in the price of labour. When steam brings all races into competition with each other, the cheaper races will extinguish the dearer, till at last some one people will inhabit the whole earth. Coal remains the only power, as it will probably always be cheaper to carry the manufactured goods than to carry the coal.

Time after time I have heard the Western farmers draw imaginary pictures of the state of America if Free Trade should gain the day, and ask of what avail it is to say that Free Trade and free circulation of people are profitable to the pocket, if they destroy the national existence of America; what good to point out the gain of weight to their purses, in the face of the destruction of their religion, their language, and their Saxon institutions.

One of the greatest of the thinkers of America defended Protection to me on the following grounds: That without Protection, America could at present have but few and limited manufactures. That a nation cannot properly be said to exist as such, unless she has manufactures of many kinds; for men are born, some with a turn to agriculture, some with a turn to mechanics; and if you force the mechanic-by-nature to become a farmer, he will make a bad farmer, and the nation will lose the advantage of all his power and invention. That the whole of the possible employments of the human race are in a measure necessary employments—necessary to the making up of a nation. That every concession to Free Trade cuts out of all chance of action some of the faculties of the American national mind, and, in so doing, weakens and debases it. That each and every class of workers is of such importance to the country, that we must make any sacrifice necessary to maintain them in full work. "The national mind is manifold," he said; "and if you do not keep up every branch of employment in every district, you waste the national force. If we were to remain a purely agricultural people, land would fall into fewer and fewer hands, and our people become more and more brutalised as the years rolled on."

It must not be supposed that Protection is entirely defended upon these strange new grounds. "Save us from the pauper-labour of Europe," is the most recent as well as the oldest of Protectionist cries. The Australians and Americans say, that by working women at 1s. a day in the mines in Wales, and by generally degrading all labourers under the rank of highly-skilled artisans, the British keep wages so low, that, in spite of the cost of carriage, they can almost invariably undersell the colonists and Americans in American and Australian markets. This state of degradation and poverty nothing can force them to introduce into their own countries, and, on the other hand, they consider manufactures necessary for the national purpose alluded to before. The alternative is Protection.

The most unavoidable of all the difficulties of Protection—namely, that no human government can ever be trusted to adjust protective taxation without corruption—is no objection to the Prohibition which the Western Protectionists demand. The New Englanders say—" Let us meet the English on fair terms ; " the Western men say that they will not meet them at all. Some of the New York Protectionists declare that their object is merely the fostering of American manufactures until they are able to stand alone, the United States not having at present reached the point which had been attained by other nations when they threw Protection to the winds. Such halting Protectionists as these manufacturers find no sympathy in Australia or the West, although the highest of all Protectionists look forward to the distant time when, local centres being everywhere established, customs will be abolished on all sides, and mankind form one family.

The chief thing to be borne in mind in discussing Protection with an Australian or an American is that he never thinks of denying that under Protection he pays a higher price for his goods than he would if he bought them from us, and that he admits at once that he temporarily pays a tax of 15 or 20 per cent. upon everything he buys in order to help set his country on the road to national unity and ultimate wealth. Without Protection, the American tells you, there will be commercial New York, sugar-growing Louisiana, the corn-growing North-West, but no America. Protection alone can give him a united country. When we talk about things being to the advantage or disadvantage of a country, the American Protectionist asks what you mean. Admitting that all you say against Protection may be true, he says that he had sooner see America supporting a hundred millions independent of the remainder of the world than two hundred millions dependent for clothes upon the British. "You, on the other hand," he says, "would prefer our custom. How can we discuss the question? The difference between us is radical, and we have no base on which to build."

It is a common doctrine in the colonies of England that a nation cannot be called "independent" if it has to cry out to another for supplies of necessaries; that true national existence is first attained when the country becomes capable of supplying to its own citizens those goods without which they cannot exist in the state of comfort which they have already reached. Political is apt to follow upon commercial dependency, they say.

The question of Protection is bound up with the wider one of whether we are to love our fellow-subjects, our race, or the world at large; whether we are to pursue our country's good at the expense of other nations? There is a growing belief in England that the noblest philosophy is to deny the existence of the moral right to benefit ourselves by harming others; that love of mankind must in time replace love of race as that has in part replaced narrow patriotism and love of self. It would seem that our Free Trade system lends itself better to these wide modern sympathies than does Protection. On the other hand, it may be argued that, if every State consults the good of its own citizens, we shall, by the action of all nations, obtain the desired happiness of the whole world, and this with rapidity, from the reason that every country understands its own interests better than it does those of its neighbour. As a rule, the colonists hold that they should not protect themselves against the sister-colonies, but only against the outer world; and while I was in Melbourne an arrangement was made with respect to the border customs between Victoria and New South Wales; but this is at present the only step that has been taken towards inter-colonial Free Trade.

It is passing strange that Victoria should be noted for the eagerness with which her people seek Protection. Possessed of little coal, they appear to be attempting artificially to create an industry which, owing to this sad lack of fuel, must languish from the moment that it is let alone. Sydney coal sells in Melbourne at thirty shillings a ton; at the pit's-mouth at Newcastle, New South Wales, it fetches only seven or eight shillings. With regard, however, to the making-up of native produce, the question in the case of Victoria is merely this: Is it cheaper to carry the wool to the coal, and then the woollen goods back again, than to carry the coal to the wool? and as long as Victoria can continue to export wheat, so that the coal-ships may not want freight, wool manufactures may prosper in Victoria.

The Victorians naturally deny that the cost of coal has much to do with the question. The French manufacturers, they point out, with dearer coal, but with cheaper labour, have in many branches of trade beaten the English out of common markets, but then under Protection there is no chance of cheap labour in Victoria.

Writing for the Englishmen of Old England, it is not necessary for me to defend Free Trade by any arguments. As far as we in our island are concerned, it is so manifestly to the pocket interest of almost all of us, and at the same time, on account of the minuteness of our territory, so little dangerous politically, that for Britain there can be no danger of a deliberate relapse into Protection; although we have but little right to talk about Free Trade so long as we continue our enormous subsidies to the Cunard liners.

The American argument in favour of Prohibition is in the main, it will be seen, political, the economical objections being admitted, but outweighed. Our action in the matter of our postal contracts, and in the case of the Factory Acts, at all events shows that we are not ourselves invariably averse to distinguish between the political and the economical aspect of certain questions.

My duty has been to chronicle what is said and thought upon the matter in our various plantations. One thing at least is clear—that even if the opinions I have recorded be as ridiculous when applied to Australia or America as they would be when applied to England, they are not supported by a selfish clique, but rest upon the generosity and self-sacrifice of a majority of the population.

CHAPTER VII.

LABOUR.

SIDE by side with the unselfish Protectionism of the diggers, there flourishes among the artisans of the Australias a self-interested desire for non-intercourse with the outside world.

In America, the working men, themselves almost without exception immigrants, though powerful in the various States from holding the balance of parties, have never as yet been able to make their voices heard in the Federal Congress. In the chief Australian colonies, on the other hand, the artisans have, more than any other class, the possession of political power. Throughout the world the grievance of the working classes lies in the fact that, while trade and profits have increased enormously within the last few years, true as distinguished from nominal wages have not risen. It is even doubtful whether the American or British handicraftsman can now live in such comfort as he could make sure of a few years back : it is certain that agricultural labourers in the south of England are worse off than they were ten years ago, although the depreciation of gold prevents us from accurately gauging their true position. In Victoria and New South Wales, and in the States of

Wisconsin, Illinois, and Missouri, where the artisans possess some share of power, they have set about the attempt to remedy by law the grievance under which they suffer. In the American States, where the suppression of immigration seems almost impossible, their interference takes the shape of eight-hour bills, and exclusion of coloured labourers. There is no trades-union in America which will admit to membership a Chinaman, or even a mulatto. In Victoria and New South Wales, however, it is not difficult quietly to put a check upon the importation of foreign labour. The vast distance from Europe makes the unaided immigration of artisans extremely rare, and since the democrats have been in power the funds for assisted immigration have been withheld, and the Chinese influx all but forbidden, while manifestoes against the ordinary European immigration have repeatedly been published at Sydney by the Council of the Associated Trades.

The Sydney operatives have always taken a leading part in opposition to immigration, from the time when they founded the Anti-Transportation Committee up to the present day. In 1847, a natural and proper wish to prevent the artificial depression of wages was at the bottom of the anti-transportation movement, although the arguments made use of in the petition to the Queen were of the most general character, and Sydney mechanics, many of them free immigrants themselves, say that there is no difference of principle between the introduction of free or assisted immigrants and that of convicts.

If we look merely to the temporary results of the policy of the Australian artisans, we shall find it hard to deny that their acts are calculated momentarily to increase their material prosperity; so far they may be selfish, but they are not blind. Admitting that wages depend on the ratio of capital to population, the Australians assert that, with them, population increases faster than capital, and that hindering immigration will restore the balance. Prudential checks on population are useless, they say, in face of Irish immigration. At the same time, it is clear that, from the discouragement of immigration and limitation to eight hours of the daily toil, there results an exceptional scarcity of labour, which cramps the development of the country, and causes a depression in trade which must soon diminish the wage-fund, and re-act upon the working men. It is unfortunately the fact, that colonial artisans do not sufficiently bear in mind the distinction between real and nominal wages, but are easily caught by the show of an extra few shillings a week, even though the purchasing power of each shilling be diminished by the change. When looked into, "higher wages" often mean that the labourer, instead of starving upon ten shillings a week, is to starve upon twenty.

As regards the future, contrasted with the temporary condition of the Australian labourer, there is no disguising the fact that mere exclusion of immigration will not in the long run avail him. It might, of course, be urged that immigration is, even in America, a small matter by the side of the natural increase of the people, and that to shut out the immigrant is but one of many checks to population; but in Australia the natural increase is not so great as in a young country might be expected. The men so largely outnumber the women in Australia, that even early marriages and large families cannot make the birth-rate very high, and fertile land being at present still to be obtained at first hand, the new agricultural districts swallow up the natural increase of the population. Still, important as is immigration at this moment, ultimately through the influx of women—to which the democrats are not opposed—or, more slowly, by the effort of nature to restore the balance of the sexes, the rate of natural increase will become far greater in Australia. Ultimately, there can be no doubt, if the Australian labourer continues to retain his present standard of comfort, prudential checks upon the birth of children will be requisite to maintain the present ratio of capital to population.

Owing to the comparatively high prices fixed for agricultural land in the three south-eastern colonies of Australia, the abundance of unoccupied tracts has not hitherto had that influence on wages in Australia which it appears to have exercised in America; but under the democratic amendments of the existing free selection system, wages will probably again rise in the colonies, to be once more reduced by immigration, or, if the democracy gains the day, more slowly lowered by the natural increase of the population.

In places where competition has reduced the reward of labour to the lowest amount consistent with the efficiency of the work, compulsory restriction of the hours of toil must evidently be an unmixed benefit to the labourer, until carried to the point at which it destroys the trade in which he is engaged. In America and Australia, however, where the labourer has a margin of luxuries which can be cut down, and where the manufacturers are still to some extent competing with European rivals, restriction of hours puts them at a disadvantage with the capitalists of the old world, and, reducing their profits, tends also to diminish the wage-fund, and ultimately to decrease the wages of their men. The colonial action in this matter may, nevertheless, like all infringements of general economic laws, be justified by proof of the existence of a higher necessity for breaking than for adhering to the rule of freedom. Our own Factory Acts, we should remember, were undoubtedly calculated to diminish the production of the country.

Were the American and Australian handicraftsmen to become sufficiently powerful to combine strict Protection, or prohibition of foreign intercourse, with reduction of hours of toil, they would ultimately drive capital out of their countries, and either lower wages, or else diminish the population by checking both immigration and natural increase. Here, as in the consideration of Protection, we come to that bar to all discussion, the question, "What is a nation's good?" It is at least doubtful whether in England we do not attach too great importance to the continuance of nations in "the progressive state." Unrestricted immigration may destroy the literature, the traditions, the nationality itself of the invaded country, and it is a question whether these ideas are not worth preserving even at a cost of a few figures in the returns of imports, exports, and population. A country in which Free Trade principles have been carried to their utmost logical development must be cosmopolitan and nationless, and for such a state of things to exist universally without danger to civilization the world is not yet prepared.

"Know-nothingism" in America, as what is now styled "native Americanism" was once called—a form of the protest against the exaggeration of Free Trade—was founded by handicraftsmen, and will in all probability find its main support within their ranks whenever the time for its inevitable resuscitation shall arrive. That there is honest pride of race at the bottom of the agitation no one can doubt who knows the history of the earlier Know-nothing movement; but class interest happens to point the same way as does the instinct of the race. The refusal of political privileges to immigrants will have some tendency to check the flow of immigration; at all events, it will check the self-assertion of the immigrants. That which does this leaves, too, the control of wages more within the hands of actual labourers, and prevents the European labourers of the eleventh hour coming in to share the heightened wages for which the American hands have struck, and suffered misery and want. No consistent republican can object to the making ten or twenty years' residence in the United States the condition for citizenship of the land.

In the particular case of the Australian colonies, they are happily separated from Ireland by seas so wide as to have a chance of preserving a distinct nationality, such as America can scarcely hope for: only 1,500 persons have come to New South Wales, unassisted, in the last five years. The burthen of proof lies upon those who propose to destroy the rising nationality by assisting the importation of a mixed multitude of negroes, Chinamen, Hill-coolies, Irish, and Germans, in order that the imports and exports of Victoria and New South Wales may be increased, and that there may be a larger number of so-called Victorians and New South Welsh to live in misery.

Owing to the fostering of immigration by the aristocratic government, the population of Queensland had, in 1866, quadrupled itself since 1860; but, even were the other colonies inclined to follow the example of their northern sister, they could not do so with success. New South Wales and Tasmania might import colonists by the thousand, but they would be no sooner landed than they would run to Queensland, or sail to the New Zealand diggings, just as the "Canadian immigrants" flock into the United States.

That phase of the labour question to which I have last alluded seems to shape itself into the question, "Shall the labourer always and everywhere be encouraged or permitted to carry his labour to the best market?" The Australians answer that they are willing to admit that additional hands in a new country mean additional wealth, but that there is but little good in our preaching moral restraint to them if European immigration is to be encouraged, Chinese allowed. The only effect, they say, that self-control can have is that of giving such children as they rear Chinamen or Irishmen to struggle against instead of brothers. It is hopeless to expect that the Australian workmen will retain their present standard of comfort if an influx of dark-skinned handicraftsmen is permitted.

Some ten or even fewer years ago, we free-traders of the Western world, first then coming to know some little about the kingdoms of the further East, paused a moment in our daily toil to lift to the skies our hands in lamentation at the blind exclusiveness which we were told had for ages past held sway within the council-chambers of Pekin. No words were too strong for our new-found laughing-stock; China became for us what we are to Parisian journalists—a Bœotia redeemed only by a certain eccentricity of folly. This vast hive swarming with two hundred million working bees was said to find its interest in shutting out the world, punishing with death the outgoing and incoming of the people. "China for the Chinese," was the common war-cry of the rulers and the ruled; "Self-contained has China been, and prospered; self-contained she shall continue," the favourite maxim of their teachers. Nothing could be conceived nobler than the scorn which mingled with half-doubting incredulity and with Pharisaic thanking of heaven that we were not as they, when the blindness of these outer barbarians of "Gog and Magog land" was drawn for us by skilful pens, and served out with all the comments that self-complacency could suggest. A conversion in the future was foretold, however; this Chinese infirmity of vision was not to last for ever; the day, would come when Studentships in Political Economy would be founded in Pekin, and Ricardo take the place of Cou-fou-chow in Thibetian schools. A conversion has taken place of late, but not that hoped for; or, if it be a conversion consistent with the truths of Economic Science, it has taken a strange shape. The wise men of Canton may be tempted, perhaps, to think that it is we who have learnt the wisdom of the sages, and been brought back into the fold of the great master. Chinese immigration is heavily taxed in California; taxed to the point of prohibition in Victoria; and forbidden under heavy penalties in Louisiana and other ex-rebel States.

The Chinaman is pushing himself to the fore wherever his presence is allowed. We find Chinese helmsmen and quartermasters in the service of the Messageries and Oriental companies receiving twice the wages paid to Indian Lascars. We hear of the importation of Chinese labourers into India for railway and for drainage works. The Chinaman has great vitality. Of the cheap races the Mongol is the most pushing, the likeliest to conquer in the fight. It would almost seem as though we were wrong in our common scales of preference; far from right in our use of the terms "superior" and "inferior" races.

A well-taught white man can outreason or can overreach a well-taught Chinaman or negro. But under some climatic conditions, the negro can outwork the white man; under almost all conditions, the Chinaman can outwork him. Where this is the case, is it not the Chinaman or the negro that should be called the better man? Call him what we may, will he not prove his superiority by working the Englishman off the soil? In Florida and Mississippi, the black is certainly the better man.

Many Victorians, even those who respect and admire the Chinese, are in favour of the imposition of a tax upon the yellow immigrants, in order to prevent the destruction of the rising Australian nationality. They fear that otherwise they will live to see the English element swamped in the Asiatic throughout Australia. It is not certain that we may not some day have to encounter a similar danger in Old England.

It will be seen from the account thus given of the state of the labour question in Australia, that the colonial handicraftsmen stand towards those of the world in much the same relative position as that held by the members of a trade-union towards the other workmen of the same trade. The limitation of immigration has much the same effects as the limitation of apprentices in a single trade in England. It is easy to say that the difference between fellow-countryman and foreigner is important; that while it is an unfairness to all English workmen that English hatters should limit apprentices, it is not unfair to English hatters that Australian hatters should limit their apprentices. For my own part, I am inclined to think that, fair or unfair—and we have no international moral rule to decide the question—

we might at least say to Australia that, while she throws upon us the chief expenses of her defence, she is hardly in a position to refuse to aid our emigrants.

Day by day, the labour question in its older aspects becomes of less and less importance. The relationship of master and servant is rapidly dying the death; cooperative farming and industrial partnerships must supersede it everywhere at no distant date. In these systems we shall find the remedy against the decline of trade with which the English-speaking countries of the earth are threatened.

The existing system of labour is anti-democratic; it is at once productive of and founded on the existence of an aristocracy of capital and a servitude of workmen; and our English democracies cannot afford that half their citizens should be dependent labourers. If manufactures are to be consistent with democracy, they must be carried on in shops in which each man shall be at once capitalist and handicraftsman. Such institutions are already in existence in Massachusetts, in Illinois, in Pennsylvania, and in Sydney; while at Troy, in New York State, there is a great iron-foundry, owned from roof to floor by the men who work in it. It is not enough that the workman should share in the profits. The change which, continuing through the Middle Ages into the present century, has at last everywhere converted the relation of lord and slave into that of master and hireling, is already giving place to the silent revolution which is steadily substituting for this relationship of capital and labour that of a perfect marriage, in which the labourer and the capitalist shall be one.

Under this system there can be no·strikes, no petty trickery, no jealousy, no waste of time. Each man's individual interest is coincident with that of all. Where the labour is that of a brotherhood, the toil becomes ennobled. Were industrial partnerships a new device, their inventor would need no monument; his would be found in the future history of the race. As it is, this latest advance of Western civilization is but a return to the earliest and noblest form of labour; the Arabs, the Don Cossacks, the Maori tribes, are all co-operative farmers; it is the mission of the English race to apply the ancient principle to manufactures.

CHAPTER VIII.

WOMAN.

IN one respect, Victoria stands at once sadly behind and strangely in advance of other democratic countries. Women, or at least some women, vote at the Lower House elections, but, on the other hand, the legal position of the sex is almost as inferior to that of man as it is in England or the East.

At an election held some few years ago, female ratepayers voted everywhere throughout Victoria. Upon examination, it was found that a new Registration Act had directed the rate-books to be used as a basis for the preparation of the electoral lists, and that women householders had been legally put on the register, although the intention of the Legislature was not expressed, and the question of female voting had not been raised during the debates. Another instance, this, of the singular way in which in truly British countries reforms are brought about by accident, and, when once become facts, are allowed to stand. There is no more sign of general adhesion in Australia than in England to the doctrine which asserts that women, as well as men, being interested in good government, should have a voice in the selection of that government to which they are forced to submit.

As far as concerns their social position, women are as badly off in Australia as in England. Our theory of marriage—which has been tersely explained thus: "the husband and wife are one, and *the husband is that one*,"—rules as absolutely at the antipodes as it does in Yorkshire. I was daily forced to remember the men of Kansas and Missouri, and the widely different view they take of these matters to that of the Australians. As they used to tell me, they are impatient of seeing their women ranked with "lunatics and idiots" in the catalogue of incapacities. They are unable to see that women are much better represented by their male friends than were the Southern blacks by their owners or overseers. They believe that the process of election would not be more purified by female emancipation than would the character of the Parliaments elected.

The Kansas people often say that if you were told that there existed in some ideal country two great sections of a race, the members of the one often gross, often vicious, often given to loud talking, to swearing, to drinking, spitting, chewing; not infrequently corrupt; those of the other branch, mild, kind, quiet, pure, devout, with none of the habitual vices of the first-named sect—if you were told that one of these branches was alone to elect rulers and to govern, you would at once say, "Tell us where this happy country is that basks in the rule of such a god-like people." "Stop a minute," says your informant, "it is the creatures I described first—the *men*—who rule; the others are only women, poor silly fools—imperfect men, I assure you; nothing more."

It is somewhat the fashion to say that the so-called "extravagancies" of the Kansas folk and other American Western men arise from the extraordinary position given to their women by the disproportion of the sexes. Now, in all the Australian colonies the men vastly outnumber the women, yet the disproportion has none of those results which have been attributed to it by some writers on America. In New South Wales, the sexes are as 250,000 to 200,000, in Victoria 370,000 to 280,000, in New Zealand 130,000 to 80,000, in Queensland 60,000 to 40,000, in Tasmania 50,000 to 40,000, in West Australia 14,000 to 8,000, and 90,000 to 80,000 in South Australia. In all our Southern colonies together, there are a million of men to only three-quarters of a million of women; yet with all this disproportion, which far exceeds that in Western America, not only have the women failed to acquire any great share of power, political or social, but they are content to occupy a position not relatively superior to that held by them at home.

The "Sewing Clubs" of the war-time are at the bottom of a good deal of the "woman movement" in America. At the time of greatest need, the ladies of the Northern States formed themselves into associations for the supply of lint, of linen, and of comforts to the army: the women of a district would meet together daily in some large room, and sew, and chat while they were sewing.

The British section of the Teutonic race seems naturally inclined, through the operation of its old interest-begotten prejudices, to rank women where Plato placed them in the "Timæus," along with horses and draught cattle, or to think of them much as he did when he said that all the brutes derived their origin from man by a series of successive degradations, of which the first was from man to woman. There is, however, one strong reason why the English should, in America, have laid aside their prejudices upon this point, retaining them in Australia, where the conditions are not the same. Among farming peoples, whose women do not work regularly in the field, the woman, to whom falls the household and superior work, is better off than she is among town-dwelling peoples. The Americans are mainly a farming, the Australians and British mainly a town-dwelling, people. The absence in all sections of our race of regular woman labour in the field seems to be a remnant of the high estimation in which women were held by our German ancestry. In Britain we have, until the last few years, been steadily retrograding upon this point.

It is a serious question how far the natural prejudice of the English mind against the labour of what we call "inferior races" will be found to extend to half the superior race itself. How will English labourers receive the inevitable competition of women in many of their fields? Woman is at present starved, if she works at all, and does not rest content in dependence upon some man, by the terrible lowness of wages in every employment open to her, and this low rate of wages is itself the direct result of the fewness of the occupations which society allows her. Where a man can see a hundred crafts in which he may engage, a woman will perhaps be permitted to find ten. A hundred times as many women as there is room for invade each of this small number of employments. In the Australian labour-field the prospects of women are no better than they are in Europe, and during my residence in Melbourne the Council of the Associated Trades passed a resolution to the effect that nothing could justify the employment of women in any kind of productive labour.

CHAPTER IX.

VICTORIAN PORTS.

ALL allowance being made for the great number of wide roads for trade, there is still a singular absence of traffic in the Melbourne streets. Trade may be said to be transacted only upon paper in the city, while the tallow, grain, and wool, which form the basis of Australian commerce, do not pass through Melbourne, but skirt it, and go by railway to Williamstown, Sandridge, and Geelong.

Geelong, once expected to rival Melbourne, and become the first port of all Australia, I found grass-grown and half deserted, with but one vessel lying at her wharf. At Williamstown, a great fleet of first-class ships was moored alongside the pier. When the gold-find at Ballarat took place, Geelong rose fast as the digging port, but her citizens chose to complete the railway line to Melbourne instead of first opening that to Ballarat, and so lost all the up-country trade. Melbourne, having once obtained the lead, soon managed to control the Legislature, and grants were made for the Echuca Railroad, which tapped the Murray, and brought the trade of Upper Queensland and New South Wales down to Melbourne, in the interest of the ports of Williamstown and Sandridge. Not content with ruining Geelong, the Melbourne men have set themselves to ridicule it. One of their stories goes that the Geelong streets bear such a fine crop of grass, that a free selector has applied to have them surveyed and sold to him, under the 42nd clause of the New Land Act. Another story tells how a Geelongee lately died, and went to heaven. Peter, opening the door to his knock, asked, "Where from?" "Geelong." "Where?" said Peter. "Geelong." "There's no such place," replied the Apostle. "In Victoria," cried the colonist. "Fetch Ham's Australian Atlas," called Peter; and when the map was brought and the spot shown to him, he replied, "Well, I beg your pardon, but I really never had any one here from that place before."

If Geelong be standing still, which in a colony is the same as rapid decline would be with us, the famed wheat country around it seems as inexhaustible as it ever was. The whole of the Barrabool range, from Ceres to Mount Moriac, is one great golden waving sheet, save where it is broken by the stunted claret-vineyards. Here and there I came upon a group of the little daughters of the German vine-dressers, tending and trenching the plants, with the round eyes, rosy cheeks, and shiny pigtails of their native Rudesheim all flourishing beneath the Southern Cross.

The colonial vines are excellent; better, indeed, than the growths of California, which, however, they resemble in general character. The wines are naturally all Burgundies, and colonial imitations of claret, port, and sherry are detestable, and the hocks but little better. The Albury Hermitage is a better wine than can be bought in Europe at its price, but in some places this wine is sold as Murray Burgundy, while the dealers foist horrible stuff upon you under the name of Hermitage. Of the wines of New South Wales, White Dallwood is a fair Sauterne, and White Cawarra a good Chablis, while for sweet wines the Chasselas is cheap; and the Tokay, the Shiraz, and the still Muscat are full of flavour.

North-west of Geelong, upon the summit of the foot hills of the dividing range, lies Ballarat, the head-quarters of deep quartz mining, and now no longer a diggers' camp, but a graceful city, full of shady boulevards and noble buildings, and with a stationary population of thirty thousand. My first visit was made in the company of the prime ministers of all the colonies, who were at Melbourne nominally for a conference, but really to enjoy a holiday and the Intercolonial Exhibition. With that extraordinary generosity in the spending of other people's money which distinguishes Colonial Cabinets, the Victorian Government placed special trains, horses, carriages, and hotels at our disposal, the result of which was that, fêted everywhere, we saw nothing, and I had to return to Ballarat in order even to go through the mines.

In visiting Lake Learmouth and Clunes, and the mining district on each side of Ballarat, I found myself able to discover the date of settlement by the names of places, as one finds the age of a London suburb by the titles of its terraces. The dates run in a wave across the country. St. Arnaud is a town between Ballarat and Castlemaine, and Alma lies near to it, while Balaklava Hill is near Ballarat, where also are Raglan and Sebastopol. Inkerman lies close to Castlemaine, and Mount Cathcart bears the name of the general killed at the Two-gun Battery, while the Malakhoff diggings, discovered doubtless towards the end of the war, lie to the northward, in the Wimmera.

Everywhere I found the interior far hotter than the coast, but free from the sudden changes of temperature that occur in Melbourne twice or thrice a week throughout the summer, and are dangerous to children and to persons of weak health. After two or three days of the hot wind, there comes a night, breathless, heavy, still. In the morning the sun rises, once more fierce and red. After such a night and dawn, I have seen the shade thermometer in the cool verandahs of the Melbourne Club standing at 95° before ten o'clock, when suddenly the sun and sky would change from red and brown to gold and blue, and a merry breeze, whistling up from the ice-packs of the South Pole and across the Antarctic seas, would lower the temperature in an hour to 60° or 65°. After a few days of cold and rain, a quiet English morning would be cut in half about eleven by a sudden slamming of doors and whirling of dust from the north across the town, while darkness came upon the streets. Then was heard the cry of "Shut the windows; here's a hot wind," and down would go every window, barred and bolted, while the oldest colonists walked out to enjoy the dry air and healthy heat. The thick walls of the clubs and private houses will keep out the heat for about three days, but if, as sometimes happens, the hot wind lasts longer, then the walls are heated through, and the nights are hardly to be borne. Up the country, the settlers know nothing of these changes. The regular irregularity is peculiar to the Melbourne summer.

CHAPTER X.

TASMANIA.

AFTER the parching heat of Australia, a visit to Tasmania was a grateful change. Steaming along Port Dalrymple and up the Tamar in the soft sunlight of an English afternoon, we were able to look upwards, and enjoy the charming views of wood and river, instead of having to stand with downcast head, as in the blaze of the Victorian sun.

The beauty of the Tamar is of a quiet kind: its scenery like that of the non-Alpine districts of the west coast of New Zealand, but softer and more smiling than is that of even the least rude portions of those islands. To one fresh from the baked Australian plains, there is likeness between any green and humid land and the last unparched country that he may have seen. Still, New Zealand cannot show fresher cheeks nor homes more cosy than those of the Tamar valley. Somersetshire cannot surpass the orchards of Tasmania, nor Devon match its flowers.

The natural resemblance of *Maria* Van Diemen's Land (as Tasman called it after his betrothed) to England seems to have struck the early settlers. In sailing up the Tamar, we had on one bank the county of Dorset, with its villages touchingly named after those at home, according to their situations, from its Lulworth Cove, Corfe Castle, and St. Alban's Head, round to Abbotsbury, and, on our right hand, Devon, with its Sidmouth, Exeter, and Torquay.

Hurrying through Launceston—a pretty little town, of which the banks and post-office are models of simple architecture—I passed at once across the island southwards to Hobarton, the capital. The scenery on the great convict road is not impressive. The Tasmanian mountains—detached and rugged masses of basaltic rock, from four to five thousand feet in height—are wanting in grandeur when seen from a distance, with a foreground of flat corn-land. It is disheartening, too, in an English colony, to see half the houses shut up and deserted, and acre upon acre of old wheat-land abandoned to mimosa scrub. The people in these older portions of the island have worked their lands to death, and even guano seems but to galvanize them into a momentary life. Since leaving Virginia, I had seen no such melancholy sight.

Nature is bountiful enough: in the world there is not a fairer climate; the gum-trees grow to 350 feet, attesting the richness of the soil; and the giant tree-ferns are never injured by heat, as in Australia, nor by cold, as in New Zealand. All the fruits of Europe are in season at the same time, and the Christmas dessert at Hobarton often consists of five-and-twenty distinct fresh fruits. Even more than Britain, Tasmania may be said to present in a small area an epitome of the globe: mountain and plain, forest and rolling prairie-land, rivers and grand capes, and the noblest harbour in the world, all are contained in a country the size of Ireland. It is unhappily not only in this sense that Tasmania is the Ireland of the South.

Beautiful as is the view of Hobarton from Mount Wellington, — the spurs in the foreground clothed with a crimson carpet by a heath-like plant; the city nestled under the basaltic columns of the crags,—even here it is difficult to avoid a certain gloom when the eye, sweeping over the vast expanse of Storm Bay and D'Entrecasteaux Sound, discovers only three great ships in a harbour fitted to contain the navies of the world.

The scene first of the horrible deeds of early convict days at Macquarie Harbour and Port Arthur, and later of the still more frightful massacres of the aboriginal inhabitants of the isle, Van Diemen's Land has never been a name of happy omen, and now the island, in changing its title, seems not to have escaped from the former blight. The poetry of the English village names met with throughout Tasmania vanishes before the recollection of the circumstances under which the harsher native terms came to be supplanted. Fifty years ago, our colonists found in Tasmania a powerful and numerous though degraded native race. At this moment, three old women and a lad who dwell on Gun-carriage Rock, in Bass's Straits, are all who remain of the aboriginal population of the island.

We live in an age of mild humanity, we are often told; but, whatever the polish of manner and of minds in the old country, in outlying portions of the empire there is no lack of the old savagery of our race. Battues of the natives were conducted by the military in Tasmania not more than twenty years ago, and are not unknown even now among the Queensland settlers. Let it not be thought that Englishmen go out to murder natives unprovoked; they have that provocation for which even the Spaniards in Mexico used to wait, and which the Brazilians wait for now—the provocation of robberies committed in the neighbourhood by natives unknown. It is not that there is no offence to punish, it is that the punishment is indiscriminate, that even when it falls upon the guilty it visits men who know no better. Where one wretched untaught native pilfers from a sheep-station, on the Queensland Downs, a dozen will be shot by the settlers "as an example," and the remainder of the tribe brought back to the district to be fed and kept, until whiskey, rum, and other devils' missionaries have done their work.

Nothing will persuade the rougher class of Queensland settlers that the "black-fellow" and his "jin" are human. They tell you freely that they look upon the native Australian as an ingenious kind of monkey, and that it is not for us to talk too much of the treatment of the "jins," or native women, while the "wrens" of the Curragh exist among ourselves. No great distance appears to separate us from the days when the Spaniards in the West Indies used to brand

on the face and arms all the natives they could catch, and gamble them away for wine.

Though not more than three or four million acres out of seventeen million acres of land in Tasmania have as yet been alienated by the Crown, the population has increased only by 15,000 in the last ten years. Such is the indolence of the settlers, that vast tracts of land in the central plain, once fertile under irrigation, have been allowed to fall back into a desert state from sheer neglect of the dams and conduits. Though iron and coal are abundant, they are seldom if ever worked, and one house in every thirty-two in the whole island is licensed for the sale of spirits, of which the annual consumption exceeds five gallons a head for every man, woman, and child in the population. Tasmania reached her maximum of revenue in 1858, and her maximum of trade in 1853.

The curse of the country is the indolence of its lotus-eating population, who, like all dwellers in climates cool but winterless, are content to dream away their lives in drowsiness to which the habits of a hotter but less equable clime—Queensland, for example—are energy itself. In addition, however, to this natural cause of decline, Van Diemen's Land is not yet free from all traces of the convict blood, nor from the evil effects of reliance on forced labour. It is, indeed, but a few years since the island was one great gaol, and in 1853 there were still 20,000 actual convicts in the country. The old free settlers will tell you that the deadly shade of slave labour has not blighted Jamaica more thoroughly than that of convict labour has Van Diemen's Land.

Seventy miles north-west of Hobarton is a sheet of water called Macquarie Harbour, the deeds wrought upon the shores of which are not to be forgotten in a decade. In 1823, there were 228 prisoners at Macquarie Harbour, to whom, in the year, 229 floggings and 9,925 lashes were ordered, 9,100 lashes being actually inflicted. The cat was, by order of the authorities, soaked in salt water and dried in the sun before being used. There was at Macquarie Harbour one convict overseer who took a delight in seeing his companions punished. A day seldom passed without five or six being flogged on his reports. The convicts were at his mercy. In a space of five years, during which the prisoners at Macquarie Harbour averaged 250 in number, there were 835 floggings and 32,723 lashes administered. In the same five years, 112 convicts absconded from this settlement, of whom ten were killed and eaten by their companions, seventy-five perished in the bush with or without cannibalism, two were captured with portions of human flesh in their possession, and died in hospital, two were shot, sixteen were hanged for murder and cannibalism, and seven are reported to have made good their escape, though this is by no means certain.

It has been stated by a Catholic missionary bishop in his evidence before a Royal Commission, that when, after a mutiny at one of the stations, he read out to his men the names of thirty-one condemned to death, they with one accord fell upon their knees, and solemnly thanked God that they were to be delivered from that horrible place. Men were known to commit murder that they might be sent away for trial, preferring death to Macquarie Harbour.

The escapes were often made with the deliberate expectation of death, the men perfectly knowing that they would have to draw lots for which should be killed and eaten. Nothing has ever been sworn to in the history of the world which, for revolting atrocity, can compare with the conduct of the Pierce-Greenhill party during their attempted escape. The testimony of Pierce is a revelation of the depths of degradation to which man can descend. The most fearful thought, when we hear of these Tasmanian horrors, is that probably many of those subjected to them were originally guiltless. If only one in a thousand was an innocent man, four human beings were consigned each year to hell on earth. We think, too, that the age of transportation for mere political offences has long gone by, yet it is but eleven or twelve years since Mr. Frost received his pardon, after serving for sixteen years amid the horrors of Port Arthur.

Tasmania has never been able to rid herself of the convict population in any great degree, for the free colonies have always kept a jealous watch upon her emigrants. Even at the time of the great gold-rush to Victoria, almost every "Tasmanian bolter" and many a suspected but innocent man was seized upon his landing, and thrown into Pentridge Gaol, to toil within its twenty-foot walls till death should come to his relief. Even now, men of wealth and station in Victoria are sometimes discovered to have been "bolters" in the digging times, and are at the mercy of their neighbours and the police, unless the Governor can be wheedled into granting pardons for their former deeds. A wealthy Victorian was arrested as a "Tasmanian bolter" while I was in the colony.

The passport system is still in force in the free colonies with regard to passengers arriving from penal settlements, and there is a penalty of 100*l.* inflicted upon captains of ships bringing convicts into Melbourne. The conditional pardons granted to prisoners in West Australia and in Tasmania generally contain words permitting the convict to visit any portion of the world except the British isles, but the clause is a mere dead letter, for none of our free colonies will receive even our pardoned convicts.

It is hard to quarrel with the course the colonies have taken in this matter, for to them the transportation system appears in the light of moral vitriol-throwing; still, there is a wide distinction to be drawn between the action of the New South Welsh and that of the New Yorkers, when they declared to a British Government of the last century, that nothing should induce them to accept the labour of "white English slaves:" the Sydney people have enjoyed the advantages of the system they now blame. Even the Victorians and South Australians, who have never had convicts in their land, can be met by argument. The Australian colonies, it might be urged, were planted for the sole purpose of affording a suitable soil for the reception of British criminals: in face of this fact, the remonstrances of the free colonists read somewhat oddly, for it would seem as though men who quitted, with open eyes, Great Britain to make their home in the spots which their Government had chosen as its giant prisons have little right to pretend to rouse themselves on a sudden, and cry out that England is pouring the scum of her soil on to a free land, and that they must rise and defend themselves against the grievous wrong. Weighing, however, calmly, the good and evil, we cannot avoid the conclusion that the Victorians have much reason to object to a system which sends to another country a man who is too bad for his own, just as Jersey rogues are transported to Southampton. The Victorian proposition of selecting the most ruffianly of the colonial expirees, and shipping them to England in exchange for the convicts that we might send to Australia, was but a plagiarism on the conduct of the Virginians in a similar case, who quietly began to freight a ship with snakes.

The only cure for Tasmania, unless one is to be found in the mere lapse of years, lies in annexation to Victoria; a measure strongly wished for by a considerable party in each of the colonies concerned. No two countries in the world are more manifestly destined by nature to be complementary to each other.

Owing to the small size of the country, and the great moral influence of the landed gentry, Tasmanian politics are singularly peaceful. For the Lower House elections, the suffrage rests upon a household, not a manhood basis, as in Victoria and New South Wales; and for the Upper House it is placed at 500*l*. in any property, or 50*l*. a year in freehold land. Tasmanian society is cast in a more aristocratic shape than is that of Queensland, with this exception the most oligarchical of all our colonies; but even here, as in the other colonies and the United States, the ballot is supported by the Conservatives. Unlike what generally happens in America, the vote in the great majority of cases is here kept secret, bribery is unknown, and, the public "nomination" of candidates having been abolished, elections pass off in perfect quiet. In the course of a dozen conversations in Tasmania, I met with one man who attacked the ballot. He was the first person, aristocrat or democrat, conservative or liberal, male or female, silly or wise, by whom I had found the ballot opposed since I left England.

The method in which the ballot is conducted is simple enough. The returning officer sits in an outer room, beyond which is an inner chamber with only one door, but with a desk. The voter gives his name to the returning officer, and receives a white ticket bearing his number on the register. On the ticket the names of the candidates are printed alphabetically, and the voter, taking the paper into the other room, makes a cross opposite to the name of each candidate for whom he votes, and then brings the paper folded to the returning officer, who puts it in the box. In New South Wales and Victoria, he runs his pen through all the names excepting those for which he intends to vote, and himself deposits the ticket in the box, the returning officer watching him, to see that he does not carry out his ticket to show it to his bribers, and then send it in again by a man on his own side. One scrutineer for each candidate watches the opening of the box. In New South Wales, the voting papers, after having been sealed up, are kept for five years, in order to allow of the verification of the number of votes said to have been cast; but in Tasmania they are destroyed immediately after the declaration of the poll.

Escaping from the capital and its Lilliputian politics, I sailed up the Derwent to New Norfolk. The river reminds the traveller sometimes of the Meuse, but oftener of the Dart, and unites the beauties of both streams. The scenery is exquisitely set in a framework of hops; for not only are all the flats covered with luxuriant bines, but the hills between which you survey the views have also each its "garden," the bines being trained upon a wire trellis.

A lovely ride was that from New Norfolk to the Panshanger salmon-ponds, where the acclimatization of the English fish has lately been attempted. The track, now cut along the river cliff, now lost in the mimosa scrub, offers a succession of prospects, each more charming than the one before it; and that from the ponds themselves is a repetition of the view along the vale of the Towy, from Steele's house near Caermarthen. Trout of a foot long, and salmon of an inch, rewarded us (in the spirit) for our ride, but we were called on to express our belief in the statement, that salmon "returned from the sea" have lately been seen in the river. Father ——, the Catholic parish priest, " that saw 'em," is the hero of the day, and his past experiences upon the Shannon are quoted as testimonies to his infallibility in fish questions. My hosts of New Norfolk had their fears lest the reverend gentleman should be lynched, if it were finally proved that he had been mistaken.

The salmon madness will at least have two results: the catalogue of indigenous birds will be reduced to a blank sheet, for every wretched Tasmanian bird that never saw a salmon egg in all its life is shot down and nailed to a post for fear it should eat the ova; and the British wasp will be acclimatized in the southern hemisphere. One is known to have arrived in the last box of ova, and to have survived with apparent cheerfulness his 100 days in ice. Happy fellow, to cross the line in so cool a fashion!

The chief drawbacks to Tasmanian picnics and excursions are the snakes, which are as numerous throughout the island as they are round Sydney. One of the convicts in a letter home once wrote: " Parrots is as thick as crows, and snakes is very bad, fourteen to sixteen feet long;" but in sober truth the snakes are chiefly small.

The wonderful "snake stories" that in the colonial papers take the place of the English "triple birth" and "gigantic gooseberry" are all written in vacation time by the students at Melbourne University, but a true one that I heard in Hobarton is too good to be lost. The Chief Justice of the island, who, in his leisure time, is an amateur naturalist, and collects specimens for European collections in his walks, told me that it was his practice, after killing a snake, to carry it into Hobarton tied to a stick by a double lashing. A few days before my visit, on entering his hall, where an hour before he had hung his stick with a rare snake in readiness for the Government naturalist, he found to his horror that the viper had been only scotched, and that he had made use of his regained life to free himself from the string which confined his head and neck. He was still tied by the tail, so he was swinging to and fro, or "squirming around," as some Americans would say, with open mouth and protruded tongue. When lassoing with a piece of twine had been tried in vain, my friend fetched a gun, and succeeded in killing the snake and much damaging the stone-work of his vestibule.

After a week's sojourn in the neighbourhood of Hobarton, I again crossed the island, but this time by a night of piercing moonlight such as can be witnessed only in the dry air of the far south. High in the heavens, and opposite the moon, was the solemn constellation of the Southern Cross, sharply relieved upon the pitchy background of the Magellanic clouds, while the weird-tinted stars which vary the night-sky of the southern hemisphere stood out from the blue firmament elsewhere. The next day I was again in Melbourne.

CHAPTER XI.

CONFEDERATION.

MELBOURNE is unusually gay, for at a shapely palace in the centre of the city the second great Intercolonial Exhibition is being held, and, as its last days are drawing to their close, fifty thousand people—a great number for the colonies—visit the building every week. There are exhibitors from each of our seven southern colonies, and from French New Caledonia, Netherlandish India, and the Mauritius. It is strange to remember now that in the colonization both of New Zealand and of Australia, we were the successful rivals of the French only after having been behind them in awakening to the advisability of an occupation of those countries. In the case of New Zealand, the French fleet was anticipated three several times by the forethought and decision of our naval officers on the station and in the case of Australia, the whole south coast was actually named "La Terre Napoléon," and surveyed for colonization by Captain Baudin in 1800. New Caledonia, on the other hand, was named and occupied by ourselves, and afterwards abandoned to the French.

The present remarkable exhibition of the products of the Australias, coming just at the time when the border customs between Victoria and New South Wales have been abolished by agreement, and when all seems to point to the formation of a customs union between the colonies, leads men to look still further forward, and to expect confederation. It is worthy of notice at this conjuncture that the Australian Protectionists, as a rule, refuse to be protected against their immediate neighbours, just as those of America protect the manufactures of the Union rather than of single states. They tell us that they can point, with regard to Europe, to pauper labour, but that they have no case as against the sister colonies; they wish, they say, to obtain a wide market for the sale of the produce of each colony; the nationality they would create is to be Australian, not provincial.

Already there is postal union, and a partial customs union, and confederation itself, however distant in fact, has been very lately brought about in the spirit by the efforts of the London press, one well-known paper having three times in a single article called the Governor of New South Wales by the sounding title of "Governor-General of the Australasian colonies," to which he has, of course, not the faintest claim.

There are many difficulties in the way of confederation. The leading merchants and squatters of Victoria are in favour of it; but not so those of the poorer or less populous colonies, where there is much fear of being swamped. The costliness of the federal government of New Zealand is a warning against over hasty confederation. Victoria, too, would probably insist upon the exclusion of West Australia, on account of her convict population. The continental theory is undreamt of by Australians, owing to their having always been inhabitants of comparatively small states, and not, like dwellers in the organized territories of America, potentially citizens of a vast and homogeneous empire.

The choice of capital will, here as in Canada, be a matter of peculiar difficulty. It is to be hoped by all lovers of freedom that some hitherto unknown village will be selected. There is in all great cities a strong tendency to Imperialism. Bad pavement, much noise, narrow lanes, blockaded streets, all these things are ill dealt with by free government, we are told. Englishmen who have been in Paris, Americans who know St. Petersburg, forgetting that without the Emperor the Préfet is impossible, cry out that London, that New York, in their turn need a Haussmann. In this tendency lies a terrible danger to free States—a danger avoided, however, or greatly lessened, by the seat of the Legislature being placed, as in Canada and the United States, far away from the great cities. Were Melbourne to become the seat of government, nothing could prevent the distant colonies from increasing the already gigantic power of that city by choosing her merchants as their representatives.

The bearing of confederation upon Imperial interests is a more simple matter. Although union will tend to the earlier independence of the colonies, yet, if federated, they are more likely to be a valuable ally than they could be if remaining so many separate countries. They would also be a stronger enemy; but distance will make all their wars naval, and a strong fleet would be more valuable to us as a friend than dangerous as an enemy, unless in the case of a coalition against us, in which it would probably not be the interest of Australia to join.

From the colonial point of view, federation would tend to secure to the Australians better general and local government than they possess at present. It is absurd to expect that colonial governors should be upon good terms with their charges when we shift men every four years—say from Demerara to New South Wales, or from Jamaica to Victoria. The unhappy governor loses half a year in moving to his post, and a couple of years in coming to understand the circumstances of his new province, and then settles down to be successful in the ruling of educated whites under democratic institutions only if he can entirely throw aside the whole of his experience, derived as it will probably have been from the despotic sway over blacks. We never can have a set of colonial governors fit for Australia until the Australian governments are made a distinct service, and entirely separated from those of the West Indies, of Africa, and Hong Kong.

Besides improving the government, confederation would lend to every colonist the dignity derived from citizenship of a great country—a point the importance of which will not be contested by any one who has been in America since the war.

It is not easy to resist the conclusion that confederation is in every way desirable. If it leads to independence, we must say to the Australians what Houmai ta Whiti said in his great speech to the progenitors of the Maori race when they were quitting Hawaiki: "Depart, and dwell in peace; let there be no quarrelling amongst you, but build up a great people."

CHAPTER XII.

ADELAIDE.

THE capital of South Australia is reputed the hottest of all the cities that are chiefly inhabited by the English race, and as I neared it through the Backstairs Passage into the Gulf of St. Vincent, past Kangaroo Island, and still more when I landed at Glenelg, I came to the conclusion that its reputation was deserved. The extreme heat which characterizes South Australia is to some extent a consequence of its lying as far north as New South Wales and Queensland, and so far inland as to escape the breeze by which their coasts are visited; for although by "South Australia" we should, in the southern hemisphere, naturally understand that portion of Australia which was furthest from the tropics, yet it is a curious fact that the whole colony of Victoria is to the south of Adelaide, and that nearly all the northernmost points of the continent now lie within the country misnamed "South Australia."

The immense northern territory, being supposed to be valueless, has generously been handed over to South Australia, which thus becomes the widest of all British colonies, and nearly as large as English

Hindostan. If the present great expenditure succeeds in causing the discovery of any good land at the north, it will of course at once be made a separate colony. The only important result that seems likely to follow from this annexation of the northern territory to South Australia is that schoolboys' geography will suffer; one would expect, indeed, that a total destruction of all principle in the next generation will be the inevitable result of so rude a blow to confidence in books and masters as the assurance from a teacher's lips that the two most remote countries of Australia are united under one colonial government, and that the northernmost points of the whole continent are situated in South Australia. Boys will probably conclude that, across the line, south becomes north and north south, and that in Australia the sun rises in the west.

Instead of gold, wheat, sheep, as in Victoria, the staples here are wheat, sheep, copper; and my introduction to South Australia was characteristic of the colony, for I found in Port Adelaide, where I first set foot, not only every store filled to overflowing, but piles of wheat-sacks in the roadways, and lines of wheat-cars on the sidings of railways, without even a tarpaulin to cover the grain.

Of all the mysteries of commerce, those that concern the wheat and flour trade are, perhaps, the strangest to the uninitiated. Breadstuffs are still sent from California and Chili to Victoria, yet from Adelaide, close at hand, wheat is being sent to England and flour to New York!

ADELAIDE.

There can be no doubt but that ultimately Victoria and Tasmania will at least succeed in feeding themselves. It is probable that neither New Zealand nor Queensland will find it to their interest to do the like. Wool-growing in the former and cotton and wool in the latter will continue to pay better than wheat in the greater portion of their lands. Their granary, and that possibly of the city of Sydney itself, will be found in South Australia, especially if land capable of carrying wheat be discovered to the westward of the settlements about Adelaide. That the Australias, Chili, California, Oregon, and other Pacific States can ever export largely of wheat to Europe is more than doubtful. If manufactures spring up on this side the world, these countries, whatever their fertility, will have at least enough to do to feed themselves.

As I entered the streets of the "farinaceous village," as Adelaide is called by conceited Victorians, I was struck with the amount of character they exhibit both in the way of buildings, of faces, and of dress. The South Australians have far more idea of adapting their houses and clothes to their climate than have the people of the other colonies, and their faces adapt themselves. The verandahs to the shops are sufficiently close to form a perfect piazza; the people rise early, and water the side-walk in front of their houses; and you never meet a man who does not make some sacrifice to the heat, in the shape of puggree, silk coat, or sun-helmet; but the women are nearly as unwise here as in the other colonies, and persist in going about in shawls and coloured dresses.

Might they but see a few of the Richmond or Baltimore ladies in their pure white muslin frocks, and die of envy, for the dress most suited to a hot dry climate is also the most beautiful under its bright sun.

The German element is strong in South Australia, and there are whole villages in the wheat-country where English is never spoken; but here, as in America, there has been no mingling of the races, and the whole divergence from the British types is traceable to climatic influences, and especially dry heat. The men born here are thin, and fine-featured, somewhat like the Pitcairn Islanders, while the women are all alike—small, pretty, and bright, but with a burnt-up look. The haggard eye might, perhaps, be ascribed to the dreaded presence of my old friend of the Rocky Mountains, the brulot sand-fly. The inhabitants of all hot dry countries speak from the head, and not the chest, and the English in Australia are acquiring this habit; you seldom find a "cornstalk" who speaks well from the chest.

The air is crisp and hot—crisper and hotter even than that of Melbourne. The shaded thermometer upon the Victorian coast seldom reaches 110°, but in the town of Adelaide, 117° has been recorded by the Government astronomer. Such is the figure of the Australian continent, that Adelaide, although a seaport town, lies, as it were, inland. Catching the heated gales from three of the cardinal points, Adelaide has a summer six months long, and is exposed to a fearful continuance of hot winds; nevertheless, 105° at Adelaide is easier borne than 95° in the shade at Sydney.

Nothing can be prettier than the outskirts of the capital. In laying out Adelaide, its founders have reserved a park about a quarter of a mile in width all round the city. This gives a charming drive nine miles long, outside which again are the olive-yards and villas of the citizens. Hedges of the yellow cactus, or of the graceful Kangaroo Island acacia, bound the gardens, and the pomegranate, magnolia, fig, and aloe grow upon every lawn. Five miles to the eastward are the cool wooded hills of the Mount Lofty Range, on the tops of which are grown the English fruits for which the plains afford no shade or moisture.

Crossing the Adelaide plains, for fifty miles by railway, to Kapunda, I beheld one great wheat-field without a break. The country was finer than any stretch of equal extent in California or Victoria, and looked as though the crops were "standing"—which in one sense they were, though the grain was long since "in." The fact is that they use the Ridley machines, by which the ears are thrashed out without any cutting of the straw, which continues to stand, and is finally ploughed in at the farmer's leisure, except in the neighbourhood of Adelaide. There would be a golden age of partridge-shooting in Old England did the climate and the price of straw allow of the adoption of the Ridley reaper. Under this system, South Australia grows on the average six times as much wheat as she can use, whereas, if reaping had to be paid for, she could only grow from one and a half times to twice as much as would meet the home demand.

In this country, as in America, "bad farming" is found to pay, for with cheap land, the Ridley reaper, and good markets, light crops without labour, except the peasant-proprietor's own toil, pay well when heavy crops obtained by the use of hired labour would not reimburse the capitalist. The amount of land under cultivation has been trebled in the last seven years, and half a million acres are now under wheat. South Australia has this year produced seven times as much grain as she can consume, and twelve acres are under wheat for every adult male of the population of the colony.

A committee has been lately sitting in New South Wales "to consider the state of the colony." To judge from the evidence taken before it, the members seemed to have conceived that their task was to inquire why South Australia prospered above New South Wales. Frugality of the people, especially of the Germans, and fertility of the soil were the reasons which they gave for the result, but it is impossible not to see that the success of South Australia is but another instance of the triumph of small proprietors, of whom there are now some seven or eight thousand in the colony, and who were brought here by the adoption of the Wakefield land system.

In the early days of the colony, land was sold at a good price in 130-acre sections, with one acre of townland to each agricultural section. Now, under rules made at home, but confirmed after the introduction of self-government, land is sold by auction, with a reserved price of 1*l.* an acre, but when once a block has passed the hammer, it can for ever be taken up at 1*l.* the acre without further competition. The Land Fund is kept separate from the other revenue, and a few permanent charges, such as that for the aborigines, being paid out of it, the remainder is divided into three portions, of which two are destined for public works, and one for immigration.

There is a marvellous contrast to be drawn between the success which has attended the Wakefield system in South Australia and the total failure, in the neighbouring colony of West Australia, of the old system, under which, vast tracts of land being alienated for small prices to the Crown, there remains no fund for introducing that abundant supply of labour without which the land is useless.

Adelaide is so distant from Europe that no immigrants come of themselves, and, in the assisted importation of both men and women, the relative proportions of English, Scotch, and Irish that exist at home are carefully preserved, by which simple precaution the colony is saved from an organic change of type, such as that which threatens all America, although it would, of course, be idle to deny that the restriction is aimed against the Irish.

The greatest difficulty of young countries lies in the want of women: not only is this a bar to the natural increase of population; it is a deficiency preventive of permanency, destructive of religion: where woman is not there can be no home, no country.

How to obtain a supply of marriageable girls is a question which Canada, Tasmania, South Australia, and New South Wales, have each in their turn attempted to solve by the artificial introduction of Irish workhouse girls. The difficulty apparently got rid of, we begin to find that it is not so much as fairly seen; we have yet to look it "squarely" in the face. The point of the matter is that we should find not girls, but honest girls, — not women merely, but women fit to bear families in a free State.

One of the colonial superintendents, writing of a lately-received batch of Irish workhouse girls, has said that, if these are the "well-conducted girls, he should be curious to see a few of the evil-disposed." While in South Australia, I read the details of the landing of a similar party of women, from Limerick workhouse, one Sunday afternoon at Point Levi, the Lambeth of Quebec. Although supplied by the city authorities with meat and drink, and ordered to leave for Montreal at early morning, nothing could be more abominable than their conduct in the meanwhile. They sold baggage, bonnets, combs, cloaks, and scarves, keeping on nothing but their crinolines and senseless finery. With the pence they thus collected they bought corn-whiskey, and in a few hours were yelling, fighting, swearing, wallowing in beastly drunkenness; and by the time the authorities came down to pack them off by train, they were as fiends, mad with rum and whiskey. At five in the morning, they reached the Catholic Home at Montreal, where the pious nuns were shocked and horrified at their grossness of conduct and lewd speech; nothing should force them, they declared, ever again to take into their peaceable asylum the Irish workhouse girls. This was no exceptional case: the reports from South Australia, from Tasmania, can show as bad; and in Canada such conduct on the part of the freshly-landed girls is common. A Tasmanian magistrate has stated in evidence before a Parliamentary Committee that once when his wife was in ill health he went to one of the immigration offices, and applied for a decent woman to attend on a sick lady. The woman was sent down, and found next day in her room lying on the bed in a state best pictured in her own words: "Here I am with my yard of clay, blowing a cloud, you *say*."

It is evident that a batch of thoroughly bad girls cost a colony from first to last, in the way of prisons, hospitals, and public morals, ten times as much as would the free passages across the seas of an equal number of worthy Irish women, free from the workhouse taint. Of one of these gangs which landed in Quebec not many years ago, it has been asserted by the immigration superintendents that the traces are visible to this day, for wherever the women went, "sin, and shame, and death were in their track." The Irish unions have no desire in the matter beyond that of getting rid of their most abandoned girls; their interests and those of the colonies they supply are diametrically opposed. No inspection, no agreements, no supervision can be effective in the face of facts like these. The class that the unions can afford to send, Canada and Tasmania cannot afford to keep. Women are sent out with babies in their arms; no one will take them into service because the children are in the way, and in a few weeks they fall chargeable on one of the colonial benevolent societies, to be kept till the children grow up or the mothers die. Even when the girls are not so wholly vicious as to be useless in service, they are utterly ignorant of everything they ought to know. Of neither domestic nor farm-work have they a grain of knowledge. Of thirteen who were lately sent to an up-country town, but one knew how to cook, or wash, or milk, or iron, while three of them had agreed to refuse employment unless they were engaged to serve together. The agents are at their wits' ends; either the girls are so notoriously infamous in their ways of life that no one will hire them, or else they are so extravagant in their new-found "independence" that they on their side will not be hired. Meanwhile the Irish authorities lay every evil upon the long sea voyage. They say that they select the best of girls, but that a few days at sea suffice to demoralize them.

The colonies could not do better than combine for the establishment of a new and more efficient emigration agency in Ireland. To avoid the evil, by as far as possible refusing to meet it face to face, South Australia has put restrictions on her Irish immigration; for there as in America it is found that the

Scotch and Germans are the best of immigrants. The Scotch are not more successful in Adelaide than everywhere in the known world. Half the most prominent among the statesmen of the Canadian Confederation, of Victoria, and of Queensland, are born Scots, and all the great merchants of India are of the same nation. Whether it be that the Scotch emigrants are for the most part men of better education than those of other nations, of whose citizens only the poorest and most ignorant are known to emigrate, or whether the Scotchman owes his uniform success in every climate to his perseverance or his shrewdness, the fact remains, that wherever abroad you come across a Scotchman, you invariably find him prosperous and respected.

The Scotch emigrant is a man who leaves Scotland because he wishes to rise faster and higher than he can at home, whereas the emigrant Irishman quits Galway or County Cork only because there is no longer food or shelter for him there. The Scotchman crosses the seas in calculating contentment; the Irishman in sorrow and despair.

At the Burra Burra and Kapunda copper-mines there is not much to see, so my last days in South Australia were given to the political life of the colony, which present one singular feature. For the elections to the Council or Upper House, for which the franchise is a freehold worth 50*l.*, or a leasehold of 20*l.* a year, the whole country forms but a single district, and the majority elect their men. In a country where party feeling runs high, such a system would evidently unite almost all the evils conceivable in a plan of representation, but in a peaceful colony it undoubtedly works well. Having absolute power in their hands, the majority here, as in the selection of a governor for an American state, use their position with great prudence, and make choice of the best men that the country can produce. The franchise for the Lower House, for the elections to which the colony is "districted," is the simple one of six months' residence, which with the ballot works irreproachably.

The day that I left Adelaide was also that upon which Captain Cadell, the opener of the Murray to trade, sailed with his naval expedition to fix upon a capital for the Northern territory; that coast of tropical Australia which faces the Moluccas. As Governor Gilpin had pressed me to stay, he pressed me to go with him, making as an inducement a promise to name after me either "a city" or a headland. He said he should advise me to select the headland, because that would remain, whereas the city probably would not. When I pleaded that he had no authority to carry passengers, he offered to take me as his surgeon. Hitherto the expeditions have discovered nothing but natives, mangroves, alligators, and sea-slugs; and the whole of the money received from capitalists at home, for 300,000 acres of land to be surveyed and handed over to them in North Australia, being now exhausted, the Government are seriously thinking of reimbursing the investors and giving up the search for land. It would be as cheap to colonize equatorial Africa from Adelaide, as tropical Australia.

If the Northern territory is ever to be rendered habitable, it must be by Queensland that the work is done.

It is not certain that North Australia may not be found to yield gold in plenty. In a little-known manuscript of the seventeenth century, the north-west of Australia is called " The land of gold;" and we are told that the fishermen of Solor, driven on to this land of gold by stress of weather, picked up in a few hours their boat full of gold nuggets, and returned in safety. They never dared repeat their voyage, on account of their dread of the unknown seas; but Manoel Godinho de Eredia was commissioned by the Portuguese Lord Admiral of India to explore this gold land, and enrich the Crown of Portugal by the capture of the treasures it contained. It would be strange enough if gold came to be discovered on the northwest coast, in the spot from which the Portuguese reported their discovery.

By dawn, after one of the most stifling of Australian nights, I left Port Adelaide for King George's Sound. A long narrow belt of a clear red-yellow light lay glowing along the horizon to the east, portending heat and drought; elsewhere the skies were of a deep blue-black. As we steamed past Kangaroo Island, and through Investigator Straits, the sun shot up from the tawny plains, and the hot wind from the northern desert, rising on a sudden after the stillness of the night, whirled clouds of sand over the surface of the bay.

CHAPTER XIII.

TRANSPORTATION.

AFTER five days' steady steaming across the great Australian bight, north of which lies the true "Terra Australis incognita," I reached King George's Sound—"Le Port du Roi Georges en Australie," as I saw it written on a letter in the gaol. At the shore end of a great land-locked harbour, the little houses of bright white stone that make up the town of Albany peep out from among geranium-covered rocks. The climate, unlike that of the greater portion of Australia, is damp and tropical, and the dense scrub is a mass of flowering bushes, with bright blue and scarlet blooms and curiously-cut leaves.

The contrast between the scenery and the people of West Australia is great indeed. The aboriginal inhabitants of Albany were represented by a tribe of filthy natives—tall, half-starved, their heads bedaubed with red ochre, and their faces smeared with yellow clay; the "colonists" by a gang of fiend-faced convicts working in chains upon the esplanade, and a group of scowling expirees hunting a monkey with bull-dogs on the pier; while the native women, half clothed in tattered kangaroo-skins, came slouching past with an aspect of defiant wretchedness. Work is never done in West Australia unless under the compulsion of the lash, for a similar degradation of labour is produced by the use of convicts as by that of slaves.

Settled at an earlier date than was South Australia, West Australia, then called Swan River, although one of the oldest of the colonies, was so soon ruined by the free gift to the first settlers of vast territories useless without labour, that in 1849 she petitioned to be made a penal settlement, and though at the instance of Victoria transportation to the Australias has now all but ceased, Freemantle Prison is still the most considerable convict establishment we possess across the seas.

At the time of my visit, there were 10,000 convicts or emancipists within the "colony," of whom 1,500 were in prison, 1,500 in private service on tickets-of-leave, while 1,500 had served out their time, and over 5,000 had been released upon conditional pardons. 600 of the convicts had arrived from England in 1865. Out of a total population, free and convict, of 20,000, the offenders in the year had numbered nearly 3,500, or more than one-sixth of the people, counting women and children.

If twenty years of convict labour seem to have done but little for the settlement, they have at least enabled us to draw the moral, that transportation and free immigration cannot exist side by side: the one element must overbear and destroy the other. In Western Australia, the convicts and their keepers form two-thirds of the whole population, and the district is a great English prison, not a colony, and exports but a little wool, a little sandal-wood, and a little cotton.

Western Australia is as unpopular with the convicts as with free settlers: fifty or sixty convicts have successfully escaped from the settlement within the last few years. From twenty to thirty escapes take place annually, but the men are usually recaptured within a month or two, although sheltered by the people, the vast majority of whom are ticket-of-leave men or ex-convicts. Absconders receive a hundred lashes and one year in the chain-gang, yet from sixty to seventy unsuccessful attempts are reported every year.

On the road between Albany and Hamilton I saw a man at work in ponderous irons. The sun was striking down on him in a way that none can fancy who have no experience of Western Australia or Bengal, and his labour was of the heaviest; now he had to prise up huge rocks with a crowbar, now to handle pick and shovel, now to use the rammer, under the eye of an armed warder, who idled in the shade by the road-side. This was an "escape-man," thus treated with a view to cause him to cease his continual endeavours to get away from Albany. No wonder that the "chain-gang" system is a failure, and the number both of attempts and actual escapes larger under it than before the introduction of this tremendous punishment.

Many of the "escapes" are made with no other view than to obtain a momentary change of scene. On the last return trip of the ship in which I sailed from Adelaide to King George's Sound, a convict coalman was found built up in the coal-heap on deck: he and his mates at Albany had drawn lots to settle which of them should be thus packed off by the help of the others "for a change." Of ultimate escape there could be no chance; the coal on deck could not fail to be exhausted within a day or two after leaving port, and this they knew. When he emerged, black, half-smothered, and nearly starved, from his hiding-place, he allowed himself to be quietly ironed, and so kept till the ship reached Adelaide, when he was given up to the authorities, and sent back to Albany for punishment. Acts of this class are common enough to have received a name. The offenders are called "bolters for a change."

A convict has been known, when marching in his gang, suddenly to lift up his spade, and split the skull of the man who walked in front of him, thus courting a certain death for no reason but to escape from the monotony of toil. Another has doubled his punishment for fun by calling out to the magistrates: "Gentlemen, pray remember that I am entitled to an iron-gang, because this is the second time of my absconding."

One of the strangest things about the advance of England is the many-sided character of the form of early settlement: Central North America we plant with Mormons, New Zealand with the runaways of our whaling ships, Tasmania and portions of Australia with our transported felons. Transportation has gone through many phases since the system took its rise in the exile to the colonies under Charles II. of the moss-troopers of Northumberland. The plan of forcing the exiles to labour as slaves on the plantations was introduced in the reign of George II., and by an Act then passed offenders were actually put up to auction, and knocked down to men who undertook to transport them, and make what they could of their labour. In 1786, an Order in Council named the eastern coast of Australia and the adjacent islands as the spot to which transportation beyond the seas should be directed, and in 1787 the black bar was drawn indelibly across the page of history which records the foundation of the colony of New South Wales. From that time to the present day the world has witnessed the portentous sight of great countries in which the major portion of the people, the whole of the handicraftsmen, are convicted felons.

There being no free people whatever in the " colonies" when first formed, the Governors had no choice but to appoint convicts to all the official situations. The consequence was robbery and corruption. Recorded sentences were altered by the convict-clerks, free pardons and grants of land were sold for money. The convict overseers forced their gangmen to labour not for Government, but for themselves, securing secresy by the unlimited supply of rum to the men, who in turn bought native women with all that they could spare. On the sheep-stations whole herds were stolen, and those from neighbouring lands driven in to show on muster-days. Enormous fortunes were accumulated by some of the emancipists, by fraud and infamy rather than by prudence, we are told, and a vast number of convicts were soon at large in Sydney town itself, without the knowledge of the police. As the settlements waxed in years and size, the sons of convict parents grew up in total ignorance, while such few free settlers as arrived—"the ancients," as they were styled, or "the ancient nobility of Botany Bay"—were wholly dependent on convict tutors for the education of their children—the "cornstalks" and "currency girls;" and cock-fighting was the chief amusement of both sexes. The newspapers were without exception conducted by gentlemen convicts, or "specials," as they were called, who were assigned to the editors for that purpose, and the police-force itself was composed of ticket-of-leave men and "emancipists." Convicts were thus the only schoolmasters, the only governesses, the only nurses, the only journalists, and, as there were even convict clergymen and convict university professors, the training of the youth of the land was committed almost exclusively to the felon's care.

A petition sent home from Tasmania in 1848 is simple and pathetic; it is from the parents and guardians resident in Van Diemen's Land. They set forth that there are 13,000 children growing up in the colony, that within six years alone 24,000 convicts have been turned into the island, and of these but 4,000 women. The result is that their children are brought up in the midst of profligacy and degradation.

The lowest depth of villany, if in such universal infamy degrees can be conceived, was to be met with in the parties working in the "chain-gangs" on the roads. "Assignees" too bad even for the whip of the harshest, or the "beef and beer" of the most lenient master, brutalised still further, if that were possible, by association with those as vile as themselves, and followed about the country by women too infamous even for service in the houses of the up-country settlers, or in the gin-palaces of the towns, worked in gangs upon the roads by day, whenever promises of spirits or the hope of tobacco could induce them to work at all, and found a compensation for such unusual toil in nightly quitting their camp, and traversing the country, robbing and murdering those they met, and sacking every homestead that lay in their track.

The clerk in charge of one of the great convict barracks was himself a convict, and had an understanding with the men under his care that they might prowl about at night and rob, on condition that they should share their gains with him, and that, if they were found out, he should himself prosecute them for being absent without leave. Juries were composed either of convicts, or of publicans dependent on the convicts for their livelihood, and convictions were of necessity extremely rare. In a plain case of murder the judge was known to say, "If I don't attend to the recommendation to mercy, these fellows will never find a man guilty again;" and jurymen would frequently hand down notes to the counsel for the defence, and bid him give himself no trouble, as they intended to acquit their friend.

The lawyers were mostly convicts, and perjury in the courts was rife. It has been given in evidence before a Royal Commission by a magistrate of New South Wales, that a Sydney free immigrant once had a tailor's bill sent in which he did not owe, he having been but a few weeks in the colony. He instructed a lawyer, and did not himself appear in court. He afterwards heard that he had won his case, for the tailor had sworn to the bill, but the immigrant's lawyer, "to save trouble," had called a witness who swore to having paid it, which settled the case. Sometimes there were not only convict witnesses and convict jurors, but convict judges.

The assignment system was supposed to be a great improvement upon the gaol, but its only certain result was that convict master and convict man used to get drunk together, while a night never passed without a burglary in Sydney. Many of the convicts' mistresses went out from England as Government free emigrants, taking with them funds subscribed by the thieves at home and money obtained by the robberies for which their "fancy men" had been convicted; and on their arrival at Sydney succeeded in getting their paramours assigned to them as convict servants. Such was the disparity of the sexes that the term "wife" was a mockery, and the Female Emigration Society and the Government vied with each other in sending out to Sydney the worst women in all London, to reinforce the ranks of the convict girls of the Paramatta factory. Even among the free settlers, marriage soon became extremely rare. Convicts were at the head of the colleges and benevolent asylums; the custom-house officials were all convicts;

one of the occupants of the office of Attorney-General took for his clerk a notorious convict, who was actually re-committed to Bathurst after his appointment, and yet allowed to return to Sydney and resume his duties.

The most remarkable peculiarity of the assignment system was its gross uncertainty. Some assigned convicts spent their time working for high wages, living and drinking with their masters; others were mere slaves. Whether, however, he be in practice well or ill treated, in the assignment or apprenticeship system the convict is, under whatever name, a slave, subject to the caprice of a master who, though he cannot himself flog his "servant," can have him flogged by writing a note or sending his compliments to his neighbour the magistrate on the next run or farm. The "whipping-houses" of Mississippi and Alabama had their parallel in New South Wales; a look or word would cause the hurrying of the servant to the post or the forge as a preliminary to a month in the chain-gang "on the roads." On the other hand, under the assignment system nothing can prevent skilled convict workmen being paid and pampered by their masters, whose interest it evidently becomes to get out of them all the work possible, by excessive indulgence, as intelligent labour cannot be produced through the machinery of the whipping-post, but may be through that of "beef and beer."

Whatever may have been the true interest of the free settlers, cruelty was in practice commoner than indulgence. Fifty and a hundred lashes, months of solitary confinement, years of labour in chains on the roads, were laid upon convicts for such petty offences as brawling, drunkenness, and disobedience. In 1835, among the 28,000 convicts then in New South Wales, there were 22,000 summary convictions for disorderly or dishonest conduct, and in a year the average was 3,000 floggings, and above 100,000 lashes. In Tasmania, where the convicts then numbered 15,000, the summary convictions were 15,000 and the lashes 50,000 a year.

The criminal returns of Tasmania and New South Wales contain the condemnation of the transportation system. In the single year of 1834, one-seventh of the free population of Van Diemen's Land were summarily convicted of drunkenness. In that year, in a population of 37,000, 15,000 were convicted before the courts for various offences. Over a hundred persons a year were at that time sentenced to death in New South Wales alone. Less than a fourth of the convicts served their time without incurring additional punishment from the police, but those who thus escaped proved in after-life the worst of all, and even Government officials were forced into admitting that transportation demoralized far more persons than it reformed. Hundreds of assigned convicts made their escape to the back country, and became bushrangers; many got down to the coast, and crossed to the Pacific islands, whence they spread the infamies of New South Wales throughout all Polynesia. A Select Committee of the House of Commons reported, in words characteristic of our race, that these convicts committed, in New Zealand and the Pacific, "outrages at which humanity shudders," and which were to be deplored as being "injurious to our commercial interests in that quarter of the globe."

Transportation to New South Wales came to its end none too soon: in fifty years 75,000 convicts had been transported to that colony, and 30,000 to the little island of Tasmania in twenty years.

Were there no other argument for the discontinuance of transportation, it would be almost enough to say that the life in the convict-ship itself makes the reformation of transported criminals impossible. Where many bad men are brought together, the few not wholly corrupt who may be among them have no opportunity for speech, and the grain of good that may exist in every heart can have no chance for life; if not inclination, pride at least leads the "old hand" to put down all acts that are not vile, all words that are not obscene. Those who have sailed in convict company say that there is something terrible in the fiendish delight that the "old hands" take in watching the steady degradation of the "new chums." The hardened criminals invariably meet the less vile with outrage, ridicule, and contempt, and the better men soon succumb to ruffians who have crime for their profession, and for all their relaxation vice.

To describe the horrors of the convict-ships, we are told, would be impossible. The imagination will scarce suffice to call up dreams so hideous. Four months of filthiness in a floating hell sink even the least bad to the level of unteachable brutality. Mutiny is unknown; the convicts are their own masters and the ship's, but the shrewd callousness of the old gaol-bird teaches all that there is nothing to be gained even by momentary success. Rage and violence are seldom seen, but there is a humour that is worse than blows,—conversation that transcends all crime in infamy.

It will be long before the last traces of convict disease disappear from Tasmania and New South Wales; the gold-find has done much to purify the air, free selection may lead to a still more bright advance, manufacturing may lend its help; but years must go by before Tasmania can be prosperous or Sydney moral. Their history is not only valuable as a guide to those who have to save West Australia, as General Bourke and Mr. Wentworth saved New South Wales, but as an example, not picked from ancient rolls, but from the records of a system founded within the memory of living man, and still existent, of what transportation must necessarily be, and what it may easily become.

The results of a dispassionate survey of the transportation system in the abstact are far from satisfactory. If deportation be considered as a punishment, it would be hard to find a worse. Punishment should be equable, reformatory, deterrent, cheap. Transportation is the most costly of all the punishments that are known to us; it is subject to variations that cannot be guarded against; it is severest to the least guilty and slightest to the most hardened; it morally destroys those who have some good remaining in them; it leaves the ruffianly malefactor worse if possible than it finds him; and, while it is frightfully cruel and vindictive in its character, it is useless as a deterrent because its nature is unknown at home. Transportation to the English thief means exile, and nothing more; it is only after conviction, when far away from his uncaught associates, that he comes to find it worse than death. Instead of deterring, transportation tempts to crime; instead of reforming, it debases the bad, and confirms in villany the already infamous. To every bad man it gives the worst companions; the infamous are to be reformed by association with the vile; while its effects upon the colonies are described in every petition of the settlers, and testified to by the whole history of our plantations in the antipodes, and by the present condition of West Australia. We have come at last to transportation in its most limited and restricted sense; the only remaining step is to be quit of it altogether.

In conjunction with all punishment, we should secure some means of separating the men one from another as soon as the actual punishment is terminated: to settle them on land, to settle them with wives where possible, should be our object. The work which really has in it something of reformation is that which a man has to do, not in order that he may avoid whipping, but that he may escape starvation; and it is from this point of view that transportation is defensible. A man, however bad, will generally become a useful member of society and a not altogether neglectful father if allowed to settle upon land away from his old companions; but morbid tendencies of every kind are strengthened by close association with others who are labouring under a like infirmity: and where the former convicts are allowed to hang together in towns, nothing is to be expected better than that which is actually found—namely, a state of society where wives speedily become as villanous as their husbands, and where children are brought up to emulate their fathers' crimes.

To keep the men separate from each other, after the expiration of the sentence, we need to send the convicts to a fairly populous country, whence arises this great difficulty: if we send convicts to a populous colony, we are met at once by a cry that we are forcing the workmen of the colony into a one-sided competition; that we are offering an unbearable insult to the free population; that, in attempting to reform the felon, by allowing him to be absorbed into the colonial society, we are degrading and corrupting the whole community on the chance of possible benefit to our English villain. On the other hand, if we send our convicts to an uninhabited land, such as New South Wales and Tasmania were, such as West Australia is now, we build up an artificial Pandemonium, whither we convey at the public cost the pick and cream of the ruffians of the world, to form a community of which each member must be sufficiently vile of himself to corrupt a nation.

If by care the difficulty of which I have spoken can be avoided, transportation might be replaced by short sentences, solitary confinement, and low diet, to be followed by forced exile, under regulations, to some selected colony, such as the Ghauts of Eastern Africa, opposite to Madagascar, or the highlands that skirt the Zambesi River. Exile after punishment may often be the only way of providing for convicts who would otherwise be forced to return to their former ways. The difficulties in the path of discharged convicts seeking employment are too terrible for them not to accept joyfully a plan for emigration to a country where they are unknown.

In Western Australia transportation has not been made subservient to colonization, and both in consequence have failed.

On going on board the *Bombay* at King George's Sound, I at once found myself in the East. The captain's crew of Malays, the native cooks in long white gowns, the Bombay serangs in dark blue turbans, red cummerbunds, and green or yellow trousers; the negro or Abyssinian stokers; the passengers in coats of China-grass; the Hindoo deck-sweepers playing on their tomtoms in the intervals of work; the punkahs below; the Hindostanee names for everything on deck; and, above all, the general indolence of everybody, all told of a new world.

A convict clerk superintended the coaling, which took place before we left the harbour for Ceylon, and I remarked that the dejection of his countenance exceeded that of the felon-labourers who worked in irons on the quay. There is a wide-spread belief in England that unfair favour is shown to "gentlemen convicts." This is simply not the case; every educated prisoner is employed at in-door work, for which he is suited, and not at road-making, in which he might be useless; but there are few cases in which he would not wish to exchange a position full of hopeless degradation for that of an out-door labourer, who passes through his daily routine drudgery (far from the prison) unknown, and perhaps in his fancy all but free. The longing to change the mattock for the pen is the result of envy, and confined to those who, if listened to, would prove incapable of pursuing the pen-driver's occupation.

Under a fair and freshening breeze, we left the port of Albany, happy to escape from a gaol the size of India, even those of us who had been forced to pass only a few days in West Australia.

CHAPTER XIV.

AUSTRALIA.

PACING the deck with difficulty, as the ship tore through the lava-covered seas, before a favouring gale that caught us off Cape Lewin, some of us discussed the prospects of the great Southland as a whole.

In Australia, it is often said, we have a second America in its infancy; but it may be doubted whether we have not become so used to trace the march of empire on a westward course, through Persia and Assyria, Greece and Rome, then by Germany to England and America, that we are too readily prepared to accept the probability of its onward course to the Pacific.

The progress of Australia has been singularly rapid. In 1830, her population was under 40,000; in 1860, it numbered 1,500,000; nevertheless, it is questionable how far the progress will continue. The natural conditions of America in Australia are exactly reversed. All the best lands of Australia are on her coast, and these are already taken up by settlers. Australia has three-quarters the area of Europe, but it is doubtful whether she will ever support a dense population throughout even half her limits. The uses of the northern territory have yet to be discovered, and the interior of the continent is far from being tempting to the settler. Upon the whole, it seems likely that almost all the imperfectly-known regions of Australia will in time be occupied by pastoral Crown tenants, but that the area of agricultural operations is not likely to admit of indefinite extension. The central district of Australia, to the extent, perhaps, of half the entire continent, lies too far north for winter rains, too far south for tropical wet seasons, and in these vast solitudes agriculture may be pronounced impossible, sheep-farming difficult. There will be no difficulty in retaining in tanks, or raising by means of wells, sufficient water for sheep and cattle-stations, and the wool, tallow, and even meat, will be carried by those railways for which the country is admirably fitted, while the construction of locks upon the Murray and its tributaries will enable steamers to carry the whole trade of the Riverina. So far, all is well, but the arable lands of Australia are limited by the rains, and apparently the limit is a sadly narrow one.

Once in a while, a heavy winter rain falls in the interior; grass springs up, the lagoons are filled, the up-country squatters make their fortunes, and all goes prosperously for a time. Accounts reach the coast cities of the astonishing fertility of the interior, and hundreds of settlers set off to the remotest districts. Two or three years of drought then follow, and all the more enterprising squatters are soon ruined, with a gain, however, sometimes of a few thousand square miles of country to civilization.

Hitherto the Australians have not made so much as they should have done of the country that is within their reach. The want of railroads is incredible. There are but some 400 miles of railway in all Australia—far less than the amount possessed by the single infant state of Wisconsin. The sums spent upon the Victorian lines have deterred the colonists from completing their railway system. 10,000,000*l.* sterling were spent upon 200 miles of road, through easy country in which the land cost nothing. The United States have made nearly 40,000 miles of railroad for less than 300,000,000*l.* sterling; Canada made her 2,000 miles for 20,000,000*l.*, or ten times as much railroad as Victoria for only twice the money. Cuba has already more miles of railroad than all Australia.

Small as are the inhabited portions of Australia when compared with the corresponding divisions of the United States, this country nevertheless is huge enough. The part of Queensland already peopled is five times larger than the United Kingdom. South Australia and West Australia are each of them nearly as large as British India, but of these colonies the greater part is desert. Fertile Victoria, the size of Great Britain, is only a thirty-fourth part of Australia.

In face of the comparatively small amount of good agricultural country known to exist in Australia, the disproportionate size of the great cities shows out more clearly than ever. Even Melbourne, when it comes to be examined, has too much the air of a magnified Hobarton, of a city with no country at its back, of a steam-hammer set up to crack nuts. Queensland is at present free from the burthen of gigantic cities, but then Queensland is subject to the greater danger of becoming what is in reality a slave republic.

Morally and intellectually, at all events, the colonies are thriving. A literature is springing up, a national character is being grafted upon the good English stock. What shape the Australian mind will take is at present somewhat doubtful. In addition to considerable shrewdness and a purely Saxon capacity and willingness to combine for local objects, we find in Australia an admirable love of simple mirth, and a serious distaste for prolonged labour in one direction, while the downrightness and determination in the pursuit of truth, remarkable in America, are less noticeable here.

The extravagance begotten of the tradition of convict times has not been without effect, and the settlers waste annually, it is computed, food which would support in Europe a population of twice their numbers. This wastefulness is, however, in some degree a consequence of the necessary habits of a pastoral people. The 8,000 tons of tallow exported annually by the Australias are said to represent the boiling down of sheep enough to feed half a million of people for a twelvemonth.

Australian manners, like the American, resemble the French rather than the British—a resemblance traceable, perhaps, to the essential democracy of Australia, America, and France. One surface point which catches the eye in any Australian ball-room, or on any racecourse, is clearly to be referred to the habit of mind produced by democracy—the fact, namely, that the women dress with great expense and care, the men with none whatever. This, as a rule, is true of Americans, Australians, and French.

Unlike as are the Australians to the British, there is nevertheless a singular mimicry of British forms and ceremonies in the colonies, which is extended to the most trifling details of public life. Twice in Australia was I invited to ministerial dinners, given to mark the approaching close of the session; twice also was I present at university celebrations, in which home whimsicalities were closely copied. The Governors' messages to the Colonial Parliaments are travesties of those which custom in England leads us to call "the Queen's." The very phraseology is closely followed. We find Sir J. Manners Sutton gravely saying: "The representatives of the Government of New South Wales and of *my* Government have agreed to an arrangement on the border duties . . ." The "my" in a democratic country like Victoria strikes a stranger as pre-eminently incongruous, if not absurd.

The imitation of Cambridge forms by the University of Sydney is singularly close. One almost expects to see the familiar blue gown of the "bulldog" thrown across the arm of the first college servant met within its precincts. Chancellor, Vice-chancellor, Senate, Syndicates, and even Proctors, all are here in the antipodes. Registrar, professors, "seniors," fees, fines, and "petitions with the University seal attached;" "Board of Classical Studies"—the whole corporation sits in borrowed plumage; the very names of the colleges are being imitated: we find already a St. John's. The Calendar reads like a parody on the volume issued every March by Messrs. Deighton. Rules upon matriculation, upon the granting of *testamurs*; prize-books stamped with college arms are named, *ad eundem* degrees are known, and we have imitations of phraseology even in the announcement of prizes to "the most distinguished candidates for honours in each of the aforesaid schools," and in the list of subjects for the Moral Science tripos. Lent Term, Trinity Term, Michaelmas Term, take the place of the Spring, Summer, and Fall Terms of the less pretentious institutions in America, and the height of absurdity is reached in the regulations upon "academic costume," and on the "respectful salutation" by undergraduates of the "fellows and professors" of the University. The situation on a hot-wind day of a member of the Senate, in "black silk gown, with hood of scarlet cloth edged with white fur, and lined with blue silk, black velvet trencher cap," all in addition to his ordinary clothing, it is to be presumed, can be imagined only by those who know what hot winds are. We English are great acclimatisers: we have carried trial by jury to Bengal, tenant-right to Oude, and caps and gowns to be worn over loongee and paejama at Calcutta University. Who are we, that we should cry out against the French for "carrying France about with them everywhere"?

The objects of the founders are set forth in the charter as "the advancement of religion and morality, and the promotion of useful knowledge;" but as there is no theological faculty, no religious test or exercise whatever, the philosophy of the first portion of the phrase is not easily understood.

In no Western institutions is the radicalism of Western thought so thoroughly manifested as in the Universities; in no English colonial institutions is Conservatism so manifest. The contrast between Michigan and Sydney is far more striking than that between Harvard and old Cambridge.

Of the religious position of Australia there is little to be said: the Wesleyans, Catholics, and Presbyterians are stronger, and the other denominations weaker, than they are at home. The general mingling of incongruous objects and of conflicting races, characteristic of colonial life, extends to religious buildings. The graceful Wesleyan church, the Chinese joss-house, and the Catholic cathedral stand not far apart in Melbourne. In Australia, the mixture of blood is not yet great. In South Australia, where it is most complete, the Catholics and Wesleyans have great strength. Anglicanism is naturally strongest where the race is most exclusively British—in Tasmania and New South Wales.

As far as the coast tracts are concerned, Australia,

as will be seen from what has been said of the individual colonies, is rapidly ceasing to be a land of great tenancies, and becoming a land of small freeholds, each cultivated by its owner. It need hardly be pointed out that, in the interests of the country and of the race, this is a happy change. When English rural labourers commence to fully realize the misery of their position, they will find not only America, but Australia also, open to them as a refuge and future home. Looming in the distance, we still, however, see the American problem of whether the Englishman can live out of England. Can he thrive except where mist and damp preserve the juices of his frame? He comes from the fogs of the Baltic shores, and from the Flemish lowlands; gains in vigour in the south island of New Zealand. In Australia and America—hot and dry—the type has already changed. Will it eventually disappear?

It is still an open question whether the change of type among the English in America and Australia is a climatic adaptation on the part of nature, or a temporary divergence produced by abnormal causes, and capable of being modified by care.

Before we had done our talk, the ship was pooped by a green sea, which, curling in over her taffrail, swept her decks from end to end, and our helmsmen, although regular old "hard-a-weather" fellows, had difficulty in keeping her upon her course. It was the last of the gale, and when we made up our beds upon the skylights, the heavens were clear of scud, though the moon was still craped with a ceaseless roll of cloud.

CHAPTER XV.

COLONIES.

WHEN a Briton takes a survey of the colonies, he finds much matter for surprise in the one-sided nature of the partnership which exists between the mother and the daughter lands. No reason presents itself to him why our artisans and merchants should be taxed in aid of populations far more wealthy than our own, who have not, as we have, millions of paupers to support. We at present tax our humblest classes, we weaken our defences, we scatter our troops and fleets, and lay ourselves open to panics such as those of 1853 and 1859, in order to protect against imaginary dangers the Australian gold-digger and Canadian farmer. There is something ludicrous in the idea of taxing St. Giles's for the support of Melbourne, and making Dorsetshire agricultural labourers pay the cost of defending New Zealand colonists in Maori wars.

It is possible that the belief obtains in Britain among the least educated classes of the community that colonial expenses are rapidly decreasing, if they have not already wholly disappeared; but in fact they have for some years past been steadily and continuously growing in amount.

As long as we choose to keep up such *propugnacula* as Gibraltar, Malta, and Bermuda, we must pay roundly for them, as we also must for such costly luxuries as our Gold Coast settlements for the suppression of the slave-trade; but if we confine the term "colonies" to English-speaking, white-inhabited, and self-governed lands, and exclude on the one hand garrisons such as Gibraltar, and on the other mere dependencies like the West Indies and Ceylon, we find that our true colonies in North America, Australia, Polynesia, and South Africa, involve us nominally in yearly charges of almost two millions sterling, and, really, in untold expenditure.

Canada is in all ways the most flagrant case. She draws from us some three millions annually for her defence, she makes no contribution towards the cost; she relies mainly on us to defend a frontier of 4,000 miles, and she excludes our goods by prohibitive duties at her ports. In short, colonial expenses which, rightly or wrongly, our fathers bore (and that not ungrudgingly) when they enjoyed a monopoly of colonial trade, are borne by us in face of colonial prohibition. What the true cost to us of Canada may be is unfortunately an open question, and the loss by the weakening of our home forces we have no means of computing; but when we consider that, on a fair statement of the case, Canada would be debited with the cost of a large portion of the half-pay and recruiting services, of Horse Guards and War Office expenses, of arms, accoutrements, barracks, hospitals, and stores, and also with the gigantic expenses of two of our naval squadrons, we cannot but admit that we must pay at least three millions a year for the hatred that the Canadians profess to bear towards the United States. Whatever may be the case, however, with regard to Canada, less fault is to be found with the cost of the Australian colonies. If they bore a portion of the half-pay and recruiting expenses as well as the cost of the troops actually employed among them in time of peace, and also paid their share in the maintenance of the British navy,—a share to increase with the increase of their merchant shipping—there would be little to desire, unless, indeed, we should wish that, in exchange for a check upon imperial braggadocio and imperial waste, the Australias should also contribute towards the expenses of imperial wars.

No reason can be shown for our spending millions on the defence of Canada against the Americans or in aiding the New Zealand colonists against the Maories that will not apply to their aiding us in case of a European war with France, control being given to their representatives over our public action in questions of imperial concern. Without any such control over imperial action, the old American colonists were well content to do their share of fighting in imperial wars. In 1689, in 1702, and in 1744, Massachusetts attacked the French, and taking from them Nova Scotia and others of their new plantations, handed them over to Great Britain. Even when the tax time came, Massachusetts, while declaring that the English Parliament had no right to tax colonies, went on to say that the king could inform them of the exigencies of the public service, and that they were ready "to provide for them if required."

It is not likely however, nowadays, that our colonists would, for any long stretch of time, engage to aid us in our purely European wars. Australia would scarcely feel herself deeply interested in the guarantee of Luxembourg, nor Canada in the affairs of Servia. The fact that we in Britain paid our share—or rather nearly the whole cost—of the Maori wars would be no argument to an Australian, but only an additional proof to him of our extraordinary folly. We have been educated into a habit of paying with complacency other people's bills—not so the Australian settler.

As far as Australia is concerned, our soldiers are not used as troops at all. The colonists like the show of the red-coats, and the military duties are made up partly of guard-of-honour work, and partly of the labours of police. The colonists well know that in time of war we should immediately withdraw our troops, and they trust wholly in their volunteers and the colonial marine.

As long as we choose to allow the system to continue, the colonists are well content to reap the benefit. When we at last decide that it shall cease, they will reluctantly consent. It is more than doubtful whether, if we were to insist to the utmost upon our rights as towards our southern colonies, they would do more than grumble and consent to our demands; and there is no chance whatever of our asking for more than our simple due.

When you talk to an intelligent Australian, you can

always see that he fears that separation would be made the excuse for the equipment of a great and costly Australian fleet—not more necessary then than now—and that, however he may talk, he would, rather than separate from England, at least do his duty by her.

The fear of conquest of the Australian colonies if we left them to themselves is on the face of it ridiculous. It is sufficient, perhaps, to say that the old American colonies, when they had but a million and a half of people, defended themselves successfully against the then all-powerful French, and that there is no instance of a self-protected English colony being conquered by the foreigner. The American colonies valued so highly their independence of the old country in the matter of defence that they petitioned the Crown to be allowed to fight for themselves, and called the British army by the plain name of "grievance."

As for our so-called defence of the colonies, in wartime we defend ourselves; we defend the colonies only during peace. In war-time they are ever left to shift for themselves, and they would undoubtedly be better fit to do so were they in the habit of maintaining their military establishments in time of peace. The present system weakens us and them—us, by taxes and by the withdrawal of our men and ships; the colonies, by preventing the development of that self-reliance which is requisite to form a nation's greatness. The successful encountering of difficulties is the marking feature of the national character of the English, and we can hardly expect a nation which has never encountered any, or which has been content to see them met by others, ever to become great. In short, as matters now stand the colonies are a source of military weakness to us, and our "protection" of them is a source of danger to the colonists. No doubt there are still among us men who would have wished to have seen America continue in union with England, on theprinciple on which the Russian conscripts are chained each to an old man—to keep her from going too fast—and who now consider it our duty to defend our colonies at whatever cost, on account of the "prestige" which attaches to the somewhat precarious tenure of these great lands. With such men it is impossible for colonial reformers to argue: the standpoints are wholly different. To those, however, who admit the injustice of the present system to the taxpayers of the mother-country, but who fear that her merchants would suffer by its disturbance, inasmuch as, in their belief, action on our part would lead to a disruption of the tie, we may plead that, even should separation be the result, we should be none the worse off for its occurrence. The retention of colonies at almost any cost has been defended—so far as it has been supported by argument at all—on the ground that the connexion conduces to trade, to which argument it is sufficient to answer that no one has ever succeeded in showing what effect upon trade the connexion can have, and that as excellent examples to the contrary we have the fact that our trade with the Ionian Islands has greatly increased since their annexation to the kingdom of Greece, and a much more striking fact than even this—namely, that while the trade with England of the Canadian Confederation is only four-elevenths of its total external trade, or little more than one-third, the English trade of the United States was in 1860 (before the war) nearly two-thirds of its total external trade, in 1861 more than two-thirds, and in 1866 (first year after the war) again four-sevenths of its total trade. Common institutions, common freedom, and common tongue have evidently far more to do with trade than union has; and for purposes of commerce and civilization, America is a truer colony of Britain than is Canada.

It would not be difficult, were it necessary, to multiply examples whereby to prove that trade with a country does not appear to be affected by union with or separation from it. Egypt (even when we carefully exclude from the returns Indian produce in transport) sends us nearly all such produce as she exports, notwithstanding that the French largely control the government, and that we have much less footing in the country than the Italians, and no more than the Austrians or Spanish. Our trade with Australia means that the Australians want something of us and that we need something of them, and that we exchange with them our produce as we do in a larger degree with the Americans, the Germans, and the French.

The trade argument being met, and it being remembered that our colonies are no more an outlet for our surplus population than they would be if the Great Mogul ruled over them, as is seen by the fact that of every twenty people who leave the United Kingdom, one goes to Canada, two to Australia, and sixteen to the United States, we come to the "argument" which consists in the word "prestige." When examined, this cry seems to mean that, in the opinion of the utterer, extent of empire is power—a doctrine under which Brazil ought to be nineteen and a half times, and China twenty-six times as powerful as France. Perhaps the best answer to the doctrine is a simple contradiction: those who have read history with most care well know that at all times extent of empire has been weakness. England's real empire was small enough in 1650, yet it is rather doubtful whether her "prestige" ever reached the height it did while the Cromwellian admirals swept the seas. The idea conveyed by the words "mother of free nations" is every bit as good as that contained in the cry "prestige," and the argument that, as the colonists are British subjects, we have no right to cast them adrift so long as they wish to continue citizens, is evidently no answer to those who merely urge that the colonists should pay their own policemen.

It may, perhaps, be contended that the possession of "colonies" tends to preserve us from the curse of small island countries, the dwarfing of mind which would otherwise make us Guernsey a little magnified. If this be true, it is a powerful argument in favour of continuance in the present system. It is a question, however, whether our real preservation from the insularity we deprecate is not to be found in the possession of true colonies—of plantations such as America, in short—rather than in that of mere dependencies. That which raises us above the provincialism of citizenship of little England is our citizenship of the greater

Saxondom which includes all that is best and wisest in the world.

From the foundation, separation would be harmless, does not of necessity follow the conclusion, separation is to be desired. This much only is clear—that we need not hesitate to demand that Australia should do her duty.

With the more enlightened thinkers of England, separation from the colonies has for many years been a favourite idea, but as regards the Australias it would hardly be advisable. If we allow that it is to the interest both of our race and of the world that the Australias should prosper, we have to ask whether they would do so in a higher degree if separated from the mother country than if they remained connected with her and with each other by a federation. It has often been said that, instead of the varying relations which now exist between Britain and America, we should have seen a perfect friendship had we but permitted the American colonies to go their way in peace; but the example does not hold in the case of Australia, which is by no means wishful to go at all.

Under separation we should, perhaps, find the colonies better emigration-fields for our surplus population than they are at present. Many of our emigrants who flock to the United States are attracted by the idea that they are going to become citizens of a new nation instead of dependents upon an old one. On the separation of Australia from England we might expect that a portion of these sentimentalists would be diverted from a colony necessarily jealous of us so long as we hold Canada, to one which from accordance of interests is likely to continue friendly or allied. This argument, however, would have no weight with those who desire the independence of Canada, and who look upon America as still our colony.

Separation, we may then conclude, though infinitely better than a continuance of the existing one-sided tie, would, in a healthier state of our relations, not be to the interest of Britain, although it would perhaps be morally beneficial to Australia. Any relation, however, would be preferable to the existing one of mutual indifference and distrust. Recognising the fact that Australia has come of age, and calling on her, too, to recognise it, we should say to the Australian colonists: "Our present system cannot continue; will you amend it, or separate?" The worst thing that can happen to us is that we should "drift" blindly into separation.

After all, the strongest of the arguments in favour of separation is the somewhat paradoxical one that it would bring us a step nearer to the virtual confederation of the English race.

PART IV.
INDIA.

A REGULAR and uniform system of spelling of native names and other words has lately been brought into common use in India, and adopted by the Government. Not without hesitation I have decided upon ignoring this improvement, and confining myself to spellings known to and used by the English in England, for whom especially I am writing.

I am aware that there is no system in the spelling, and that it is scientifically absurd; nevertheless, the new Government spelling is not yet sufficiently well understood in England to warrant its use in a book intended for general circulation. The scientific spelling is not always an improvement to the eye, moreover: Talookdars of Oude may not be right, but it is a neater phrase than "Taâlulehdars of Awdh;" and it will probably be long before we in England write "kuli" for coolie, or adopt the spelling "Tátá hordes."

CHAPTER I.

MARITIME CEYLON.

WE failed to sight the Island of Cocoas, a territory where John Ross is king—a worthy Scotchman, who having settled down in mid-ocean, some hundreds of miles from any port, proceeded to annex himself to Java and the Dutch. On being remonstrated with, he was made to see his error; and, being appointed governor of and consul to himself and labourers, now hoists the union-jack, while his island has a red line drawn under its name upon the map. Two days after quitting John Ross's latitudes, we crossed the line in the heavy noonday of the equatorial belt of calms. The sun itself passed the equator the same day; so, after having left Australia at the end of autumn, I suddenly found myself in Asia in the early spring. Mist obscured the skies except at dawn and sunset, when there was a clear air, in which floated cirro-cumuli with flat bases—clouds cut in half, as it seemed—and we were all convinced that Homer must have seen the Indian Ocean, so completely did the sea in the equatorial belt realize his epithet "purple" or "wine-dark." All day long the flying fish—"those good and excellent creatures of God," as Drake styled them—were skimming over the water on every side. The Elizabethan captain, who knew their delicacy of taste, attributed their freedom from the usual slime of fish, and their wholesome nature, to "their continued exercise in both air and water." The heat was great, and I made the discovery that Australians as well as Americans can put their feet above their heads. It may be asserted that the height above the deck of the feet of passengers on board ocean steamers varies directly as the heat, and inversely as the number of hours before dinner.

In the afternoon of the day we crossed the line, we sighted a large East Indiaman lying right in our course, and so little way was she making that, on coming up with her, we had to port our helm, in order not to run her down. She hailed us, and we lay-to while she sent a boat aboard us with her mail; for although she was already a month out from Calcutta and bound for London, our letters would reach home before she was round the Cape—a singular commentary upon the use of sailing ships in the Indian seas. Before the boat had left our side, the ships had floated so close together, through attraction, that we had to make several revolutions with the screw in order to prevent collision.

When we, who were all sleeping upon deck, were aroused by the customary growl from the European quartermaster of "Four o'clock, sir! Going to swab decks, sir! Get up, sir!" given with the flare of the lantern in our eyes, we were still over a hundred miles from Galle; but before the sun had risen, we caught sight of Adam's Peak, a purple mass upon the northern sky, and soon we were racing with a French steamer from Saigon, and with a number of white-sailed native craft from the Maldives. Within a few hours, we were at anchor in a small bay, surrounded with lofty cocoa palms, in which were lying, tossed by a rolling swell, some dozen huge steamers, yard-arm to yard-arm—the harbour of Point du Galle. Every ship was flying her ensign, and in the damp hot air the old tattered union-jacks seemed brilliant crimson, and the dull green of the cocoa palms became a dazzling emerald. The scene wanted but the bright plumage of the Panama macaws.

Once seated in the piazza of the Oriental Company's hotel, the best managed in the East, I had before me a curious scene. Along the streets were pouring silent crowds of tall and graceful girls, as we at the first glance supposed, wearing white petticoats and bodices; their hair carried off the face with a decorated hoop, and caught at the back by a high tortoise-shell comb. As they drew near, moustaches began to show, and I saw that they were men, whilst walking with them were women naked to the waist, combless, and far more rough and "manly" than their husbands. Petticoat and chignon are male institutions in Ceylon, and time after time I had to look twice before I could fix the passer's sex. My rule at last became to set down everybody that was womanly as a man, and everybody that was manly as a woman. Cinghalese, Kandians,

Tamils from South India, and Moormen with crimson caftans and shaven crowns, formed the body of the great crowd; but, besides these, there were Portuguese, Chinese, Jews, Arabs, Parsees, Englishmen, Malays, Dutchmen, and half-caste burghers, and now and then a veiled Arabian woman or a Veddah—one of the aboriginal inhabitants of the isle. Ceylon has never been independent, and in a singular mixture of races her ports bear testimony to the number of the foreign conquests.

Two American missionaries were among the passers-by, but one of them, detecting strangers, came up to the piazza in search of news. There had been no loss of national characteristics in these men;—they were brim-full of the mixture of earnestness and quaint profanity which distinguishes the New England puritan: one of them described himself to me as "just a kind of journeyman soul-saver, like."

The Australian strangers were not long left unmolested by more serious intruders than grave Vermonters. The cry of "baksheesh"—an Arabian word that goes from Gibraltar to China, and from Ceylon to the Khyber Pass, and which has reached us in the form of "boxes" in our phrase Christmas-boxes —was the first native word I heard in the East, at Galle, as it was afterwards the last, at Alexandria. One of the beggars was an Albino, fair as a child in a Hampshire lane; one of those strange sports of nature from whom Cinghalese tradition asserts the European races to be sprung.

The beggars were soon driven off by the hotel

servants, and better licensed plunderers began their work. "Ah safeer, ah rupal, ah imral, ah mooney stone, ah opal, ah amtit, ah!" was the cry from every quarter, and jewel-sellers of all the nations of the East descended on us in a swarm. "Me givee you written guarantee dis real stone;" "Yes, dat real stone; but dis *good* stone—dat no good stone—no water. Ah, see!" "Dat no good stone. Ah, sahib, you tell good stone; all dese bad stone, reg'lar England stone. You go by next ship? No? Ah, den you come see me shop. Dese ship-passenger stone—humbuk stone. Ship gone, den you come me shop; see good stone. When you come? eh? when you come?" "Ah safeer, ah catty-eye, ah pinkee collal!" Meanwhile every Galle-dwelling European, at the bar of the hotel, was adding to the din by shouting to the native servants, "Boy, turn out these fellows, and stop their noise." This cry of "boy" is a relic of the old Dutch times: it was the Hollander's term for his slave, and hence for every member of the inferior race. The first servant that I heard called "boy" was a tottering, white-haired old man.

The gems of Ceylon have long been famed. One thousand three hundred and seventy years ago, the Chinese records tell us that Ceylon, then tributary to the empire, sent presents to the Brother of the Moon, one of the gifts being a "lapis-lazuli spittoon." It is probable that some portion of the million and a half pounds sterling which are annually absorbed in this small island, but four-fifths the size of

Ireland, is consumed in the setting of the precious stones for native use; every one you meet wears four or five heavy silver rings, and sovereigns are melted down to make gold ornaments.

Rushing away from the screaming crowd of pedlars, I went with some of my Australian friends to stroll upon the ramparts, and enjoy the evening salt breeze. We met several bodies of white-faced Europeans, sauntering like ourselves, and dressed like us in white trousers and loose white jackets and pith hats. What we looked like I do not know, but they resembled ships' stewards. At last it struck me that they were soldiers, and upon inquiring I found that these washed-out dawdlers represented a British regiment of the line. I was by this time used to see linesmen out of scarlet, having beheld a parade in bushranger-beards, and blue-serge "jumpers" at Taranaki in New Zealand; but one puts up easier with the soldier-bushranger, than with the soldier-steward.

The climate of the day had been exquisite with its bright air and cooling breeze, and I had begun to think that those who knew Acapulco and Echuca could afford to laugh at the East, with its thermometer at 88°. The reckoning came at night, however, for by dark all the breeze was gone, and the thermometer, instead of falling, had risen to 90° when I lay down to moan and wait for dawn. As I was dropping off to sleep at about four o'clock, a native came round and closed the doors, to shut out the dangerous land-breeze that springs up at that hour. Again, at half-past five, it was cooler, and I had begun to doze, when a cannon-shot, fired apparently under my bed, brought me upon my feet with something more than a start. I remembered the saying of the Western boy before Petersburg, when he heard for the first time the five o'clock camp-gun, and called to his next neighbour at the fire, "Say, Bill, did you hap to hear how partic'lar loud the day broke just now?" for it was the morning-gun, which in Ceylon is always fired at the same time, there being less than an hour's difference between the longest and shortest days. Although it was still pitch dark, the bugles began to sound the *réveille* on every side—in the infantry lines, the artillery barracks, and the lines of the Malay regiment, the well-known Ceylon Rifles. Ten minutes afterwards, when I had bathed by lamplight, I was eating plantains and taking my morning tea in a cool room lit by the beams of the morning sun, so short is the April twilight in Ceylon.

It is useless to consult the thermometer about heat: a European can labour in the open air in South Australia with the thermometer at 110° in the shade, while, with a thermometer at 88°, the nights are unbearable in Ceylon. To discover whether the climate of a place be really hot, examine its newspapers; and if you find the heat recorded, you may make up your mind that it is a variable climate, but if no "remarkable heat" or similar announcements appear, then you may be sure that you are in a permanently hot place. It stands to reason that no one in the tropics ever talks of "tropical heat."

In so equable a climate, the apathy of the Cinghalese is not surprising; but they are not merely lazy, they are a cowardly, effeminate, and revengeful race. They sleep and smoke, and smoke and sleep, rousing themselves only once in the day to snatch a bowl of curry and rice, or to fleece a white man; and so slowly do the people run the race of life that even elephantiasis, common here, does not seem to put the sufferer far behind his fellow-men. Buddhism is no mystery when expounded under this climate. See a few Cinghalese stretched in the shade of a cocoa-palm, and you can conceive Buddha sitting cross-legged for ten thousand years contemplating his own perfection.

The second morning that I spent in Galle, the captain of the *Bombay* was kind enough to send his gig for me to the landing-steps at dawn, and his Malay crew soon rowed me to the ship, where the captain joined me, and we pulled across the harbour to Watering-place Point, and bathed in the shallow sea, out of the reach of sharks. When we had dressed, we went on to a jetty, to look into the deep water just struck by the rising sun. I should have marvelled at the translucency of the waters had not the awful clearness with which the bottom of the Canadian lakes stand revealed in evening light been fresh within my memory, but here the bottom was fairly paved with corallines of inconceivable brilliancy of colour, and tenanted by still more gorgeous fish. Of the two that bore the palm, one was a little fish of mazarine blue, without a speck of any other colour, and perfect too in shape; the second, a silver fish, with a band of soft brown velvet round its neck, and another about its tail. In a still more sheltered cove the fish were so thick that dozens of Moors were throwing into the water, with the arm-twist of a fly-fisher, bare hooks, which they jerked through the shoal and into the air, never failing to bring them up clothed with a fish, caught most times by the fin.

In the evening, two of us tried a native dinner, at a house where Cinghalese gentlemen dine when they come into Galle on business. Our fare was as follows:—First course: a curry of the delicious seir-fish, a sort of mackerel; a prawn curry; a bread-fruit and cocoa-nut curry; a Brinjal curry, and a dish made of jack-fruit, garlic, and mace; all washed down by iced water. Second course: plantains, and very old arrack in thimble-glasses, followed by black coffee. Of meat there was no sign, as the Cinghalese rarely touch it; and, although we liked our vegetarian dinner, my friend passed a criticism in action on it by dining again at the hotel-ordinary one hour later. We agreed, too, that the sickly smell of cocoa-nut would cleave to us for weeks.

Starting with an Australian friend, at the dawn of my third day in the island, I took the coach by the coast road to Columbo. We drove along a magnificent road in an avenue of giant cocoa-nut palms, with the sea generally within easy sight, and with a native hut at each few yards. Every two or three miles, the road crossed a lagoon, alive with bathers, and near the bridge was generally a village, bazaar, and Buddhist temple, built pagoda-shape, and filled with worshippers. The road was thronged with gaily-dressed Cinghalese; and now and again we would pass a Buddhist priest in saffron-coloured robes, hastening along, his umbrella borne over him by a boy clothed from top to toe in white. The umbrellas of the priests are of yellow silk, and shaped like ours, but other natives carry flat-topped umbrellas, gilt, or coloured red and black. The Cinghalese farmers we met travelling to their temples in carts drawn by tiny bullocks. Such was the brightness of the air, that the people, down to the very beggars, seemed clad in holiday attire.

As we journeyed on, we began to find more variety in the scenery and vegetation, and were charmed with the scarlet-blossomed cotton-tree, and with the areca, or betel-nut palm. The cocoa-nut groves, too, were carpeted with an undergrowth of orchids and ipecacuanha, and here and there was a bread-fruit tree or an hibiscus.

In Ceylon we have retained the Dutch posting system, and small light coaches, drawn by four or six small horses at a gallop, run over excellent roads, carrying, besides the passengers, two boys behind, who shout furiously whenever vehicles or passengers obstruct the mails, and who at night carry torches high in the air, to light the road. Thus we dashed through the bazaars and cocoa groves, then across the golden sands covered with rare shells, and fringed on the one side with the bright blue dancing sea, dotted with many a white sail, and on the other side with deep green jungle, in which were sheltered dark lagoons. Once in a while, we would drive out on to a plain, varied by clumps of fig and tulip trees, and, looking to the east, would sight the purple mountains of the central range; then, dashing again into the thronged bazaars, would see little but the bright palm trees relieved upon an azure sky. The road is one continuous village, for the population is twelve times as dense in the western as in the eastern provinces of Ceylon. No wonder that ten thousand natives have died of cholera within the last few months! All this dense coast population is supported by the cocoa-nut, for there are in Ceylon 200,000 acres under cocoa palms, which yield from seven to eight hundred million cocoa-nuts a year, and are worth two millions sterling.

Near Bentotté, where we had lunched off horrible oysters of the pearl-yielding kind, we crossed the Kaluganga river, densely fringed with mangrove, and in its waters saw a python swimming bravely towards the shore. Snakes are not so formidable as land-leeches, the Cinghalese and planters say, and no one hears of many persons being bitten, though a great reward for an antidote to the cobra bite has lately been offered by the Rajah of Travancore.

As we entered what the early maps style "The Christian Kyngdom of Colombo," though where they found their Christians no one knows, our road lay through the cinnamon gardens, which are going out of cultivation, as they no longer pay, although the cinnamon laurel is a spice-grove in itself, giving cinnamon from its bark, camphor from the roots, clove oil from its leaves. The plant grows wild about the island, and is cut and peeled by the natives at no cost save that of children's labour, which they do not count as cost at all. The scene in the gardens that still remain was charming: the cinnamon-laurel bushes contrasted well with the red soil, and the air was alive with dragon-flies, moths, and winged-beetles, while the softness of the evening breeze had tempted out the half-caste Dutch "burgher" families of the city, who were driving and walking clothed in white, the ladies with their jet hair dressed with natural flowers. The setting sun threw brightness without heat into the gay scene.

A friend who had horses ready for us at the hotel where the mail-coach stopped, said that it was not too late for a ride through the fort, or European town inside the walls; so, cantering along the esplanade, where the officers of the garrison were enjoying their evening ride, we crossed the moat, and found ourselves in what is perhaps the most graceful street in the world:—a double range of long low houses of bright white stone, with deep piazzas, buried in masses of bright foliage, in which the fire-flies were beginning to play. In the centre of the fort is an Italian campanile, which serves at once as a belfry, a clock-tower, and a lighthouse. In the morning, before sunrise, we climbed this tower for the view. The central range stood up sharply on the eastern sky, as the sun was still hid behind it, and to the south-east there towered high the peak where Adam mourned his son a hundred years. In colour, shape, and height, the Cinghalese

Alps resemble the Central Apennines, and the view from Columbo is singularly like that from Pesaro on the Adriatic. As we looked landwards from the campanile, the native town was mirrored in the lake, and outside the city the white-coated troops were marching by companies on to the parade-ground, whence we could faintly hear the distant bands.

Driving back in a carriage, shaped like a street cab, but with fixed venetians instead of sides and windows, we visited the curing establishment of the Ceylon Coffee Company, where the coffee from the hills is dried and sorted. Thousands of native girls are employed in coffee-picking at the various stores, but it is doubted whether the whole of this labour is not wasted, the berries being sorted according to their shape and size—characteristics which seem in no way to affect the flavour. The Ceylon exporters say that if we choose to pay twice as much for shapely as for ill-shaped berries, it is no business of theirs to refuse to humour us by sorting.

The most remarkable institution in Columbo is the steam factory where the Government make or mend such machinery as their experts certify cannot be dealt with at any private works existing in the island. The Government elephants are kept at the same place, but I found them at work up country on the Kandy road.

In passing through the native town upon Slave Island, we saw some French Catholic priests in their working jungle dresses of blue serge. They have met with singular successes in Ceylon, having made

150,000 converts, while the English and American missions have between them only 30,000 natives. The Protestant missionaries in Ceylon complain much of the planters, whom they accuse of declaring when they wish to hire men, that "no Christian need apply;" but it is a remarkable fact that neither Protestants nor Catholics can make converts among the self-supported "Moormen," the active pushing inhabitants of the ports, who are Mohamedans to a man. The chief cause of the success of the Catholics among the Cinghalese, seems to be the remarkable earnestness of the French and Italian missionary priests. Our English missionaries in the East are too often men incapable of bearing fatigue or climate; ignorant of every trade, and inferior even in teaching and preaching powers to their rivals. It is no easy matter to spread Christianity among the Cinghalese, the inventors of Buddhism, the most ancient and most widely spread of all the religions of the world. Every Buddhist firmly believes in the potential perfection of man, and is incapable of understanding the ideas of original sin and redemption; and a Cinghalese Buddhist—passionless himself—cannot comprehend the passionate worship that Christianity requires. The Catholics, however, do not neglect the Eastern field for missionary labour. Four of their bishops from Cochin China and Japan were met by me in Galle, upon their way to Rome.

Our drive was brought to an end by a visit to the old Dutch quarter—a careful imitation of Amsterdam; indeed, one of its roads still bears the portentous Batavian name of Dam Street. Their straight canals, and formal lines of trees, the Hollanders have carried with them throughout the world; but in Columbo, not content with manufacturing imitation canals, that began and ended in a wall, they dug great artificial lakes to recall their well-loved Hague.

The same evening, I set off by the new railway for Kandy and Nuwara Ellia (pronounced Nooralia) in the hills. Having no experience of the climate of mountain regions in the tropics, I expected a merely pleasant change, and left Columbo wearing my white kit, which served me well enough as far as Ambe Pusse—the railway terminus, which we reached at ten o'clock at night. We started at once by coach, and had not driven far up the hills in the still moonlight before the cold became extreme, and I was saved from a severe chill only by the kindness of the coffee-planter who shared the back seat with me, and who, being well clad in woollen, lent me his great-coat. After this incident, we chatted pleasantly without fear of interruption from our sole companion—a native girl, who sat silently chewing betel all the way—and reached Kandy before dawn. Telling the hotel servants to wake me in an hour, I wrapped myself in a blanket—the first I had seen since I left Australia—and enjoyed a refreshing sleep.

CHAPTER II.

KANDY.

THE early morning was foggy and cold as an October dawn in an English forest; but before I had been long in the gardens of the Government House, the sun rose, and the heat returned once more. After wandering among the petunias and fan-palms of the gardens, I passed on into the city, the former capital of the Kandian or highland kingdom, and one of the holiest of Buddhist towns. The kingdom was never conquered by the Portuguese or Dutch while they held the coasts, and was not overrun by us till 1815, while it has several times been in rebellion since that date. The people still retain their native customs in a high degree: for instance, the Kandian husband does not take his wife's inheritance unless he lives with her on her father's land: if she lives with him, she forfeits her inheritance. Kandian law, indeed, is expressly maintained by us except in the matters of polygamy and polyandry, although the maritime Cinghalese are governed, as are the English in Ceylon and at the Cape, by the civil code of Holland.

The difference between the Kandian and coast Cinghalese is very great. At Kandy, I found the men wearing flowing crimson robes and flat-topped caps, while their faces were lighter in colour than those of the coast people, and many of them had beards. The women also wore the nose-ring in a different way, and were clothed above as well as below the waist. It is possible that some day we may unfortunately hear more of this energetic and warlike people.

The city is one that dwells long in the mind. The Upper Town is one great garden, so numerous are the sacred groves, vocal with the song of the Eastern orioles, but here and there are dotted about pagoda-shaped temples, identical in form with those of Tartary two thousand miles away, and from these there proceeds a roar of tomtoms that almost drowns the song. One of these temples contains the holiest of Buddhist relics, the tooth of Buddha, which is yearly carried in a grand procession. When we first annexed the Kandian kingdom, we recognised the Buddhist Church, made our officers take part in the procession of the Sacred Tooth, and sent a State offering to the shrine. Times are changed since then, but the Buddhist priests are still exempt from certain taxes. All round the sacred enclosures are ornamented walls, with holy sculptured figures; and in the Lower Town are fresh-water lakes and tanks, formed by damming the Mavaliganga River, and also, in some measure, holy. An atmosphere of Buddhism pervades all Kandy.

From Kandy, I visited the coffee-district of which it is the capital and centre, but I was much disappointed with regard to the amount of land that is still open to coffee-cultivation. At the Government Botanic Garden at Peredenia (where the jalap plant, the castor-oil plant, and the ipecacuanha were growing side by side), I was told that the shrub does not flourish under 1,500, nor over 3,000 or 4,000 feet above sea-level, and that all the best coffee-land is already planted. Coffee-growing has already done so much for Ceylon that it is to be hoped that it has not reached its limit: in thirty-three years, it has doubled her trade ten times, and to England alone she now sends two millions worth of coffee every year. The central district of the island, in which lie the hills and coffee-country, is, with the exception of the towns, politically not a portion of Ceylon: there are English capital, English management, and Indian labour, and the cocoa-palm is unknown; Tamil labourers are exclusively employed upon the plantations, although the carrying trade, involving but little labour, is in the hands of the Cinghalese. No such official discouragement is shown to the European planters in Ceylon as that which they experience in India; and were there but more good coffee-lands and more capital, all would be well. The planters say that, after two years' heavy expenditure and dead loss, 20 per cent. can be made by men who take in sufficient capital, but that no one ever does take capital enough for the land he buys, and that they all have to borrow from one of the Columbo companies at 12 per cent., and are then bound to ship their coffee through that company alone. It is regarded as an open question by many disinterested friends of Ceylon whether it might not be wise for the local Government to advance money to the planters; but besides the fear of jobbery, there is the objection to this course, that the Government, becoming interested in the success of coffee-planting, might also come to connive at the oppression of the native labourers. This oppression of the people lies at the bottom of that Dutch system which is often held up for our imitation in Ceylon.

Those who narrate to us the effects of the Java system forget that it is not denied that in the tropical islands, with an idle population and a rich soil, compulsory labour may be the only way of developing the resources of the countries, but they fail to show the justification for our developing the resources of the country by such means. The Dutch culture-system puts a planter down upon the Crown lands, and, having made advances to him, leaves it to him to find out how he shall repay the Government. Forced labour —under whatever name—is the natural result.

The Dutch, moreover, bribe the great native chiefs by princely salaries and vast per-centage upon the crops their people raise, and force the native agriculturists to grow spices for the Royal Market of Amsterdam. Of the purchase of these spices the Government has a monopoly: it buys them at what price it will, and, selling again in Europe to the world, clears annually some 4,000,000*l.* sterling by the job. That plunder, slavery, and famine often follow the extension of their system is nothing to the Dutch. Strict press-laws prevent the Dutch at home from hearing anything of the discontent in Java, except when famine or insurrection call attention to the isle; and 4,000,000*l.* a year profit, and half the expenses of their navy paid for them by one island in the Eastern seas, make up for many deaths of brown-faced people by starvation.

The Dutch often deny that the Government retains the monopoly of export; but the fact of the matter is that the Dutch Trading Company, who have the monopoly of the exports of the produce of Crown lands—which amount to two-thirds of the total exports of the isle—are mere agents of the Government.

It is hard to say that, apart from the nature of the culture-system, the Dutch principle of making a profit out of the countries which they rule is inconsistent with the position of a Christian nation. It is the ancient system of countries having possessions in the East, and upon our side we are not able to show any definite reasons in favour of our course of scrupulously keeping separate the Indian revenue, and spending Indian profits upon India and Cinghalese in Ceylon, except such reasons as would logically lead to our quitting India altogether. That the Dutch should make a profit out of Java is perhaps not more immoral than that they should be there. At the same time, the character of the Dutch system lowers the tone of the whole Dutch nation, and especially of those who have any connexion with the Indies, and effectually prevents future amendment. With our system, there is some chance of right being done, so small is our self-interest in the wrong. From the fact that no surplus is sent home from Ceylon, she is at least free from that bane of Java,—the desire of the local authorities to increase as much as possible the valuable productions of their districts, even at the risk of famine, provided only that they may hope to put off the famine until after their time—a desire that produces the result that subaltern Dutch officers who observe in their integrity the admirable rules which have been made for the protection of the native population are heartily abused for their ridiculous scrupulosity, as it is styled.

Not to be carried away by the material success of the Dutch system, it is as well to bear in mind its secret history. A private company—the Dutch Trading Society—was founded at Amsterdam in 1824, the then King being the largest shareholder. The company was in difficulties in 1830, when the King, finding he was losing money fast, sent out as Governor-General of the Dutch East Indies his personal friend Van den Bosch. The next year, the culture-system, with all its attendant horrors, was introduced into Java by Van den Bosch, the Dutch Trading Society being made agents for the Government. The result was the extraordinary prosperity of the company, and the leaving by the merchant-king of a private fortune of fabulous amount.

The Dutch system has been defended by every conceivable kind of blind misrepresentation; it has even been declared, by writers who ought certainly to know better, that the four millions of surplus that Holland draws from Java, being profits on trade, are not taxation! Even the blindest admirers of the system are forced, however, to admit that it involves the absolute prohibition of missionary enterprise, and total exclusion from knowledge of the Java people.

The Ceylon planters have at present political as well as financial difficulties on their hands. They have petitioned the Queen for "self-government for Ceylon," and for control of the revenue by "representatives of the public"—excellent principles, if "public" meant public, and "Ceylon," Ceylon; but, when we inquire of the planters what they really mean, we find that by "Ceylon" they understand Galle and Columbo Fort, and by "the public" they mean themselves. There are at present six unofficial members of the Council: of these, the whites have three members, the Dutch burghers one, and the natives two; and the planters expect the same proportions to be kept in a Council to which supreme power shall be entrusted in the disposition of the revenues. They are, indeed, careful to explain that they in no way desire the extension of representative institutions to Ceylon.

The first thing that strikes the English traveller in Ceylon is the apparent slightness of our hold upon the country. In my journey from Galle to Columbo, by early morning and mid-day, I met no white man; from Columbo to Kandy, I travelled with one, but met none; at Kandy, I saw no whites; at Nuwara Ellia, not half-a-dozen. On my return, I saw no whites between Nuwara Ellia and Ambe Pusse, where there was a white man in the railway-station; and on my return by evening from Columbo to Galle, in all the thronging crowds along the roads there was not a single European. There are hundreds of Cinghalese in the interior who live and die, and never see a white man. Out of the two and a quarter millions of people who dwell in what the planters call the "colony of Ceylon," there are but 3,000 Europeans, of whom 1,500 are our soldiers, and 250 our civilians. Of the European non-official class, there are but 1,300 persons, or about 500 grown-up men. The proposition of the Planters' Association is that we should confide the despotic government over two and a quarter millions of Buddhist, Mohamedan, and Hindoo labourers to these 500 English Christian employers. It is not the Ceylon planters who have a grievance against us, but we who have a serious complaint against them; so flourishing a dependency should certainly provide for all the costs of her defence.

Some of the mountain views between Kandy and Nuwara Ellia are full of grandeur, though they lack the New Zealand snows; but none can match, for variety and colour, that which I saw on my return from the ascent to the Kaduganava Pass, where you look over a foreground of giant-leaved talipot and slender areca palms and tall bamboos, lit with the scarlet blooms of the cotton-tree, on to a plain dotted with banyan-tree groves and broken by wooded hills. On either side, the deep valley-bottoms are carpeted with bright green—the wet rice-lands, or terraced paddy-fields, from which the natives gather crop after crop throughout the year.

In the union of rich foliage with deep colour and grand forms, no scenery save that of New Zealand can bear comparison with that of the hill country of Ceylon, unless, indeed, it be the scenery of Java, and the far Eastern isles.

CHAPTER III.

MADRAS TO CALCUTTA.

SPENDING but a single day in Madras—an inferior Columbo—I passed on to Calcutta with a pleasant remembrance of the air of prosperity that hangs about the chief city of what is still called by Bengal civilians "The Benighted Presidency." Small as are the houses, poor as are the shops, every one looks well-to-do, and everybody happy, from the not undeservedly famed cooks at the club to the catamaran men on the shore. Coffee and good government have of late done much for Madras.

The surf consists of two lines of rollers, and is altogether inferior to the fine-weather swell on the west coast of New Zealand, and only to be dignified and promoted into surfship by men of that fine imagination which will lead them to sniff the spices a day before they reach Ceylon, or the pork and molasses when off Nantucket light-ship. The row through the first roller in the lumbering Massullah boat, manned by a dozen sinewy blacks, the waiting for a chance between the first and second lines of spray, and then the dash for shore, the crew singing their measured "Ah! lah! lálala!—ah! lah! lálala!" the stroke coming with the accented syllable, and the helmsman shrieking with excitement, is a more pretentious ceremony than that which accompanies the crossing of Hokitika bar, but the passage is a far less dangerous one. The Massullah boats are like empty hay-barges on the Thames, but built without nails, so that they "give" instead of breaking up when battered by the sand on one side and the seas upon the other. This is a very wise precaution in the case of boats which are always made to take the shore broadside on. The first sea that strikes the boat either shoots the passenger on to the dry sand, or puts him where he can easily be caught by the natives on the beach, but the Massullah boat herself gets a terrible banging before the crew can haul her out of reach of the seas.

Sighting the Temple of Juggernauth and one palm-tree, but seeing no land, we entered the Hoogly, steaming between light-houses, guard-ships, and buoys, but not catching a glimpse of the low land of the Sunderabunds till we had been many hours in "the river." After lying right off the tiger-infested island of Saugur, we started on our run up to Calcutta before the sun was risen. Compared with Ceylon, the scene was English; there was nothing tropical about it except the mist upon the land; and low villas and distant factory chimneys reminded one of the Thames between Battersea and Fulham. Coming into Garden Reach, where large ships anchor before they sail, we had a long, low building on our right, gaudy and architecturally hideous, but from its vast size almost imposing : it was the palace of the dethroned King of Oude, the place where, it is said, are carried on deeds become impossible in Lucknow. Such has been the extravagance of the King that the Government of India has lately interfered, and appointed a commission to pay his debts, and deduct them from his income of 120,000*l.* a year ; for we pay into the privy purse of the dethroned Vizier of Oude exactly twice the yearly sum that we set aside for that of Queen Victoria. Whatever income is allowed to native princes, they always spend the double. The experience of the Dutch in Java and our own in India is uniform in this respect. Removed from that slight restraint upon expenditure which the fear of bankruptcy or revolution forces upon reigning kings, native princes supported by European Governments run recklessly into debt. The commission which was sitting upon the debts of the King of Oude while I was in Calcutta warned him that, if he offended a second time, Government would for the future spend his income for him. It is not the King's extravagance alone, however, that is complained of. Always notorious for debauchery, he has now become infamous for his vices. One of his wives was arrested while I was in Calcutta for purchasing girls for the harem, but the King himself escaped. For nine years he has never left his palace, yet he spends, we are told, from 200,000*l.* to 250,000*l.* a year.

In his extravagance and immorality the King of Oude does not stand alone in Calcutta. His mode of life is imitated by the wealthy natives ; his vices are mimicked by every young Bengalee baboo. It is a question whether we are not responsible for the tone which has been taken by "civilization" in Calcutta. The old philosophy has gone, and left nothing in its place; we have by moral force destroyed the old religions in Calcutta, but we have set up no new. Whether the character of our Indian Government, at once levelling and paternal, has not much to do with the spread of careless sensuality is a question before answering which it would be well to look to France, where a similar government has for sixteen years prevailed. In Paris, at least, democratic despotism is fast degrading the French citizen to the moral level of the Bengalee baboo.

The first thing in Calcutta that I saw was the view of the Government House from the Park Reserve—a miniature Sahara since its trees were destroyed by the great cyclone. The Viceroy's dwelling, though crushed by groups of lions and unicorns of gigantic stature and astonishing design, is an imposing building; but it is the only palace in the "city of palaces"—a name which must have been given to the pestiferous city by some one who had never seen any other towns but Liverpool and London. The true city of palaces is Lucknow.

In Calcutta, I first became acquainted with that unbounded hospitality of the great mercantile houses in the East of which I have since acquired many pleasing remembrances. The luxury of "the firm" impresses the English traveller; the huge house is kept as an hotel; every one is welcome to dinner, breakfast, and bed in the verandah, or in a room, if he can sleep under a roof in the hot weather. Sometimes two and sometimes twenty sit down to the meals, and always without notice to the butlers or the cooks, but every one is welcome, down to the friend of a friend's friend; and junior clerks will write letters of introduction to members of the firm, which secure the bearer a most hospitable welcome from the other clerks, even when all the partners are away. "If Brown is not there, Smith will be, and if he's away, why then Johnson will put you up," is the form of invitation to the hospitalities of an Eastern firm. The finest of fruits are on table between five and six, and tea and iced drinks are ready at all times, from dawn to breakfast —a ceremony which takes place at ten. To the regular meals you come in or not as you please, and no one trained in Calcutta or Bombay can conceive offence being taken by a host at his guest accepting, without consulting him, invitations to dine out in the city, or to spend some days at a villa in its outskirts. Servants are in the corridors by day and night at the call of guests, and your entertainers tell you that, although they have not time to go about with you, servants will always be ready to drive you at sunset to the bandstand in the carriage of some member of the firm.

The population of Calcutta is as motley as that of Galle, though the constituents are not the same. Greeks, Armenians, and Burmese, besides many Eurasians, or English-speaking half-castes, mingle with the mass of Indian Mohamedans and Hindoos. The hot weather having suddenly set in, the Calcutta officials, happier than the merchants—who, however, care little about heat when trade is good—were starting for Simla in a body, "just as they were warming to their work," as the Calcutta people say, and, finding that there was nothing to be done in the stifling city, I, too, determined to set off.

The heat was great at night, and the noisy native crows and whistling kites held durbars inside my window in the only cool hour of the twenty-four—namely, that which begins at dawn—and thus hastened my departure from Calcutta by preventing me from taking rest while in it. Hearing that at Patna there was nothing to be seen or learnt, I travelled from Calcutta to Benares—500 miles—in the same train and railway carriage. Our first long stoppage was at Chandernagore, but, as the native baggage-coolies, or porters, howl the station names in their own fashion, I hardly recognised the city in the melancholy moan of "Orn-dorn-orn-gorne," which welcomed the train, and it was not till I saw a French infantry uniform upon the platform that I remembered that Chandernagore, a village belonging to the French, lies hard by Calcutta, to which city it was once a dangerous rival. It is said that the French retain their Indian dependencies instead of selling them to us as did the Dutch, in order that they may ever bear in mind the fact that we once conquered them in India; but it would be hard to find any real ground for their retention, unless they are held as centres for the Catholic missions. We will not even permit them to be made smuggling depôts, for which purpose they would be excellently adapted. The whole of the possessions in India of the French amount together to only twenty-six leagues square. Even Pondicherry, the largest and only French Indian dependency of which the name is often heard in Europe, is cut into several portions by strips of British territory, and the whole of the French-Indian dependencies are mere specks of land isolated in our vast territories. The officer who was lounging in the station was a native; indeed, in the territory of Chandernagore there are but 230 Europeans, and but 1,500 in all French India. He made up to my compartment as though he would have got in, which I wished that he would have done, as natives in the French service all speak French, but seeing a European, he edged away to a dark uncomfortable compartment. This action was, I fear, a piece of silent testimony to the prejudice which makes our people in India almost invariably refuse to travel with a native, whatever may be his rank.

As we passed through Burdwan and Rajmahal, where the East Indian Railway taps the Ganges, the station scenes became more and more interesting. We associate with the word "railway" ideas that are peculiarly English:—shareholders and directors, guards in blue, policemen in dark green, and porters in brown corduroy; no English institution, however, assumes more readily an Oriental dress. Station-masters and sparrows alone are English; everything else on a Bengal railway is purely Eastern. Sikh irregulars jostle begging fakeers in the stations; palkees and doolies—palankeens and sedans, as we should call them—wait at the back doors; ticket-clerks smoke water-pipes; an ibis drinks at the engine tank; a sacred cow looks over the fence, and a tame elephant reaches up with his trunk at the telegraph wire, on which sits a hoopoe, while an Indian vulture crowns the post.

When we came opposite to the Monghyr Hills, the only natural objects which for 1,600 miles break the level of the great plain of Hindostan, people of the central tribes, small-headed and savage-looking, were mingled with the Hindoos at the stations. In blackness there was not much difference between the races, for low-caste Bengalees are as black as Guinea negroes.

As the day grew hot, a water-carrier with a well-filled skin upon his back appeared at every station, and came running to the native cars in answer to the universal long-drawn shout of "Ah ! ah ! Bheestie—e !"

The first view of the Ganges calls up no enthusiasm. The Thames below Gravesend half dried up would be not unlike it; indeed, the river itself is as ugly as the Mississippi or Missouri, while its banks are more hideous by far than theirs. Beyond Patna, the plains, too, become as monotonous as the river,—flat, dusty, and treeless, they are no way tropical in their character; they lie, indeed, wholly outside the tropics. I afterwards found that a man may cross India from the Irawaddy to the Indus, and see no tropical scenery, no tropical cultivation. The aspect of the Ganges valley is that of Cambridgeshire, or of parts of Lincoln seen after harvest time, and with flocks of strange and brilliant birds and an occasional jackal thrown in. The sun is hot—not, indeed, much hotter than in Australia, but the heat is of a different kind to that encountered by the English in Ceylon or the West Indies. From a military point of view, the plains may be described as a parade-ground continued to infinity; and this explains the success of our small forces against the rebels in 1857, our cavalry and artillery having in all cases swept their infantry from these levels with the utmost ease.

A view over the plains by daylight is one which in former times some old Indians can never have enjoyed. Many a lady in the days of palki-dawk has passed a life in the Deccan table-land without ever seeing a mountain, or knowing she was on the top of one. Carried up and down the ghauts at night, it was only by the tilting of her palki that she could detect the rise or fall, for day travelling for ladies was almost unknown in India before it was introduced with the railways.

At Patna, the station was filled with crowds of railway coolies, or navvies, as we should say, who, with their tools and baggage, were camped out upon the platform, smoking peacefully. I afterwards found that natives have little idea of time-tables and departure hours. When they want to go ten miles by railway, they walk straight down to the nearest station, and there smoke their hookahs till the train arrives—at the end of twenty-four hours or ten minutes, as the case may be. There is but one step that the more ignorant among the natives are in a hurry to take, and that is to buy their tickets. They are no sooner come to the terminus than with one accord they rush at the native ticket-clerk, yelling the name of the station to which they wish to go. In vain he declares that, the train not being due for ten or fifteen hours, there is plenty of time for the purchase. Open-mouthed, and wrought up almost to madness, the passengers dance round him, screaming "Burdwan!" or "Serampoor!" or whatever the name may be, till at last he surrenders at discretion. There is often no room for all who wish to go; indeed, the worst point about the management of the railways lies in the defective accommodation for the native passengers, and their treatment by the English station-masters is not always good: I saw them on many occasions terribly kicked and cuffed; but Indian station-masters are not very highly paid, and are too often men who cannot resist the temptations to violence which despotic power throws in their way. They might ask with the Missourian in the United States army when he was accused of drunkenness, "Whether Uncle Sam expected to get all the cardinal virtues for fifteen dollars a month?"

The Indian railways are all made and worked by companies; but as the Government guarantees the interest of five per cent., which only the East Indian, or Calcutta and Delhi, line can pay, it interferes much in the management. The telegraph is both made and worked by Government; and the reason why the railways were not put upon the same footing is that the Government of India was doubtful as to the wisdom of borrowing directly the vast sum required, and doubtful also of the possibility of borrowing it without diminishing its credit.

The most marked among the effects of railways

upon the state of India are, as a moral change, the weakening of caste ties—as a physical, the destruction of the Indian forests. It is found that if a rich native discovers that he can, by losing caste in touching his inferiors, travel a certain distance in a comfortable second-class carriage for ten rupees, while a first-class ticket costs him twenty, he will often risk his caste to save his pound; still, caste yields but slowly to railways and the telegraph. It is but a very few years since one of my friends received a thousand rupees for pleading in a case which turned on the question whether the paint-spot on Krishna's nose, which is also a caste sign, should be drawn as a plain horizontal crescent, or with a pendant from the centre. It is only a year since, in Orissa, it was seen that Hindoo peasants preferred cannibalism, or death by starvation, to defilement by eating their bullocks.

As for the forests, their destruction has already in many places changed a somewhat moist climate to one of excessive drought, and planting is now taking place, with a view both to supplying the railway engines, and bringing back the rains. On the East Indian line, I found that they burnt mixed coal and wood, but the Indian coal is scarce and bad, and lies entirely in shallow "pockets."

The train reached Mogul-Serai, the junction for Benares, at midnight of the day following that on which it left Calcutta, and, changing my carriage at once, I asked how long it would be before we started, to which the answer was, "half an hour;" so I went to sleep. Immediately, as it seemed, I was awakened by whispering, and, turning, saw a crowd of boys and baggage-coolies at the carriage-door. When I tried to discover what they wanted, my Hindostanee broke down, and it was some time before I found that I had slept through the short journey from Mogul-Serai, and had dozed on in the station till the lights had been put out, before the coolies woke me. Crossing the Ganges by the bridge of boats, I found myself in Benares, the ancient Varanasi, and sacred capital of the Hindoos.

CHAPTER IV.

BENARES.

IN the comparative cool of early morning, I sallied out on a stroll through the outskirts of Benares. Thousands of women were stepping gracefully along the crowded roads, bearing on their heads the water-jars, while at every few paces there was a well, at which hundreds were waiting along with the bheesties their turn for lowering their bright gleaming copper cups to the well-water to fill their skins or vases. All were keeping up a continual chatter, women with women, men with men : all the tongues were running ceaselessly. It is astonishing to see the indignation that a trifling mishap creates—such gesticulation, such shouting, and loud talk, you would think that murder at least was in question. The world cannot show the Hindoo's equal as a babbler; the women talk while they grind corn, the men while they smoke their water-pipes; your true Hindoo is never quiet; when not talking, he is playing on his tomtom.

The Doorgha Khond, the famed Temple of the Sacred Monkeys, I found thronged with worshippers, and garlanded in every part with roses: it overhangs one of the best holy tanks in India, but has not much beauty or grandeur, and is chiefly remarkable for the swarms of huge, fat-paunched, yellow-bearded, holy monkeys, whose outposts hold one quarter of the city, and whose main body forms a living roof to the temple. A singular contrast to the Doorgha Khond was the Queen's College for native students, built in a mixture of Tudor and Hindoo architecture. The view from the roof is noticeable, depending as it does for its beauty on the mingling of the rich green of the timber with the gay colours of the painted native huts. Over the trees are seen the minarets at the river-side, and an unwonted life was given to the view by the smoke and flames that were rising from two burning huts, in widely-separated districts of the native town. It is said that the natives, whenever they quarrel with their neighbours, always take the first opportunity of firing their huts; but in truth the huts in the hot weather almost fire themselves, so inflammable are their roofs and sides.

When the sun had declined sufficiently to admit of another excursion, I started from my bungalow, and, passing through the elephant-corral, went down with a guide to the ghauts, the observatory of Jai Singh, and the Golden Temple. From the minarets of the mosque of Aurungzebe I had a lovely sunset view of the ghauts, the city, and the Ganges; but the real sight of Benares, after all, lies in a walk through the tortuous passages that do duty for streets. No carriages can pass them, they are so narrow.

You walk preceded by your guide, who warns the people, that they may stand aside, and not be defiled by your touch, for that is the real secret of the apparent respect paid to you in Benares; but the sacred cows are so numerous and so obstinate that you cannot avoid sometimes jostling them. The scene in the passages is the most Indian in India. The gaudy dresses of the Hindoo princes spending a week in purification at the holy place, the frescoed fronts of the shops and houses, the deafening beating of the tomtoms, and, above all, the smoke and sickening smell from the "burning ghauts" that meets you, mingled with a sweeter smell of burning spices, as you work your way through the vast crowds of pilgrims who are pouring up from the river's bank —all alike are strange to the English traveller, and fill his mind with that indescribable awe which everywhere accompanies the sight of scenes and ceremonies that we do not understand. When once you are on the Ganges bank itself, the scene is wilder still:— a river front of some three miles, faced with lofty ghauts, or flights of river stairs, over which rise, pile above pile, in sublime confusion, lofty palaces with oriel windows hanging over the sacred stream; observatories with giant sun-dials, gilt domes (*golden*, the story runs), and silver minarets. On the ghauts, rows of fires, each with a smouldering body; on the river, boat-loads of pilgrims, and fakeers praying while they float; under the houses, lines of prostrate bodies—those of the sick—brought to the sacred Ganges to die—or, say our Government spies, to be murdered by suffocation with sacred mud; while prowling about are the wolf-like fanatics who feed on putrid flesh. The whole is lit by a sickly sun fitfully glaring through the smoke, while the Ganges stream is half obscured by the river fog and reek of the hot earth.

The lofty pavilions that crown the river front are ornamented with paintings of every beast that walks and bird that flies, with monsters, too—pink and green and spotted—with griffins, dragons, and elephant-headed gods embracing dancing-girls. Here and there are representations of red-coated soldiers—English, it would seem, for they have white faces, but so, the Maories say, have the New Zealand fairies, who are certainly not British. The Benares taste for painting leads to the decoration with pink and yellow spots of the very cows. The tiger is the commonest of all the figures on the walls—indeed, the explanation that the representations are allegorical, or that gods are pictured in tiger shape, has not removed from my mind the belief that the tiger must have been worshipped in India at some early date. All Easterns are inclined to worship the beasts that eat them: the Javanese light floating sacrifices to their river crocodiles; the Scindees at Kurrachee venerate the sacred muggur, or man-eating alligator; the hill-tribes pray to snakes; indeed, to a new comer, all Indian religion has the air of devil-worship, or worship of the destructive principle in some shape: the gods are drawn as grinning fiends, they are propitiated by infernal music, they are often worshipped with obscene and hideous rites.

There is even something cruel in the monotonous roar of the great tomtoms; the sound seems to connect itself with widow-burning, with child-murder, with Juggernauth processions. Since the earliest known times, the tomtom has been used to drown the cries of tortured fanatics; its booming is bound up with the thousand barbarisms of false religion. If the scene on the Benares ghauts is full of horrors, we must not forget that Hindooism is a creed of fear and horror, not of love.

The Government of India has lately instituted an inquiry into the alleged abuses of the custom of taking sick Hindoos to the Ganges-side to die, with a view to regulating or suppressing the practice which prevails in the river-side portion of Lower Bengal. At Benares, Bengal people are still taken to the river-side, but not so other natives, as Hindoos dying anywhere in the sacred city have all the blessings which the most holy death can possibly secure; the Benares Shastra, moreover, forbids the practice, and I saw but two cases of it in the city, although I had seen many near Calcutta. Not only are aged people brought from their sick-rooms, laid in the burning sun, and half suffocated with the Ganges water poured down their throats, but, owing to the ridicule which follows if they recover, or the selfishness of their relatives, the water is often muddier than it need be: hence the phrase "ghaut murder," by which this custom is generally known. Similar customs are not unheard of in other parts of India, and even in Polynesia and North America.

The Veddahs, or black aborigines of Ceylon, were, up to very lately, in the habit of carrying their dying parents or children into the jungle, and, having placed a chatty of water and some rice by their side, leaving them to be devoured by wild beasts. Under pressure from our officials, they are believed to have ceased to act thus, but they continue, we are told, to throw their dead to the leopards and crocodiles. The Maories, too, have a way of taking out to die alone those whom their seers have pronounced doomed men, but it is probable that, among the rude races, the custom which seems to be a relic of human sacrifice has not been so grossly abused as it has been by the Bengal Hindoos. The practice of Ganjatra is but one out of many similar barbarities that disgrace the religion of the Hindoos, but it is fast sharing the fate of suttee and infanticide.

As I returned through the bazaar, I met many most unholy-looking visitors to the sacred town. Fierce Rajpoots, with enormous turbans ornamented with zig-zag stripes; Bengal bankers, in large purple turbans, curling their long white moustaches, and bearing their critical noses high aloft as they daintily picked their way over the garbage of the streets; and savage retainers of the rajahs staying for a season at their city palaces, were to the traveller's eye no very devout pilgrims. In truth, the immoralities of the "holy city" are as great as its religious virtues, and it is the chosen ground of the loose characters as well as of the pilgrims of the Hindoo world.

In the whole of the great throng in the bazaar,

hardly the slightest trace of European dressing was to be perceived: the varnished boots of the wealthier Hindoos alone bore witness to the existence of English trade — a singular piece of testimony, this, to the essential conservatism of the Oriental mind. With any quantity of old army clothing to be got for the asking, you never see a rag of it on a native back—not even on that of the poorest coolie. If you give a blanket to an outdoor servant, he will cut it into strips, and wear them as a puggree round his head; but this is about the only thing he will accept, unless to sell it in the bazaar.

As I stopped to look for a moment at the long trains of laden camels that were winding slowly through the tortuous streets, I saw a European soldier cheapening a bracelet with a native jeweller. He was the first *topee-wallah* ("hat-fellow," or "European") that I had seen in Benares city. Calcutta is the only town in Northern India in which you meet Europeans in your walks or rides, and, even there, there is but one European to every sixty natives. In all India, there are, including troops, children, and officials of all kinds, far less than as many thousands of Europeans as there are millions of natives.

The evening after that on which I visited the native town, I saw in Secrole cantonments, near Benares, the India hated and dreaded by our troops—by day a blazing deadly heat and sun, at night a still more deadly fog—a hot white fog, into which the sun disappears half an hour before his time for setting, and out of which he shoots soon after seven in the morning, to blaze and kill again—a pestiferous fever-breeding ground-fog, out of which stand the tops of the palms, though their stems are invisible in the steam. Compared with our English summer climate, it seems the atmosphere of another planet.

Among the men in the cantonments, I found much of that demoralization that heat everywhere produces among Englishmen. The newly-arrived soldiers appear to pass their days in alternate trials of hard drinking and of total abstinence, and are continually in a state of nervous fright, which in time must wear them out, and make them an easy prey to fever. The officers who are fresh from England often behave in much the same manner as the men, though with them "belatee pawnee" takes the place of plain water with the brandy. "Belatee pawnee" means, being translated, "English water," but, when interpreted, it means "soda-water"—the natives once believing that this was English river-water, bottled and brought to India by us as they carry Ganges water to the remotest parts. The superstition is now at an end, owing to the fact that natives are themselves largely employed in the making of soda-water, which is cheaper in India than it is at home; but the name remains.

Our men kill themselves with beer, with brandy and soda-water, and with careless inattention to night chills, and then blame the poor climate for their fevers, or die cursing "India." Of course, long residence in a climate winterless and always hot at midday produces or intensifies certain diseases;

but brandy and soda water produces more, and intensifies all. They say it is "soda-and-brandy" the first month, and then "brandy-and-soda," but that men finally take to putting in the soda-water first, and then somehow the brandy always kills them. If a man wears a flannel belt and thick clothes when he travels by night, and drinks hot tea, he need not fear India.

In all ways, Benares is the type of India: in the Secrole cantonments, you have the English in India, intelligent enough, but careless, and more English than they are at home, with garrison chaplains, picnics, balls, and champagne suppers; hard by, in the native town, the fierce side of Hindooism, and streets for an Englishman to show himself in which ten years ago was almost certain death. Benares is the centre of all the political intrigues of India, but the great mutiny itself was hatched there without being heard of at Secrole. Except that our policemen now perambulate the town, change in Benares there has been none. Were missionaries to appear openly in its streets, their fate would still very possibly be the same as that which in this city befell St. Thomas.

CHAPTER V.

CASTE.

ONE of the greatest difficulties with which the British have to contend in Hindostan is how to discover the tendencies, how to follow the changes, of native opinion. Your Hindoo is so complaisant a companion, that, whether he is your servant at threepence a day, or the ruler of the State in which you dwell, he is perpetually striving to make his opinions the reflex of your own. You are engaged in a continual struggle to prevent your views from being seen, in order that you may get at his: in this you always fail; a slight hint is enough for a Hindoo, and, if he cannot find even that much of suggestion in your words, he confines himself to commonplace. We should see in this, not so much one of the forms assumed by the cringing slavishness born of centuries of subjection, not so much an example of Oriental cunning, as of the polish of Eastern manners. Even in our rude country, it is hardly courteous, whatever your opinions, flatly to contradict the man with whom you happen to be talking; with the Hindoo, it is the height of ill-breeding so much as to differ from him. The results of the practice are deplorable; our utter ignorance of the secret history of the rebellion of 1857 is an example of its working, for there must have been a time, before discontent ripened into conspiracy, when we might have been advised and warned. The native newspapers are worse than useless to us ; accepted as exponents of Hindoo views by those who know no better, and founded mostly by British capital, they are at once incapable of directing and of acting as indexes to native opinion, and express only the sentiments of half-a-dozen small merchants at the presidency towns, who give the tone to some two or three papers, which are copied and followed by the remainder.

The result of this difficulty in discovering native opinion is that our officers, however careful, however considerate in their bearing towards the natives, daily wound the feelings of the people who are under their care by acts which, though done in a praiseworthy spirit, appear to the natives deeds of gross stupidity or of outrageous despotism. It is hopeless to attempt to conciliate, it is impossible so much as to govern unless by main force continually displayed, an Eastern people in whose religious thought we are not deeply learned.

Not only are we unacquainted with the feelings of the people, but we are lamentably ignorant of the simplest facts about their religions, their wealth, and their occupations, for no census of all India has yet been taken. A complete census had, indeed, been taken, not long before my visit, in Central India, and another in the North-West Provinces, but none in Madras, Bombay, the Punjaub, or Bengal. The difficulties in the way of the officials who carried through the arrangements for the two that had been taken were singularly great. In the Central Provinces, the census-papers had to be prepared in five languages; both here and in the North-West, the purely scientific nature of the inquiry had to be brought home to the minds of the people. In Central India, the hill tribes believed that our object in the census was to pave the way for the collection of the unmarried girls as companions for our wifeless soldiers, so all began marrying forthwith. In the North-West, the natives took it into their heads that our object was to see how many able-bodied men would be available for a war against Russia, and to collect a poll-tax to pay for the expedition. The numerous tribes that are habitually guilty of infanticide threw every difficulty in the way; Europeans disliked the whole affair, on account of the insult offered to their dignity in ranking them along with natives. It must be admitted, indeed, that the provisions for recording caste distinctions gave an odd shape to the census-papers left at the houses at Secrole, in which European officers were asked to state their "caste or tribe." The census of the Central Provinces was imperfect enough, but that of the North-West was the second that had been taken there, and showed signs of scientific arrangement and great care.

The North-West Provinces include the great towns of Benares, Agra, and Allahabad, and the census fell into my hands at Benares itself, at the Sanscrit College. It was a strange production, and seemed to have brought together a mass of information respecting castes and creeds which was new even to those who had lived long in the North-West Provinces. All callings in India being hereditary, there were entries recording the presence in certain towns of "hereditary clerks who pray to their inkhorns," "hereditary beggars," "hereditary planters of slips or cuttings," "hereditary gravediggers," "hereditary hermits," and "hereditary hangmen," for in India a hangmanship descends with as much regularity as a crown. In the single district of the Dehra Valley, there are 1,500 "hereditary tomtom men"—drummers at the festivals; 234 Brahmins of Bijnour returned themselves as having for profession "the receipt of presents to avert the influence of evil stars." In Bijnour, there are also fifteen people of a caste which professes "the pleasing of people by assuming disguises," while at Benares there is a whole caste—the Bhâts—whose hereditary occupation is to "satirise the enemies of the rich, and to praise their friends." In the North-West Provinces, there are 572 distinct castes in all.

The accounts which some castes gave of their origin read strangely in a solemn governmental document: the members of one caste described themselves as "descended from Maicasur, a demon;" but some of the records are less legendary and more historic. One caste in the Dehra Valley sent in a note that they came in 1,000 A.D. from the Deccan; another that they emigrated from Arabia 500 years ago. The Gour Brahmins claim to have been in the district of Moozuffernuggur for 5,000 years.

Under the title of "occupations," the heads of families alone were given, and not the number of those dependent on them, whence it comes that in the whole province only "11,000 tomtom players" were set down. The habits and tastes of the people are easily seen in the entries: "3,600 firework manufacturers," "45 makers of crowns for idols," "4,353 gold-bangle makers," "29,136 glass-bangle makers," "1,123 astrologers." There are also 145 "ear-cleaners," besides "kite-makers," "ear-piercers," "pedigree-makers," "makers of caste-marks," "cow-dung sellers," and "hereditary painters of horses with spots." There was no backwardness in the followers of maligned pursuits: 974 people in Allahabad described themselves as "low blackguards," 35 as "men who beg with threats of violence," 25 as "hereditary robbers," 479,015 as "beggars," 29 as "howlers at funerals," 226 as "flatterers for gain;" "vagabonds," "charmers," "informers" were all set down, and 1,100 returned themselves as "hereditary buffoons," while 2,000 styled themselves "conjurers," 4,000 "acrobats," and 6,372 "poets." In one district alone, there were 777 "soothsayers and astrologers" by profession.

It is worthy of notice that, although there are in the North-West Provinces half a million of beggars in a population of thirty millions, they seem never to beg of Europeans—at least, I was not once asked for alms during my stay in India. If the smallest service be performed, there comes a howl of "O Bauks-heece!" from all quarters, but at other times natives seem afraid to beg of Englishmen.

The number of fakeers, soothsayers, charmers, and other "religious" vagabonds is enormous, but the dense ignorance of the people renders them a prey to witchcraft, evil-eye, devil-influence, and all such folly. In Central India, there are whole districts which are looked upon as witch-tracts or haunted places, and which are never approached by man, but set aside as homes for devils. A gentleman who was lately engaged there on the railroad survey found that night after night his men were frightened out of their wits by "fire-fiends," or blazing demons. He insisted that they should take him to the spot where these strange sights were seen, and to his amazement he, too, saw the fire-devil; at least, he saw a blaze of light moving slowly through the jungle. Gathering himself up for a chase, he rushed at the devil with a club, when the light suddenly disappeared, and instantly shone out from another spot, a hundred yards from the former place. Seeing that there was some trickery at work, he hid himself, and after some hours caught his devil, who, to escape from a sound drubbing, gave an explanation of the whole affair. The man said that the natives of the surveyor's party had stolen his mangoes for several nights, but that at last he had hit on a plan for frightening them away. He and his sons went out at dark with pots of blazing oil upon their heads, and, when approached by thieves, the leading one put a cover on his pot, and became invisible, while the second uncovered his. The surveying party got the drubbing, and the devil escaped scot-free; but the surveyor, with short-sighted wisdom, told his men, who had not seen him catch the fire-bearer, that he had had the honour of an interview with the devil himself, who had joyfully informed him of the thefts committed by the men. The surveyor did not admit that he was from this time forward worshipped by his party, but it is not unlikely that such was the case. One of the hill-tribes of Madras worships Colonel Palmer, a British officer who died some seventy years ago, just as Drake was worshipped in America, and Captain Cook in Hawaii. It was one of these tribes that invented the well-known worshipping machine, or "praying-wheel."

The hill-tribes are less refined, but hardly more ignorant in their fanaticism than are the Hindoos. At Bombay, upon the beach where the dead are buried, or rather tossed to the wild beasts, I saw a filthy and holy Hindoo saint, whose claim to veneration consists in his having spent the whole of the days and portions of the nights for twenty years in a stone box in which he can neither stand, nor lie, nor sit, nor sleep. These saintly fakeers have still much influence with the Hindoo mass, but in old times their power and their insolence were alike unbounded. Agra itself was founded to please one of them. The great Emperor Akbar, who, although a lax Mohamedan, was in no sense a Hindoo, kept nevertheless a Hindoo saint for political purposes, and gave him the foremost position in his train. When the Emperor was beginning to fortify Futtehpore Sikri, where he lived, the saint sent for him, and said that the work must be stopped, as the noise disturbed him at his prayers. The Emperor offered him new rooms away from the site of the proposed walls, but the saint replied that, whether

Akbar went on with his works or no, he should leave Futtehpore. To pacify him, Akbar founded Agra, and dismantled Futtehpore Sikri.

From the census it appears that there are, in the North-West Provinces, no less than twenty-two newspapers under Government inspection, of which five are published at Agra. The circulation of these papers is extremely small, and as the Government itself takes 3,500 of the 12,000 copies which they issue, its hold over them, without exertion of force, is great. Of the other 8,500, 8,000 go to native and 500 to European subscribers. All the native papers are skilful at catering for their double public, but those which are printed half in a native tongue and half in English stand in the first rank for unscrupulousness. One of these papers gave, while I was in India, some French speech in abuse of the English. This was headed on the English side "*Interesting* Account of the English," but on the native side "*Excellent* Account of the English." The "English correspondence" and English news of these native papers is so absurdly concocted by the editors out of their own brains that it is a question whether it would not be advisable to send them weekly a column of European news, and even to withhold Government patronage from them unless they gave it room, leaving them to qualify and explain the facts as best they could. Their favourite statements are that Russia is going to invade India forthwith, that the Queen has become a Catholic or a Mohamedan, and that the whole population of India is to be converted to Christianity by force. The external appearance of the native papers is sometimes as comical as their matter. The *Umritsur Commercial Advertiser*, of which nothing is English but the title, gives, for instance, the time-tables of the Punjaub Railway on its back sheet. The page, which is a mere maze of dots and crooked lines, has at the top a cut of a railway train, in which guards apparently cocked-hatted, but probably meant to be wearing pith helmets, are represented sitting on the top of each carriage with their legs dangling down in front of the windows.

Neither Christianity nor native reformed religions make much show in the North-Western census. The Christians are strongest in the South of India, the Hindoo reformers in the Punjaub. The Sikhs themselves, and the Kookhas, Nirunkarees, Goolab Dasseas, Naukeeka-punth, and many other Punjaubee sects, all show more or less hostility to caste; but in the North-West Provinces caste distinctions flourish, although in reality they have no doubt lost strength. The high-caste men are beginning to find their caste a drawback to their success in life, and are given to concealing it. Just as with ourselves kings go *incognito* when they travel for pleasure, so the Bengal sepoy hides his Brahminical string under his cloth, in order that he may be sent on foreign service without its being known that by crossing the seas he will lose caste.

Judging by the unanimous opinion of the native press on the doings of the Maharajahs of Bombay, and on the licentiousness of the Koolin Brahmins, many of our civilians have come to think that Hindooism in its present shape has lost the support of a large number of the more intelligent Hindoos, but there is little real reason to believe that this is the case. In Calcutta, the Church of Hindoo Deists is gaining ground, and one of their leaders is said to have met with some successes during a recent expedition to the North-West, but of this there is no proof. The little regard that many high-caste natives show for caste except as a matter of talk merely means that caste is less an affair of religion than of custom, but that it is a matter of custom does not show that its force is slight; on the contrary, custom is the lord of India.

The success of Mohamedanism in India should show that caste has never been strong except so far as caste is custom. It is true that the peasants in Orissa starved by the side of the sacred cows, but this was custom too: any one man killing the cow would have been at once killed by his also starving neighbours for breaking custom; but once change the custom by force, and there is no tendency to return to the former state of things. The Portuguese and the Mohamedans alike made converts by compulsion, yet when the pressure was removed, there was no return to the earlier faith. Of the nature of caste we had an excellent example in the behaviour of the troopers of a Bengal cavalry regiment three weeks before the outbreak of the mutiny of 1857, when they said that for their part they knew that their cartridges were not greased with the fat of cows, but that, as they looked as though they were, it came to the same thing, for they should lose caste if their friends saw them touch the cartridges in question.

It was the cry of infringement of custom that was raised against us by the mutineers: "They aim at subverting our institutions; they have put down the suttee of the Brahmins, the infanticide of the Marattas, caste and adoption are despised; they aim at destroying all our religious customs," was the most powerful cry that could be raised. It is one against which we shall never be wholly safe; but it is the custom and not the religion which is the people's especial care.

There is one point in which caste forms a singular difficulty in our way, which has not yet been brought sufficiently home to us. The comparatively fair treatment which is now extended to the low-caste and no-caste men is itself an insult to the high-caste nobility; and while the no-caste men care little how we treat them provided we pay them well, and the bunnya, or shop-keeping class, encouraged by the improvement, cry out loudly that the Government wrongs them in not treating them as Europeans, the high-caste men are equally disgusted with our good treatment both of middle-class and inferior Hindoos. These things are stumbling-blocks in our way chiefly because no amount of acquaintance with the various phases of caste feeling is sufficient to bring home its importance to Englishmen. The Indian is essentially the caste man, the Saxon as characteristically the no-caste man, and it is difficult to produce a mutual understanding. Just as in England the people are too democratic for the Government, in India the Government is too democratic for the people.

Although caste has hitherto been but little shaken, there are forces at work which must in time produce the most grave results. The return to their homes of natives who have emigrated and worked at sugar-planting in Mauritius and coffee-growing in Ceylon, mixing with negroes and with Europeans, will gradually aid in the subversion of caste distinctions, and the Parsees will give their help towards the creation of a healthier feeling. The young men of the merchant-class—who are all pure deists—set an example of doing away with caste distinctions which will gradually affect the whole population of the towns; railways will act upon the labourers and agriculturists; a closer intercourse with Europe will possibly go hand in hand with universal instruction in the English tongue, and the indirect results of Christian teaching will continue to be, as they have been, great.

The positive results of missionary work in India have hitherto been small. Taking the census as a guide, in the district of Mooradabad we find but 107 Christians in 1,100,000 people; in Budaon, 64 " Christians, Europeans, and Eurasians " (half-castes) out of 900,000 people; in Bareilly, 137 native Christians in a million and a half of people; in Shajehanpoor, 98 in a million people; in Turrai, none in a million people; in Etah, no native Christians, and only twenty Europeans to 614,000 people; in the

Banda district, thirteen native Christians out of three-quarters of a million of people; in Goruckpoor, 100 native Christians out of three and a half millions of people. Not to multiply instances, this proportion is preserved throughout the whole of the districts, and the native Christians in the North-West are proved to form but an insignificant fraction of the population.

The number of native Christians in India is extremely small. Twenty-three societies, having three hundred Protestant missionary stations, more than three hundred native missionary churches, and five hundred European preachers, costing with their assistants two hundred thousand pounds a year, profess to show only a hundred and fifty thousand converts, of whom one-seventh are communicants. The majority of the converts who are not communicants are converts only upon paper, and it may be said that of real native non-Catholic Christians there are not in India more than 40,000, of whom half are to be found among the devil-worshippers of Madras. The so-called "aboriginal" hill-tribes, having no elaborate religious system of their own, are not tied down to the creed of their birth in the same way as are Mohamedans and Hindoos, among whom our missionaries make no way whatever. The native Protestant's position is a fearful one, except in such a city as Madras, for he wholly loses caste, and becomes an outlaw from his people. The native Catholic continues to be a caste man, and sometimes an idol-worshipper, and the priests have made a million converts in Southern India.

Besides revealing the fewness of the native Christians, the North-Western census has shown us plainly the weakness of the Europeans. In the district of Mooradabad, 1,100,000 people are ruled by thirty-eight Europeans. In many places, two Europeans watch over 200,000 people. The Eurasians are about as numerous as the Europeans, to which class they may for some purposes be regarded as belonging, for the natives reject their society, and refuse them a place in every caste. The Eurasians are a much-despised race, the butt of every Indian story, but as a community they are not to be ranked high. That they should be ill-educated, vain, and cringing, is perhaps only what we might expect of persons placed in their difficult position; nevertheless, that they are so tends to lessen, in spite of our better feelings, the pity that we should otherwise extend towards them.

The census had not only its revelations, but its results. One effect of the census-taking is to check the practice of infanticide, by pointing out to the notice of our officers the castes and the districts in which it exists. The deaths of three or four hundred children are credited to the wolves in the Umritsur district of the Punjaub alone, but it is remarked that the "wolves" pick out the female infants. The great disproportion of the sexes is itself partly to be explained as the result of infanticide.

One weighty drawback to our influence upon Hindoo morals, is that in the case of many abuses we legislate without effect, our laws being evaded where they are outwardly obeyed. The practice of infanticide exists in all parts of India, but especially in Rajpootana, and the girls are killed chiefly in order to save the cost of marrying them—or, rather, of buying husbands for them. Now we have "suppressed" infanticide—which means that children are smothered or starved, instead of being exposed. It is no easy task to bring about reforms in the customs of the people of India.

The many improvements in the moral condition of the people which the census chronicles are steps in a great march. Those who have known India long are aware that a remarkable change has come over the country in the last few years. Small as have been the positive visible results of Christian teaching, the indirect effects have been enormous. Among the Sikhs and Marattas, a spirit of reflection, of earnest thought, unusual in natives, has been aroused; in Bengal it has taken the form of pure deism, but then Bengal is not India. The spirit rather than the doctrinal teaching of Christianity has been imbibed: a love of truth appeals more to the feelings of the upright natives than do the whole of the nine-and-thirty Articles. Here, as elsewhere, the natives look to deeds, not words; the example of a Frere is worth the teaching of a hundred missionaries, painstaking and earnest though they be.

CHAPTER VI.

MOHAMEDAN CITIES.

THROUGH Mirzapore, Allahabad, and Futtehpore, I passed on to Cawnpore, spending but little time at Allahabad; for though the city is strategically important, there is in it but little to be seen. Like all spots of the confluence of rivers, Allahabad is sacred with the Hindoos, for it stands, they say, at the meeting-point of no less than three great streams —the Ganges, the Jumna, and a river of the spirit-land. To us poor pagans, the third stream is invisible; not so to the faithful. Catching a glimpse of Marochetti's statue at the Cawnpore well, as I hurried through that city, I diverged from the East Indian Railway, and took dawk-carriage to Lucknow.

As compared with other Indian cities, the capital of Oude is a town to be seen in driving rather than in walking; the general effects are superior in charm and beauty to the details, and the vast size of the city makes mere sight-seeing a work of difficulty. More populous before 1857 than either Calcutta or Bombay, it is still twice as large as Liverpool. Not only, however, is Lucknow the most perfect of the modern or Italianised Oriental towns, but there are in it several buildings that have each the charm of an architecture special to itself. Of these, the Martinière is the most singular, and it looks like what it is—the freak of a wealthy madman. Its builder was General Martine, a Frenchman in the service of the Kings of Oude. Not far behind the Martinière is the Dilkousha—a fantastic specimen of an Oriental hunting-lodge. The ordinary show-building of the place, the Kaiser-Bagh, or Palace of the Kings of Oude, is a paltry place enough, but there is a certain grandeur in the view of the great Imaumbara and the Hooseinabád from a point whence the two piles form to the eye but one. The great Imaumbara suffered terribly in 1858 from the wanton destruction which our troops committed everywhere during the war of the mutiny. Had they confined themselves to outrages such as these, however, but little could have been said against the conduct of the war. There is too much fear that the English, unless held in check, exhibit a singularly strong disposition towards cruelty, wherever they have a weak enemy to meet.

The stories of the Indian mutiny and of the Jamaica riot are but two out of many—two that we happen to have heard; but the Persian war in 1857 and the last of the Chinese campaigns are not without their records of deliberate barbarity and wrong. From the first officer of one of the Peninsular and Oriental steamers, which was employed in carrying troops up the Euphrates during the Persian war, I heard a story that is the type of many such. A Persian drummer-boy of about ten years old was seen bathing from the bank one morning by the officers on deck. Bets were made as to the chance of hitting him with an Enfield rifle, and one of the betters killed him at the first shot.

It is not only in war-time that our cruelty comes out; it is often seen in trifles during peace. Even a traveller, indeed, becomes so soon used to see the natives wronged in every way by people of quiet manner and apparent kindness of disposition, that he ceases to record the cases. In Madras roads, for instance, I saw a fruit-seller hand up some limes to a lower-deck port, just as we were weighing anchor. Three Anglo-Indians (men who had been out before) asked in chorus "How much?" "One quarter rupee." "Too much." And, without more ado, paying nothing, they pelted the man with his own limes, of which he lost more than half. In Ceylon, near Bentotté rest-house, a native child offered a handsome cowrie (of a kind worth in Australia about five shillings, and certainly worth something in Ceylon) to the child of a Mauritius coffee-planter who was travelling with us to Columbo, himself an old Indian officer. The white child took it, and would not give it up. The native child cried for money, or to have his shell back, but the mother of the white child exclaimed, "You be hanged; it's worth nothing;" and off came the shell with us in the dawk. Such are the small but galling wrongs inflicted daily upon the Indian natives. It was a maxim of the Portuguese Jesuits that men who live long among Asiatics seldom fail to learn their vices, but our older civilians treat the natives with strict justice, and Anglo-Indian ladies who have been reared in the country are generally kind to their own servants, if somewhat harsh towards other natives. It is those who have been in the country from five to ten years, and especially soldiers, who treat the natives badly. Such men I have heard exclaim that the new penal code has revolutionised the country. "Formerly," they say, "you used to send a man to a police-officer or a magistrate with a note:—'My dear ——. Please give the bearer twenty lashes.' But now the magistrates are afraid to act, and your servant can have you fined for beating him." In spite of the lamentations of Anglo-Indians over the good old days, I noticed in all the hotels in India the significant notice, " Gentlemen are earnestly requested not to strike the servants."

The jokes of a people against themselves are not worth much, but may be taken in aid of other evidence. The two favourite Anglo-Indian stories are that of the native who, being asked his religion, said, " Me Christian—me get drunk like massa ;" and that of the young officer who, learning Hindostanee in 1858, had the difference between the negative "né" and the particle "ne" explained to him by the moonshee, when he exclaimed: "Dear me! I hanged lots of natives last year for admitting that they had not been in their villages for months. I suppose they meant to say that they had not left their villages for months." It is certain that in the suppression of the mutiny hundreds of natives were hanged by Queen's officers who, unable to speak a word of any native language, could neither understand evidence nor defence.

It is in India, when listening to a mess-table conversation on the subject of looting, that we begin to remember our descent from Scandinavian sea-king robbers. Centuries of education have not purified the blood: our men in India can hardly set eyes upon a native prince or a Hindoo palace before they cry, "What a place to *break up!*" "What a fellow to *loot!*" When I said to an officer who had been stationed at Secrole in the early days of the mutiny, "I suppose you were afraid that the Benares people would have attacked you," his answer was, "Well, for my part, I rather hoped they would, because then we should have thrashed them, and looted the city. It hadn't been looted for two hundred years."

Those who doubt that Indian military service makes soldiers careless of men's lives, reckless as to the rights of property, and disregardful of human dignity, can hardly remember the letters which reached home in 1857, in which an officer in high command during the march upon Cawnpore reported, "Good bag to-day; polished off —— rebels," it being borne in mind that the "rebels" thus hanged or blown from guns were not taken in arms, but villagers apprehended "on suspicion." During this march, atrocities were committed in the burning of villages, and massacre of innocent inhabitants, at which Mohamed Togluk himself would have stood ashamed, and it would be to contradict all history to assert that a succession of such deeds would not prove fatal to our liberties at home.

The European officers of native regiments, and many officers formerly in the Company's service, habitually show great kindness to the natives, but it is the benevolent kindness of the master for a favourite slave, of the superior for men immeasurably beneath him; there is little of the feeling which a common citizenship should bestow, little of that equality of man and man which Christianity would seem to teach, and which our Indian Government has for some years favoured.

At Lucknow, I saw the Residency, and at Cawnpore, on my return to the East Indian Railway, the entrenchments which were, each of them, the scene in 1857 of those defences against the mutineers generally styled "glorious" or "heroic," though made by men fighting with ropes about their necks. The successful defences of the fort at Arrah and of the Lucknow Residency were rather testimonies to the wonderful fighting powers of the English than to their courage,—for cowards would fight when the alternative was, fight or die. As far as Oude was concerned, the "rebellion" of 1857 seems to have been rather a war than a mutiny; but the habits of the native princes would probably have led them to have acted as treacherously at Lucknow in the case of a surrender as did the Nana at Cawnpore, and our officers wisely determined that in no event would they treat for terms. What is to be regretted is that we as conquerors should have shown the Oude insurgents no more mercy than they would have shown to us, and that we should have made use of the pretext that the rising was a mere mutiny of our native troops, as an excuse for hanging in cold blood the agriculturists of Oude. Whatever the duplicity of their rulers, whatever the provocation to annexation may have been, there can be no doubt that the revolution in the land-laws set on foot by us resulted in the offer of a career as native policemen or railway ticket-clerks to men whose ancestors were warriors and knights when ours wore woad; and we are responsible before mankind for having treated as flagrant treason and mutiny a legitimate war on the part of the nobility of Oude. In the official papers of the Government of the North-West Provinces, the so-called "mutiny" is styled more properly "a grievous civil war."

There is much reason to fear, not that the mutiny will be too long remembered, but that it will be too soon forgotten. Ten years ago, Monghyr was an ash-heap, Cawnpore a name of horror, Delhi a stronghold of armed rebels, yet now we can travel without change of cars through peaceful and prosperous Monghyr and Cawnpore—a thousand and twenty miles—in forty hours, and find at the end of our journey that shaded boulevards have already taken the place of the walls of Delhi.

Quitting the main line of the East India Railway at

Toondla Junction, I passed over a newly-made branch road to Agra. The line was but lately opened, and birds without number sat upon the telegraph-posts, and were seemingly too astonished to fly away from the train, while, on the open barrens, herds of Indian antelopes grazed fearlessly, and took no notice of us when we passed.

Long before we entered Akbarabad, as the city should be called, by the great new bridge across the Jumna, I had sighted in the far distance the majestic, shining dome of the famed Taj Mahal; but when arrived within the city, I first visited the citadel and ramparts. The fort and palace of Akbar are the Moslem creed in stone. Without—turned towards the unbeliever and the foe—the far-famed triple walls, frowning one above the other with the frown that a hill fanatic wears before he strikes the infidel; within is the secure paradise of the believing "Emperor of the world"—delicious fountains pouring into basins of the whitest marble, beds of rose and myrtle, balconies and pavilions; part of the zenana, or women's wing, overhanging the river, and commanding the distant snow-dome of the Taj. Within, too, the "Motee Musjid"—"Pearl of Mosques" in fact as well as name— a marble-cloistered court, to which an angel architect could not add a stone, nor snatch one from it without spoiling all. These for believers; for non-believers the grim old Saracenic "Hall of the Seat of Judgment." The palace, except the mosque, which is purity itself, is overlaid with a crust of gems. There is one famed chamber—a woman's bath-house—the roof and sides of which are covered with tiny silver-mounted mirrors, placed at such angles as to reflect to infinity the figures of those who stand within the bath ; and a court is near at hand, paved with marble squares in black and white, over which Akbar and his vizier used to sit, and gravely play at draughts with dancing girls for " pieces."

On the river bank, a mile from Akbar's palace, in the centre of a vast garden entered through the noblest gateways in the world, stands the Taj Mahal, a terrace rising in dazzling whiteness from a black mass of cypresses, and bearing four lofty, delicate minars, and the central pile that gleams like an Alp against the deep-blue sky—minars, terrace, tomb, all of spotless marble, and faultless shape. Its Persian builders named the Taj "the palace floating in the air."

Out of the fierce heat and blazing sunlight you enter into chill and darkness, but soon begin to see the hollow dome growing into form above your head, and the tomb itself—that of Noor Mahal, the favourite queen of Shah Jehan — before you, and beside it her husband's humbler grave. Though within and without the Taj is white, still here you find the walls profusely jewelled, and the purity retained. Flowers are pictured on every block in mosaic of cinnamon-stone, cornelian, turquoise, amethyst, and emerald ; the corridors contain the whole Koran, inlaid in jet black stone, yet the interior as a whole exceeds in chastity the spotlessness of the outer dome. Oriental, it is not barbaric, and a sweet melancholy is the effect the Taj produces on the mind, when seen by day; in the still moonlight, the form is too mysterious to be touching.

In a Persian manuscript, there still remains a catalogue of the prices of the gems made use of in the building of the Taj, and of the places from which they came. Among those named are coral from Arabia, sapphires from Moldavia, amethysts from Persia, crystal from China, turquoises from Thibet, diamonds from Bundelcund, and lapis-lazuli from Ceylon. The stones were presents or tribute to the Emperor, and the master masons came mostly from Constantinople and Bagdad—a fact which should be remembered when we are discussing the intellectual capacity of the Bengal Hindoos. That a people who paint their cows pink with green spots, and their horses orange or bright red, should be the authors of the Pearl Mosque and the Taj, would be too wonderful for our belief, but the Mohamedan conquerors brought with them the chosen artists of the Moslem world. The contrast between the Taj and the Monkey Temple at Benares reminds one of that between a Cashmere and a Norwich shawl.

It is not at Agra alone that we meet the works of Mogul emperors. Much as we have ourselves done in building roads and bridges, there are many parts of Upper India where the traces of the Moslem are still more numerous than are at present those of the later conquerors of the unfortunate Hindoos. Mosques, forts, conduits, bridges, gardens—all the works of the

Moguls are both solid and magnificent, and it was with almost reverential feelings that I made my pilgrimage to the tomb at Secundra of the great Emperor Akbar, grandfather of Shah Jehan, son of Hoomayoon, and founder of Agra city.

It is to be remarked that the Mohamedans in India make a considerable show for their small numbers. Of the great cities of India, the three Presidency towns are English; and the three gigantic cities of Delhi, Agra, and Lucknow, chiefly Mohamedan. Benares alone is a Hindoo city, and even in Benares the Mohamedans have their temples. All the great buildings of India are Mohamedan; so are all the great works that are not English. Yet even in the Agra district, the Mohamedans are only one-twelfth of the population, but they live chiefly in the towns.

The history of the Mogul empire of India from the time of the conquest of the older empire by Tamerlane in the fourteenth century, and the forced conversion to Mohamedanism of a vast number of Hindoos, and that of Akbar's splendour and enormous power down to the transportation of the last emperor in 1857 to Rangoon, and the shooting of his sons in a dry ditch by Captain Hodson, is one for us to ponder carefully. Those who know what we have done in India, say that even in our codes—and they are allowed to be our best claim to the world's applause—we fall short of Akbar's standard.

Delhi, the work of Shah Jehan, founder of the Taj and the Pearl Mosque, was built by himself in a wilderness, as was Agra by the Emperor Akbar. We who have seen the time that has passed since its foundation by Washington before the capital of the United States has grown out of the village shape, cannot deny that the Mogul emperors, if they were despots, were at least tyrants possessed of imperial energy. Akbar built Agra twenty or thirty miles from Futtehpore Sikri, his former capital, but Jehan had the harder task of forcing his people to quit an earlier site not five miles from modern Delhi, while Akbar merely moved his palace, and let the people follow.

Delhi suffered so much at our hands during the storm in 1857, and has suffered so much since in the way of Napoleonic boulevards intended to prevent the necessity of storming it again, that it must be much changed from what it was before the war. The walls which surround the whole city are nearly as grand as those of the fort at Agra, and the gate towers are very Gibraltars of brick and stone, as we found to our cost when we battered the Cashmere Gate in 1857. The palace and the Motee Musjid are extremely fine, but inferior to their namesakes at Agra; and the Jumna Musjid—reputed the most beautiful as it is the largest mosque in the world—impressed me only by its size. The view, however, from its minars is one of the whole North-West. The vast city becomes an ant-heap, and you instinctively peer out into space, and try to discern the sea towards Calcutta or Bombay.

The historical memories that attach to Delhi differ from those that we associate with the name of Agra. There is little pleasure in the contemplation of the zenana, where the miserable old man, the last of the Moguls, dawdled away his years.

CHAPTER VII.

SIMLA.

AFTER visiting Nicholson's tomb at the Cashmere Gate, I entered my one-horse dawk—the regulation carriage of India—and set off for Kurnaul and Simla, passing between the sand-hills, gravel-pits, and ruined mosques through which the rebel cavalry made their famous sortie upon our camp. It was evening when we started, and as the dawk-gharrees are so arranged that you can lie with comfort at full-length, but cannot sit without misery, I brought my canvas bag into service as a pillow, and was soon asleep.

When I woke, we had stopped; and when I drew the sliding shutter that does duty for door and window, and peered out into the darkness, I discovered that there was no horse in the shafts, and that my driver and his horse syce—or groom—were smoking their hubble-bubbles at a well in the company of a passing friend. By making free use of the strongest language that my dictionary contained, I prevailed upon the men to put in a fresh horse, but starting was a different matter. The horse refused to budge an inch, except, indeed, backwards, or sideways towards the ditch. Six grooms came running from the stable, and placed themselves one at each wheel, and one on each side of the horse, while many boys pushed behind. At a signal from the driver, the four wheelmen threw their whole weight on the spokes, and one of the men at the horse's head held up the obstinate brute's off fore-leg, so that he was fairly run off the ground, and forced to make a start, which he did with a violent plunge, for which all the grooms were, however, well prepared. As they yelled with triumph, we dashed along for some twenty yards, then swerved sideways, and came to a dead stop. Again and again the starting process was repeated, till at last the horse went off at a gallop, which carried us to the end of the stage. This is the only form of starting known to up-country horses, as I soon found; but sometimes even this ceremony fails to start the horse, and twice in the Delhi-to-Kalka journey we lost a quarter of an hour over horses, and had finally to get others from the stable.

About midnight, we reached a Government bungalow, or roadside inn, where I was to sup, and five minutes produced a chicken curry which, in spite of its hardness, was disposed of in as many more. Meanwhile a storm had come rumbling and roaring across the skies, and when I went to the door to start, the bungalow butler and cook pointed to the gharree, and told me that driver and horse were gone. Not wishing the bungalow men to discover how small was my stock of Hindostanee, I paid careful attention to their conversation, and looked up each time that I heard "sahib," as I knew that then they must be talking about me. Seeing this, they seemed to agree that I was a thorough Hindostanee scholar, but too proud to answer when they spoke. Whilst they were humbly requesting that I would bow to the storm and sleep in the bungalow, which was filled with twittering sparrows, waked by the thunder or the lights, I was reading my dictionary by the faint glimmer of the cocoa-nut oil-lamp, and trying to find out how I was to declare that I insisted on going on at once. When at last I hit upon my phrase, the storm was over, and the butler soon found both horse and driver. After this adventure, my Hindostanee improved fast.

A remarkable misapprehension prevails in England concerning the languages of India. The natives of India, we are inclined to believe, speak Hindostanee, which is the language of India as English is that of Britain. The truth is that there are in India a multitude of languages, of which Hindostanee is not even one. Besides the great tongues, Urdu, Maratti, and Tamil, there are dozens, if not hundreds, of local languages, and innumerable dialects of each. Hindostanee is a camp language, which contains many native words, but which also is largely composed of imported Arabic and Persian words, and which is not without specimens of English and Portuguese. "Saboon," for soap, is the latter; "glassie," for a tumbler, and "istubul," for a stable, the former: but almost every common English phrase and English word of command forms in a certain measure part of the Hindostanee tongue. Some terms have been ingeniously perverted; for instance, "Who comes there?" has become "Hookum dar?" "Stand at ease!" is changed to "Tundel tis," and "Present arms!" to "Furyunt ram!" The Hindostanee name for a European lady is "mem sahib," a feminine formed from "sahib"—lord, or European—by prefixing to it the English servants' "mum," or corruption of "madam." Some pure Hindostanee words have a comical sound enough to English ears, as "hookm," an order, pronounced "hook'em;" "misri," sugar, which sounds like "misery;" "top," fever; "molly," a gardener; and "dolly," a bundle of vegetables.

Dawk travelling in the Punjaub is by no means unpleasant; by night you sleep soundly, and by day there is no lack of life in the mere traffic on the road, while the general scene is full of charm. Here and there are *serais*, or corrals, built by the Mogul emperors or by the British Government for the use of native travellers. Our word "caravansery" is properly "caravan-serai," an enclosure for the use of those travelling in caravans. The keeper of the serai supplies water, provender, and food, and at night the serais along the road glow with the cooking fires and resound with the voices of thousands of natives, who when on journeys never seem to sleep. Throughout the plains of India, the high roads pass villages, serais, police-stations, and groups of trees at almost equal intervals. The space between clump and clump is generally about three miles, and in this distance you never see a house, so compact are the Indian villages. The North-West Provinces are the most densely-peopled countries of the world, yet between village and village you often see no trace of man, while jackals and wild blue-cows roam about as freely as though the country were an untrodden wilderness.

Each time you reach a clump of banyans, tamarind and tulip trees, you find the same tenants of its shades: village police-station, Government posting-stable, and serai are always enclosed within its limits. All the villages are fortified with lofty walls of mud or brick, as are the numerous police-stations along the road, where the military constabulary, in their dark-blue tunics, yellow trousers, and huge puggrees of bright red, rise up from sleep or hookah as you pass, and, turning out with tulwárs and rifles, perform the military salute—due in India to the white face from all native troops. Your skin here is your patent of aristocracy and your passport, all in one.

It is not only by the police and troops that you are saluted: the natives all salaam to you—except mere coolies, who do not think themselves worthy even to offer a salute—and many Anglo-Indians refuse to return their bow. Every Englishman in India ought to act as though he were an ambassador of the Queen and people, and regulate accordingly his conduct in the most trifling things; but too often the low bow and humble "Salaam sahib" is not acknowledged even by a curt "Salaam."

In the drier portions of the country, women were busy with knives digging up little roots of grass for horse-food; and four or five times a day a great bugling would be heard and answered by my driver, while the mail-cart shot by us at full speed. The astonishment with which I looked upon the Indian plains grew even stronger as I advanced up country. Not only is bush scarce, and forest never seen, but where there is jungle, it is of the thinnest and least tropical kind. It would be harder to traverse, on horse or foot, the thinnest coppice in the south of England than the densest jungle in the plain country of all India.

Both in the villages and in the desert portions of the road, the ground-squirrels galloped in troops before the dawk, and birds without number hopped fearlessly beside us as we passed; hoopoes, blue-jays, and minas were the commonest, but there were many paddy-birds and graceful golden egrets in the lower grounds.

Between Delhi and Kurnaul were many ruins, now green with the pomegranate leaf, now scarlet with the bloom of the peacock-tree, and, about the ancient villages, acre after acre of plantain-garden, irrigated by the conduits of the Mohamedan conquerors; at last, Kurnaul itself—a fortified town—seen through a forest of date, wild mango, and banyan, with patches of wheat about it, and strings of laden camels winding along the dusty road. After a bheestie had poured a skinful of water over me, I set off again for Kalka, halting in the territory of the Puttiala Rajah to see his gardens at Pinjore, and then passed on towards the base of the Himalayan foot-hills. The wheat harvest was in progress in the Kalka country, and the girls, reaping with the sickle, and carrying away the sheaves upon their heads, bore themselves gracefully, as Hindoo women ever do, and formed a contrast to the coarse old landowners as these rode past, each followed by his pipe-bearer and his retinue.

A Goorkha battalion and a Thibetan goat-train had just entered Kalka when I reached it, and the confusion was such that I started at once in a jampan up the sides of the brown and desolate hills. A jampan, called tonjon in Madras, is an arm-chair in shafts, and built more lightly than a sedan; it is carried at a short trot by four men, while another four, and a mate or chief, make their way up the hills before you, and meet you here and there to relieve guard. The hire of the jampan and nine men is less than that of a pony and groom—a curious illustration of the cheapness of labour in the East. When you first reach India, this cheapness is a standing wonder. At your hotel at Calcutta you are asked, "You wish boy pull punkah all night? Boy pull punkah all day and all night for two annas" (3*d.*). On some parts of the railway lines, where there is also a good road, the natives find it cheaper to travel by palanqueen than to ride in a third-class railway carriage. It is cheaper in Calcutta to be carried by four men in a palki than to ride in a "second-class gharry," or very bad cab; and the streets of the city are invariably watered by hand by bheesties with skins. The key to Indian politics lies in these facts.

At Wilson's at Calcutta, the rule of the hotel obliges one to hire a kitmutghar, who waits at table. This I did for the magnificent wage of 11*d.* a day, out of which Cherry—the nearest phonetic spelling of my man's name—of course fed and kept himself. I will do him the justice to add that he managed to make about another shilling a day out of me, and that he always brought me small change in copper, on the chance that I should give it him. Small as seemed these wages, I could have hired him for one-fifth the rate that I have named had I been ready to retain him in my service for a month or two. Wages in India are somewhat raised by the practice of dustooree—a custom by which every native, high or low, takes toll of all money that passes through his hands. My first introduction to this institution struck me forcibly, though afterwards I came to look upon it as tranquilly as old Indians do. It was in the gardens of the Taj, where, to relieve myself from importunity, I had bought a photograph of the dome: a native servant of the hotel, who accompanied me much against my will, and who, being far more ignorant of English than I was of Hindostanee, was of absolutely no use, I had at last succeeded in warning off from my side, but directly I bought the photograph for half a rupee, he rushed upon the seller, and claimed one-fourth of the price, or two annas, as his share, I having transgressed his privilege in buying directly instead of through him as intermediary. I remonstrated, but to my amazement the seller paid the money quietly, and evidently looked on me as a meddling sort of fellow enough for interfering with the institution of dustooree. Customs, after all, are much the same throughout the world. Our sportsmen follow the habit of Confucius, whose disciples two or three thousand years ago proclaimed that "he angled, but did not use a net; he shot, but not at birds perching;" our servants, perhaps, are not altogether innocent of dustooree. However much wages may be supplemented by dustooree, they are low enough to allow of the keeping of a tribe of servants by persons of moderate incomes. A small family at Simla "require" three body servants, two cooks, one butler, two grooms, two gardeners, two messengers, two nurses, two washermen, two water-carriers, thirteen jampan-men, one sweeper, one lamp-cleaner, and one boy, besides the European lady's maid, or thirty-five in all; but if wages were doubled, perhaps fewer men would be "absolutely needed." At the house where I stayed at Simla, ten jampan-men and two gardeners were supposed to be continuously employed in a tiny flower-garden round the house. To a European fresh from the temperate climates there is something irksome in the restraint produced by the constant presence of servants in every corner of an Indian house. To pull off one's own socks or pour out the water into the basin for oneself becomes a much-longed-for luxury. It is far from pleasant to have three or four natives squatting in front of your door, with nothing to do unless you find such odd jobs for them as holding the heel of your boot while you pull it on, or brushing your clothes for the fourteenth time.

The greater or less value of the smallest coin in common use in a country is a rough test of the wealth or poverty of its inhabitants, and by the application of it to India we find that country poor indeed. At Agra, I had gone to a money-changer in the bazaar, and asked him for change, in the cowrie-shells which do duty as money, for an anna, or 1½*d*. piece. He gave me handful after handful, till I cried enough. Yet when in the afternoon of the same day I had a performance on my threshold of "Tasa-ba-tasa"— that singular tune which reigns from Java to the Bosphorus, with Sanscrit words in Persia, and Malay words in the Eastern islands—the three players seemed grateful for half-a-dozen of the cowries, for they treated me to a native version of "Vee vont gah ham tall mardid, vee vont gah ham tall mardid," by way of thanks. Many strange natural objects pass as uncoined money in the East: tusks in Africa, women in Arabia, human skulls in Borneo; the Red Indians of America sell their neighbours' scalps for money, but have not yet reached the height of civilization which would be denoted by their keeping them to use as such; cowrie-shells, however, pass as money in almost every ancient trading country of the world.

The historical cheapness of labour in India has led to such an obstinate aversion to all labour-saving expedients that such great works as the making of railway embankments and the boulevard construction at Delhi are conducted by the scraping together of earth with the hands, and the collected pile is slowly placed in tiny baskets, much like strawberry pottles, and borne away on women's heads to its new destination. Wheelbarrows, water-carts, picks, and shovels are in India all unknown.

If, on my road from Kalka to Simla, I had an example of the cheapness of Indian labour, I also had one of its efficiency. The coolie who carried my baggage on his head trotted up the hills for twenty-one hours, without halting for more than an hour or two, and this for two days' pay.

During the first half-hour after leaving Kalka, the heat was as great as on the plains, but we had not gone many miles before we came out of the heat and dust into a new world, and an atmosphere every breath of which was life. I got out, and walked for miles; and when we halted at a rest-house on the first plateau, I thoroughly enjoyed a cup of the mountain tea, and was still more pleased at the sight of the first red-coated English soldiers that I had seen since I left Niagara. The men were even attempting bowls and cricket, so cool were the evenings at this station. There is grim satire in the fact that the director-general of military gymnastics has his establishment at Simla, in the cold of the snowy range, and there invents running drills and such like summer diversions, to be executed by the unfortunates in the plains below. Bowls, which are an amusement at Kussoolie, would in the hot weather be death at Kalka, only ten miles away; but so short is the memory of climate that you are no more able to conceive the heat of the plains when in the hills than the cold of the hills when at Calcutta.

There is no reason except a slight and temporary increase of cost to prevent the whole of the European troops in India being concentrated in a few cool and healthy stations. Provided that all the artillery be retained in the hands of the Europeans, almost the whole of the English forces might be kept in half-a-dozen hill stations, of which Darjeeling and Bangalore would be two, and some place near Bombay a third. It has been said that the men would be incapable, through want of acclimatisation, of acting on the plains if retained in hill stations except when their services were needed; but it is notoriously the fact that new comers from England—that is, men with health—do not suffer seriously from heat during the first six months which they pass upon the plains.

Soon after dark, a terrific thunderstorm came on, the thunder rolling round the valleys and along the ridges, while the rain fell in short, sharp showers. My men put me down on the lee-side of a hut, and squatted for a long smoke. The custom common to all the Eastern races of sitting round a fire smoking all night long explains the number and the excellence of their tales and legends. In Europe we see the Swedish peasants sitting round their hearths chatting during the long winter evenings: hence follow naturally the Thor legends; our sailors are with us the only men given to sitting in groups to talk: they are noted story-tellers. The word "yarn" exemplifies the whole philosophy of the matter. We meet, however, here the eternal difficulty of which is cause and which is effect. It is easy to say that the long nights of Norway, the confined space of the ship, making the fo'castle the sailor's only lounge, each in their way necessitate the story-telling; not so in India, not so in Egypt, in Arabia, in Persia: there can here be no necessity for men sitting up all night to talk, short of pure love of talk for talking's sake.

When the light came in the morning, we were ascending the same strangely-ribbed hills that we had been crossing by torchlight during the night, and were meeting Chinese-faced Thibetans, with hair done into many pig-tails, who were laboriously bringing over the mountain passes Chinese goods in tiny sheep-loads. For miles I journeyed on, up mountain sides and down into ravines, but never for a single moment upon a level, catching sight sometimes of portions of the Snowy Range itself, far distant, and half mingled with the clouds, till at last a huge mountain mass rising to the north and east blocked out all view save that behind me over the sea of hills that I had crossed, and the scene became monotonously hideous, with only that grandeur which hugeness carries with it—a view, in short, that would be fine at sunset, and at no other time. The weather, too, grew damp and cold—a cruel cold, with driving rain—and the landscape was dreariness itself.

Suddenly we crossed the ridge, and began to descend, when the sky cleared, and I found myself on the edge of the rhododendron forest—tall trees with dark green leaves and masses of crimson flowers; ferns of a hundred different kinds marking the beds of the rivulets that coursed down through the woods, which were filled with troops of chattering monkeys.

Rising again slightly, I began to pass the European bungalows, each in its thicket of deodar, and few with flat ground enough for more than half a rose-bed, or a quarter of a croquet-ground. On either side the ridge was a deep valley, with terraced rice-fields five thousand feet below, and, in the distance, on the one side the mist-covered plains lit by the single silvery ribbon of the distant Sutlej, on the other side the Snowy Range.

The first Europeans whom I met in Simla were the Viceroy's children and their nurses, who formed with their escort a stately procession. First came a tall native in scarlet, then a jampan with a child, then one with a nurse and viceregal baby, and so on, the bearers wearing scarlet and grey. All the residents at Simla have different uniforms for their jampanees, some clothing their men in red and green, some in purple and yellow, some in black and white. Before reaching the centre of the town, I had met several Europeans riding, although the sun was still high and hot, but before evening a hailstorm came across the range, and filled the woods with a chilling mist, and night found me toasting my feet at a blazing fire in an Alpine room of polished pine—a real room, with doors and casement; not a section of a street with a bed in it, as are the rooms in the Indian plains. Two blankets were a luxury in this "tropical climate of Simla," as one of our best-informed London newspapers once called it. The fact is that Simla, which stands at from seven to eight thousand feet above the sea, and in latitude 31°, or 7° north of the boundary of the tropics, has a climate cold in everything except its sun, which is sometimes strong. The snow lies on the ground at intervals for five months of the year; and during what is by courtesy styled "the hot weather," cold rains are of frequent occurrence.

The climate of Simla is no mere matter of curiosity: it is a question of serious interest in connexion with the retention of our Indian empire. When the Government seeks refuge here from the Calcutta heat, the various departments are located in tiny cottages and bungalows up on the mountain and down in the valley, practically as far from each other as London from Brighton; and, moreover, Simla itself is forty miles from Kalka by the shortest path, and sixty by the better bridle path. There is clearly much loss of time in sending despatches for half the year to and from a place like this, and there is no chance of the railway ever coming nearer to it than Kalka, even if it reaches that. On the other hand, the telegraph is replacing the railway day by day, and mountain heights are no bar to wires. This poor little, uneven hill village has been styled the "Indian Capua" and nicknamed the "Hill Versailles;" but so far from enervating the ministers or enfeebling the administration, Simla gives vigour to the Government, and a hearty English tone to the State papers issued in the hot months. English ministers are not in London all the year long, and no men, ministers or not, could stand four years' continual brainwork in Calcutta. In 1866, the first year of the removal of the Government as a whole and publication of the *Gazette* at

Simla during the summer, all the arrears of work in all the offices were cleared off for the first time since the occupation by us of any part of India.

Bengal, the North-West Provinces, and the Punjaub must soon be made into "governorships," instead of "lieutenant-governorships," so that the Viceroy may be relieved from tedious work, and time saved by the Northern Governors reporting straight home, as do the Governors of Madras and Bombay, unless a system be adopted under which all shall report to the Viceroy. At all events, the five divisions must be put upon the same footing one with another. This being granted, there is no conceivable reason for keeping the Viceroy at Calcutta—a city singularly hot, unhealthy, and out of the way. On our Council of India, sitting at the capital, we ought to have natives picked from all India for their honesty, ability, and discretion; but so bad is the water at Calcutta, that the city is deadly to water-drinkers; and although they value the distinction of a seat at the Council more than any other honour within their reach, many of the most distinguished natives in India have chosen to resign their places rather than pass a second season at Calcutta.

It is not necessary that we should argue about Calcutta's disadvantages. It is enough to say that, of all Indian cities, we have selected for our capital the most distant and the most unhealthy. The great question is, Shall we have one capital, or two? Shall we keep the Viceroy all the year round in a central but hot position, such as Delhi, Agra, Allahabad, or Jubbelpore, or else at a less central but cooler station, such as Nassuck, Poonah, Bangalore, or Mussoorie? or shall we keep him at a central place during the cool, and a hill place during the hot weather? There can be but little doubt that Simla is a necessity at present, but with a fairly healthy city, such as Agra, for the head-quarters of the Government, and the railway open to within a few miles of Mussoorie, so that men could run to the hills in six or seven hours, and even spend a few days there in each summer month, an efficient government could be maintained in the plains. We must remember that Agra is now within twenty-three days of London; and that, with the Persian Gulf route open, and a railway from Kurrachee (the natural port of England in India), leave for home would be a matter still more simple than it has become already. With some such central town as Poonah for the capital, the Bombay and Madras commander-in-chiefships could be abolished, with the result of saving a considerable expense, and greatly increasing the efficiency of the Indian army. It is probable that Simla will not continue to be the chosen station of the Government in the hills. The town is subject to the ravages of dysentery; the cost of draining it would be immense, and the water supply is very limited: the bheesties have often to wait whole hours for their turn.

Mussoorie has all the advantages and none of the drawbacks of Simla, and lies compactly in ground on which a small city could be built, whereas Simla straggles along a narrow mountain ridge, and up and down the steep sides of an Alpine peak. It is questionable, however, whether, if India is to be governed from at home, the seat of Government should not be at Poonah, within reach of London. The telegraph has already made viceroys of the ancient kind impossible.

The sunrise view of the Snowy Range from my bungalow was one rather strange from the multitude of peaks in sight at once than either beautiful or grand. The desolate ranges of foot-hills destroy the beauty that the contrast of the deodars, the crimson rhododendrons, and the snow would otherwise produce, and the height at which you stand seems to dwarf the distant ranges; but from one of the spots which I reached in a mountain march, the prospect was widely different. Here we saw at once the sources of the Jumna, the Sutlej, and the Ganges, the dazzling peaks of Gungootrie, of Jumnotrie, and of Kamet; while behind us in the distant plains we could trace the Sutlej itself, silvered by the hazy rays of the half-risen sun. We had in sight not only the 26,000 feet of Kamet, but no less than twenty other peaks of over 20,000 feet, snow-clad to their very bases, while between us and the nearest outlying range were valleys from which the ear caught the humble murmur of fresh-risen streams.

CHAPTER VIII.

COLONIZATION.

CONNECTED with the question of the site of the future capital is that of the possibility of the colonization by Englishmen of portions of the peninsula of India.

Hitherto the attempts at settlement which have been made have been mainly confined to six districts —Mysore, where there are only some dozen planters; the Neilgherries proper, where coffee-planting is largely carried on; Oude, where many Europeans have taken land as zemindars, and cultivate a portion of it, while they let out the remainder to natives on the Metayer plan; Bengal, where indigo-planting is gaining ground; the Himalayan valleys, and Assam. Settlement in the hot plains is limited by the fact that English children cannot there be reared, so to the hill districts the discussion must be confined.

One of the commonest of mistakes respecting India consists in the supposition that there is available land in large quantities on the slopes of the Himalayas. There are no Himalayan slopes; the country is all straight up and down, and for English colonists there is no room—no ground that will grow anything but deodars, and those only moderately well. The hot sun dries the ground, and the violent rains follow, and cut it through and through with deep channels, in this way gradually making all the hills both steep and ribbed. Mysore is still a native State, but, in spite of this, European settlement is increasing year by year, and there, as in the Neilgherries proper, there is room for many coffee-planters, though fever is not unknown; but when India is carefully surveyed, the only district that appears to be thoroughly suited to English settlement, as contrasted with mere planting or landholding, is the valley of Cashmere, where the race would probably not suffer deterioration. With the exception of Cashmere, none of the deep mountain valleys are cool enough for permanent European settlement. Family life is impossible where there is no home; you can have no English comfort, no English virtues in a climate which forces your people to live out of doors, or else in rocking-chairs or hammocks. Nightwork and reading are all but impossible in a climate where multitudes of insects haunt the air. In the Himalayan valleys, the hot weather is terribly scorching, and it lasts for half the year, and on the hillsides there is but little fertile soil.

The civilians and rulers of India in general are extremely jealous of the "interlopers," as European settlers are termed; and, although tea cultivation was at first encouraged by the Bengal Government, recent legislation, fair or unfair, has almost ruined the tea-planters of Assam. The native population of that district is averse to labour, and coolies from a distance have to be brought in; but the Government of India, as the planters say, interferes with harsh and narrow regulations, and so enormously increases the cost of imported labour as to ruin the planters, who, even when they have got their labourers on the ground, cannot make them work, as there exist no means of compelling specific performance of a contract to work. The remedy known to the English law is an action for damages brought by the employer against the labourer, so with English obstinacy we declare that an action for damages shall be the remedy in Burmah or Assam. A provision for attachment of goods and imprisonment of person of labourers refusing to perform their portion of a contract to work was inscribed in the draft of the proposed Indian "Code of Civil Procedure," but vetoed by the authorities at home.

The Spanish Jesuits themselves were not more afraid of free white settlers than is our Bengal Government. An enterprising merchant of Calcutta lately obtained a grant of vast tracts of country in the Sunderbunds—the fever-haunted jungle near Calcutta—and had already completed his arrangements for importing Chinese labourers to cultivate his acquisitions, when the jealous civilians got wind of the affair, and forced Government into a most undignified retreat from their agreement.

The secret of this opposition to settlement by Europeans lies partly in a horror of "low-caste Englishmen," and a fear that they will somewhat debase Europeans in native eyes, but far more in the wish of the old civilians to keep India to themselves as a sort of "happy hunting ground"—a wish which has prompted them to start the cry of "India for the Indians"—which of course means India for the Anglo-Indians.

Somewhat apart from the question of European colonization, but closely related to it, is that of the holding by Europeans of landed estates in India. It will perhaps be conceded that the European should, on the one hand, be allowed to come into the market and purchase land, or rent it from the Government or from individuals, on the same conditions as those which would apply to natives, and, on the other hand, that special grants should not be made to Europeans as they were by us in Java in old times. In Eastern countries, however, government can hardly be wholly neutral, and, whatever the law, if European landholders be encouraged, they will come; if discouraged, they will stop away. From India they stop away, while such as do reach Hindostan are known in official circles by the significant name of "interlopers."

Under a healthy social system, which the presence of English planters throughout India, and the support which would thus be given to the unofficial press, would of itself do much to create, the owning of land by Europeans could produce nothing but good. The danger of the use of compulsion towards the natives would not exist, because in India—unlike what is the case in Dutch Java—the interest of the ruling classes would be the other way. If it be answered that, once in possession of the land, the Europeans would get the government into their own hands, we must reply that they could never be sufficiently numerous to have the slightest chance of doing anything of the kind. As we have seen in Ceylon, the attempt on the part of the planters to usurp the government is sternly repressed by the English people, the moment that its true bearing is understood, and yet in Ceylon the planters are far more numerous in proportion to the population than they can ever be in India, where the climate of the plains is fatal to European children, and where there is comparatively little land upon the hills; while in Ceylon the coffee-tracts, which are mountainous and healthy, form a sensible proportion of the whole lands of the island. It is true that the press, when once completely in the planters' hands, may advocate their interests at the expense of those of the natives, but in the case of Queensland we have seen that this is no protection to the planters against the inquisitive home eye, which would be drawn to India as it has been to Queensland by the reports of independent travellers, and of interested but honest missionaries.

The infamies of the foundation of the indigo-plantations in Bengal, and of many of the tea-plantations in Assam, in which violence was freely used to make the natives grow the selected crop, and in some cases the land actually stolen from its owners, have gone far to make European settlement in India a by-word among the friends of the Hindoo, but it is clear that an efficient police would suffice to restrain these illegalities and hideous wrongs. It might become advisable in the interest of the natives to provide that not only the officers, but also the sub-officers and some constables of the police, should be Europeans in districts where the plantations lay, great care being taken to select honest and fearless men, and to keep a strict watch on their conduct.

The two great securities against that further degradation of the natives which has been foretold as a result of the expected influx of Europeans are the general teaching of the English language, and the grant of perfect freedom of action (the Government standing aloof) to missionaries of every creed under heaven. The bestowal of the English tongue upon the natives will give the local newspapers a larger circulation among them than among the planter classes, and so, by the powerful motive of self-interest, force them to the side of liberty; while the honesty of some of the missionaries and the interest of others will certainly place the majority of the religious bodies on the side of freedom. It is needless to say that the success of a policy which would be opposed by the local press and at the same time by the chief English Churches is not an eventuality about which we need give ourselves concern, and it is therefore probable that on the whole the encouragement of European settlement upon the plains would be conducive to the welfare of the native race.

That settlement or colonization would make our tenure of India more secure is very doubtful, and, if certain, would be a point of little moment. If, when India has passed through the present transition stage from a country of many peoples to a country of only one, we cannot continue to rule her by the consent of the majority of her inhabitants, our occupation of the country must come to an end, whether we will or no. At the same time, the union of interests and community of ideas which would rise out of well-ordered settlement would do much to endear our Government to the great body of the natives. As a warning against European settlement as it is, every Englishman should read the drama "Nil Darpan."

During my stay at Simla, I visited a pretty fair in one of the neighbouring valleys. There was much buffoonery and dancing—among other things, a sort of jig by a fakeer, who danced himself into a fit, real or pretended; but the charm of this, as of all Hindoo gatherings, lay in the colour. The women of the Punjaub dress very gaily for their fêtes, wearing tight-fitting trousers of crimson, blue, or yellow, and a long thin robe of white, or crimson-grounded Cashmere shawl; bracelets and anklets of silver, and a nose-ring, either huge and thin, or small and nearly solid—complete the dress.

At the fair were many of the Goorkhas (of whom there is a regiment at Simla), who danced, and seemingly enjoyed themselves immensely; indeed, the natives of all parts of India, from Nepaul to the Deccan, possess a most enviable faculty of amusement, and they say that there is a professional buffoon attached to every Goorkha regiment. Their full-dress is like that of the French *chasseurs à pied*, but in their undress uniform of white, the trousers worn so tight as to wrinkle from stretching—these dashing little fellows, with their thin legs, broad shoulders, bullet heads, and flat faces, look extremely like a corps of jockeys. A general inspecting one of these regiments once said to the colonel: "Your men are small, sir." "Their pay is small, sir!" growled the colonel, in a towering passion.

There were unmistakeable traces of Buddhist architecture in the little valley Hindoo shrine. Of the Chinese pilgrimages to India in the Buddhist period there are many records yet extant, and one of these, we are told, relates how, as late as the fourteenth century, the Emperor of China asked leave of the Delhi ruler to rebuild a temple at the southern base of the Himalayas, inasmuch as it was visited by his Tartar people.

CHAPTER IX.

THE *GAZETTE*.

OF all printed information upon India, there is none which, either for value or interest, can be ranked with that contained in the Government *Gazette*, which during my stay at Simla was published at that town, the Viceroy's Council having moved there for the hot weather. Not only are the records of the mere routine business interesting from their variety, but almost every week there is printed along with the *Gazette* a supplement, which contains memoranda from leading natives or from the representatives of the local governments upon the operations of certain customs, or on the probable effects of a proposed law, or similar communications. Sometimes the circulars issued by the Government are alone reprinted, " with a view to elicit opinions," but more generally the whole of the replies are given.

It is difficult for English readers to conceive the number and variety of subjects upon which a single number of the *Gazette* will give information of some kind. The paragraphs are strung together in the order in which they are received, without arrangement or connexion. "A copy of a treaty with his

Highness the Maharajah of Cashmere" stands side by side with a grant of three months' leave to a lieutenant of Bombay Native Foot; while above is an account of the suppression of the late murderous outrages in the Punjaub, and below a narrative of the upsetting of the Calcutta mails into a river near Jubbelpore. "A khureta from the Viceroy to his Highness the Rao Oomaid Singh Bahadoor" orders him to put down crime in his dominions, and the humble answer of the Rao is printed, in which he promises to do his best. Paragraphs are given to "the floating dock at Rangoon;" "the disease among mail horses;" "the Suez canal;" "the forests of Oude;" and "polygamy among the Hindoos." The Viceroy contributes a "note on the administration of the Khetree chieftainship;" the Bengal Government sends a memorandum on "bribery of telegraph clerks;" and the Resident of Kotah an official report of the ceremonies attending the reception of a viceregal khureta restoring the honours of a salute to the Maha Rao of Kotah. The khureta was received in state, the letter being mounted alone upon an elephant magnificently caparisoned, and saluted from the palace with 101 guns. There is no honour that we can pay to a native prince so great as that of increasing his salute, and, on the other hand, when the Guicodar of Baroda allows a suttee, or when Jung Bahadoor of Nepaul expresses his intention of visiting Paris, we punish them by docking them of two guns, or abolishing their salute, according to the magnitude of the offence.

An Order in Council confers upon the High Priest of the Parsees in the Deccan, "in consideration of his services during the mutiny of 1857," the honorary title of "Khan Bahadoor." A paragraph announces that an official investigation has been made into the supposed desecration by Scindia and the Viceroy of a mosque at Agra, and that it has been found that the place in question was not a mosque at all. Scindia had given an entertainment to the Viceroy at the Taj Mahal, and supper had been laid out at a building in the grounds. The native papers said the building was a mosque, but the Agra officials triumphantly demonstrated that it had been used for a supper to Lord Ellenborough after the capture of Cabool, and that its name meant "Feast-place." "Report on the lighthouses of the Abyssinian coast;" "Agreement with the Governor of Leh," Thibet, in reference to the trans-Himalayan caravans; the promotion of one gentleman to be "Commissioner of Coorg," and of another to be "Superintendent of the teak forests of Lower Burmah;" "Evidence on the proposed measures to suppress the abuses of polyandry in Travancore and Cochin (by arrangement with the Rajah of Travancore);" "Dismissal of Policeman Juggernauth Ramkam—Oude division, No. 11 company—for gross misconduct;" "Report on the Orissa famine;" "Plague in Turkey;" "Borer insects in coffee plantations;" "Presents to gentlemen at Fontainebleau for teaching forestry to Indian officers;" "Report on the Cotton States of America," for the information of native planters; "Division of Calcutta into postal districts" (in Bengalee as well as English); "Late engagement between the Punjaub cavalry and the Afghan tribes;" "Pension of 3rs. per mensem to the widow (aged 12) of Jamram Chesà, Sepoy, 27th Bengal N. I." are other headings. The relative space given to matters of importance and to those of little moment is altogether in favour of the latter. The government of two millions of people is transferred in three lines, but a page is taken up with a list of the caste-marks and nose-borings of native women applying for pensions as soldiers' widows, and two pages are full of advertisements of lost currency notes.

The columns of the *Gazette*, or at all events its supplements, offer to Government officials whose opinion has been asked upon questions on which they possess valuable knowledge, or in which the people of their district are concerned, an opportunity of attacking the acts or laws of the Government itself—a chance of which they are not slow to take advantage. One covertly attacks the licence-tax; a second, under pretence of giving his opinion on some proposed change in the contract law, backs the demands of the indigo-planters for a law that shall compel specific performance of labour-contracts on the part of the workman, and under penalty of imprisonment; another lays all the ills under which India can be shown to suffer at the door of the Home Government, and points out the ruinous effects of continual changes of Indian Secretaries in London.

It would be impossible to overrate the importance of the supplements to the *Gazette*, viewed either as a substitute for a system of communicated articles to the native papers, or as material for English statesmen, whether in India or at home, or as a great experiment in the direction of letting the people of India legislate for themselves. The results of no less than three Government inquiries were printed in the supplement during my stay in India, the first being in the shape of a circular to the various local governments requesting their opinion on the proposed extension to natives of the testamentary succession laws contained in the Indian Civil Code; while the second related to the "ghaut murders," and the third to the abuses of polygamy among the Hindoos. The second and third inquiries were conducted by means of circulars addressed by Government to those most interested, whether native or European.

The evidence in reply to the "ghaut murder" circular was commenced by a letter from the Secretary to the Government of Bengal to the Secretary to the Government of India, calling the attention of the Viceroy in Council to an article written in Bengalee by a Hindoo in the *Dacca Prokash* on the practice of taking sick Hindoos to the riverside to die. It appears from this letter that the local governments pay careful attention to the opinions of the native papers—unless, indeed, we are to accept the view that "the Hindoo" was a Government clerk, and the article written to order—a supposition

favoured by its radical and destructive tone. The
Viceroy answered that the local officers and native
gentlemen of all shades of religious opinion were to
be privately consulted. A confidential communication was then addressed to eleven English and four
Hindoo gentlemen, and the opinions of the English
and native newspapers were unofficially invited. The
Europeans were chiefly for the suppression of the
practice; the natives—with the exception of one,
who made a guarded reply—stated that the abuses
of the custom had been exaggerated, and that they
could not recommend its suppression. The Government agreed with the natives, and decided that
nothing should be done—an opinion in which the
Secretary of State concurred.

In his reply to the "ghaut murder" circular, the
representative of the orthodox Hindoos, after pointing
out that the *Dacca Prokash* is the Dacca organ of
the Brahmos, or Bengal Deists, and not of the true
Hindoos, went on to quote at length from the Hindoo
scriptures passages which show that to die in the
Ganges water is the most blessed of all deaths.
The quotations were printed in native character as
well as in English in the *Gazette*. One of the
officials in his reply pointed out that the discouragement of a custom was often as effective as its prohibition, and instanced the cessation of the practice
of "hook-swinging" and "self-mutilation."

Valuable as is the correspondence as a sample of
the method pursued in such inquiries, the question
under discussion has not the importance that attaches

to the examination into the abuses of the practice of polygamy.

To prevent an outcry that the customs of the Hindoo people were being attacked, the Lieutenant-Governor of Bengal stated in his letters to the Government of India that it was his wish that the inquiry should be strictly confined to the abuses of Koolin polygamy, and that there should be no general examination into ordinary polygamy, which was not opposed even by enlightened Hindoos. The polygamy of the Koolin Brahmins is a system of taking a plurality of wives as a means of subsistence: the Koolins were originally Brahmins of peculiar merit, and such was their sanctity that there grew up a custom of payments being made to them by the fathers of the forty or fifty women whom they honoured by marriage. So greatly has the custom grown that Koolins have sometimes as many as eighty wives, and the husband's sole means of subsistence consists in payments from the fathers of his wives, each of whom he visits, however, only once in three or four years. The Koolin Brahmins live in luxury and indolence, their wives exist in misery, and the whole custom is plainly repugnant to the teachings of the Hindoo scriptures, and is productive of vice and crime. The committee appointed for the consideration of the subject by the Lieutenant-Governor of Bengal—which consisted of two English civilians and five natives—reported that the suggested systems of registration of marriages, or of fines increasing in amount for every marriage after the first, would limit the general liberty of the Hindoos to take many wives, which they were forbidden to touch. On the other hand, to recommend a declaratory law on plural marriages would be to break their instructions, which ordered them to refrain from giving the sanction of English law to Hindoo polygamy. One native dissented from the report, and favoured a declaratory law.

The English idea of "not recognising" customs or religions which exist among a large number of the inhabitants of English countries is a strange one, and productive of much harm. It is not necessary, indeed, that we should countenance the worship of Juggernauth by ordering our officials to present offerings at his shrine, but it is at least necessary that we should recognise native customs by legislating to restrain them within due limits. To refuse to "recognise" polygamy, which is the social state of the vast majority of the citizens of the British empire, is not less ridiculous than to refuse to recognise that Hindoos are black.

Recognition is one thing, interference another. How far we should interfere with native customs is a question upon which no general rule can be given, unless it be that we should in all cases of proposed interference with social usages or religious ceremonies consult intelligent but orthodox natives, and act up to their advice. In Ceylon, we have prohibited polygamy and polyandry, although the law is not enforced; in India, we "unofficially recognise" the custom; in Singapore, we have distinctly recognised it by an amendment to the Indian Succession Law, which there applies to natives as well as Europeans. In India, we put down suttee; while, in Australia, we tolerate customs at least as barbarous.

One of the social systems which we recognise in India is far more revolting to our English feelings than is that of polygamy—namely, the custom of polyandry, under which each woman has many husbands at a time. This custom we unofficially recognise as completely as we do polygyny, although it prevails only on the Malabar coast, and among the hill-tribes of the Himalaya, and not among the strict Hindoos. The Thibetan frontier tribes have a singular form of the institution, for with them the woman is the wife of all the brothers of a family, the eldest brother choosing her, and the eldest son succeeding to the property of his mother and all her husbands. In Southern India, the polyandry of the present day differs little from that which in the middle of the fifteenth century Nicolo de Conti found flourishing in Calicut. Each woman has several husbands, some as many as ten, who all contribute to her maintenance, she living apart from all of them; and the children are allotted to the husbands at the will of the wife.

The toleration of polygyny, or common polygamy, is a vexed question everywhere. In India, all authorities are in favour of respecting it; in Natal, opinion is the other way. While we suppress it in Ceylon, even among black races conquered by us with little pretext only fifty years ago, we are doubtful as to the propriety of its suppression by the United

States among white people, who, whatever was the case with the original leaders, have for the most part settled down in Utah since it has been the territory of a nation whose imperial laws prohibit polygamy in plain terms.

The inquiries into the abuses of polygamy which have lately been conducted in Bengal and in Natal have revealed singular differences between the polygamy of the Hindoos and of the hill-tribes, between Indian and Mormon polygamy, and between both and the Mohamedan law. The Hindoo laws, while they limit the number of legal wives, allow of concubines, and, in the Maharajah case, Sir Joseph Arnould went so far as to say that polygamy and courtezanship are always found to flourish side by side, although the reverse is notoriously the case at Salt Lake City, where concubinage is punishable, in name at least, by death. Again, polygamy is somewhat discouraged by Mohamedan and Hindoo laws, and the latter even lay down the sum which in many cases is to be paid to the first wife as compensation for the wrong done her by the taking of other wives. Among the Mormons, on the other hand, polygamy is enjoined upon the faithful, and, so far from feeling herself aggrieved, the first wife herself selects the others, or is at the least consulted. Among some of the hill-tribes of India, such as the Paharis of Bhaugulpoor, polygamy is encouraged, but with a limitation to four wives.

Among the Mohamedans, the number of marriages is restricted, and divorce is common; among the

Mormons, there is no limit—indeed, the more wives the greater a man's glory—and divorce is all but unknown. The greatest, however, of all the many differences between Eastern and Mormon polygamy lies in the fact that, of the Eastern wives, one is the chief, while Mormon wives are absolutely equal in legitimacy and rank.

Not only is equality the law, but the first wife has recognised superiority of position over the others in the Mormon family. By custom she is always consulted by her husband in reference to the choice of a new wife, while the other wives are not always asked for their opinion; but this is a matter of habit, and the husband is in no way bound by her decision. Again, the first wife—if she is a consenting party—often gives away the fresh wives at the altar; but this, too, is a mere custom. The fact that in India one of the wives generally occupies a position of far higher dignity than that held by the others will make Indian polygamy easy to destroy by the lapse of time and operation of social and moral causes. As the city-dwelling natives come to mix more with the Europeans, they will find that only one of their wives will be generally recognised. This will tend of itself to repress polygamy among the wealthy native merchants and among the rajahs who are members of our various councils, and their example will gradually react upon the body of the natives. Already a majority of the married people of India are monogamists by practice, although polygamists in theory; their marriages being limited by poverty, although not by law. The classes which have to be reached are the noble families, the merchants, and the priests; and over the two former European influence is considerable, while the inquiry into Koolinism has proved that the leading natives will aid us in repressing the abuses of polygamy among the priests.

CHAPTER X.

UMRITSUR.

At Umbala, I heard that the Sikh pilgrims returning from the sacred fair, or great Hindoo camp-meeting, at Hurdwar, had been attacked by cholera, and excluded from the town; and as I quitted Umbala in the evening, I came upon the cholera-stricken train of pilgrims escaping by forced marches towards their homes, in many cases a thousand miles away. Tall, lithe, long-bearded men with large hooked noses, high foreheads, and thin lips, stalked along, leading by one hand their veiled women, who ran behind, their crimson and orange trousers stained with the dust of travel, while bullock-carts decked out with jingling bells bore the tired and the sick. Many children of all ages were in the throng. For mile after mile I drove through their ranks, as they marched with a strange kind of weary haste, and marched, too, with few halts, with little rest, if any. One great camp we left behind us, but only one; and all night long we were still passing ranks of marching men and women. The march was silent; there was none of the usual chatter of an Indian crowd; gloom was in every face, and the people marched like a beaten army flying from a destroying foe.

The disease, indeed, was pressing on their heels. Two hundred men and women, as I was told at the Umbala lines, had died among them in the single day. Many had dropped from fright alone, but the pestilence was in the horde, and its seeds were carried into whatever villages the pilgrims reached.

The gathering at Hurdwar had been attended by a million people drawn from every part of the Punjaub and North-West; not only Hindoos and Sikhs, but Scindhees, Beloochees, Pathans, and Afghans had their representatives in this great throng. As we neared the bridge of boats across the Sutlej, I found that a hurried quarantine had been set up on the spot. Only the sick or dying and bearers of corpses were detained, however; a few questions were asked of the remainder, and ultimately they were allowed to cross: but driving on at speed, I reached Jullundur in the morning, only to find that the pilgrims had been denied admittance to the town. A camp had been formed without the city, to which the pilgrims had to go, unless they preferred to straggle on along the roads, dropping and dying by the way; and the villagers throughout the country had risen on the wretched people, to prevent them returning to their homes.

It is not strange that the Government of India should lately have turned its attention to the regulation or suppression of these fairs, for the city-dwelling people of North India will not continue long to tolerate enormous gatherings at the commencement of the hot weather, by which the lives of thousands must ultimately be lost. At Hurdwar, at Juggernauth, and at many other holy spots, hundreds of thousands— millions, not unfrequently—are collected yearly from all parts of India. Great princes come down travelling slowly from their capitals with trains of troops and followers so long that they often take a day or more to pass a given spot. The Maharajah of Cashmere's camp between Kalka and Umbala occupied when I saw it more space than that of Aldershot. Camels, women, suttlers without count, follow in the train, so that a body of five thousand men is multiplied until it occupies the space and requires the equipments of a vast army. A huge multitude of cultivators, of princes, of fakeers, and of roisterers met for the excitement and the pleasures of the camp, is gathered about the holy spot. There is religion, and there is trade; indeed, the religious pilgrims are for the most part shrewd traders, bent on making a good profit from their visit to the fair.

The gathering at Hurdwar in 1867 had been more than usually well attended and successful, when suddenly a rumour of cholera was heard; the police procured the break-up of the camp, and Government thought fit to prohibit the visit to Simla of the Maharajah of Cashmere. The pilgrims had hardly left the camp upon their journey home when cholera broke out, and by the time I passed them hundreds were already dead, and a panic had spread through India. The cholera soon followed the rumour, and spread even to the healthiest hill-towns, and 6,000 deaths occurred in the city of Srinuggur, after the Maharajah's return with his infected escort from Hurdwar. A Government which has checked infanticide and suppressed suttee could not fail to succeed, if it interfered, in causing these fairs to be held in the cold weather.

At Jullundur, I encountered a terrible dust-storm. It came from the south and west, and, to judge from its fierceness, must have been driven before the wind from the great sandy desert of Northern Scinde. The sun was rising for a sultry day, when from the south there came a blast which in a minute covered the sky with a leaden cloud, while from the horizon there advanced, more slowly, a lurid mass of reddish-brown. It soon reached the city, and then, from the wall where I sought shelter, nothing could be seen but driving sand of ochre colour, nothing heard but the shrieking of the wind. The gale ceased as suddenly as it began, but left a day which, delightful to travellers upon the Indian plains, would elsewhere have been called by many a hard name—a day of lowering sky and dropping rain, with chilling cold—in short, a day that felt and looked like an English thaw, though the thermometer must have stood at 75°. Another legacy from the storm was a view of the Himalayas such as is seldom given to the dwellers on the plains. Looking at the clouds upon the northern horizon I suddenly caught sight of the Snowy Range hanging, as it seemed, above them, half-way up the skies

Seen with a foreground of dawk jungle in bright bloom, the scene was beautiful; but the view too distant to be grand, except through the ideas of immensity called up by the loftiness of the peaks. While crossing the Beeas (the ancient Hyphasis, and eastern boundary of the Persian empire in the days of Darius), as I had crossed the Sutlej, by a bridge of boats, I noticed that the railway viaduct, which was being built for the future Umritsur and Delhi line, stood some way from the deep water of the river; indeed, stood chiefly upon dry land. The rivers change their course so often that the Beeas and Sutlej bridges will each have to be made a mile long. There has lately been given us in the Punjaub a singular instance of the blind confidence in which Government orders are carried out by the subordinates. The order was that the iron columns on which the Beeas bridge was to rest should each be forty-five feet long. In placing them, in some cases the bottom of the forty-five feet was in the shifting sand—in others, it was thirty feet below the surface of the solid rock; but a boring which was needless in the one case and worse than useless in the other has been persevered in to the end, the story runs, because it was the "hook'm." The Indian rivers are the great bars to road and railway making; indeed, except on the Grand Trunk road, it may be said that the rivers of India are still unbridged. On the chief mail-roads stone causeways are built across the river-beds, but the streams are all but impassable during the rains. Even on the road from Kalka to Umbala, however, there is one riverbed without a causeway, across which the dawk-gharree is dragged by bullocks, who struggle slowly through the sand; and, in crossing it, I saw a steam-engine lying half-buried in the drift.

In India, we have been sadly neglectful of the roads. The Grand Trunk road and the few great railroads are the only means of communication in the country. Even between the terminus of the Bengal lines at Jubbelpore and of the Bombay railroad at Nagpore there was at the time of my visit no metalled road, although the distance was but 200 miles, and the mails already passed that way. Half a day at least was lost upon all the Calcutta letters, and Calcutta passengers for Bombay or England were put to an additional expense of some £30 and a loss of a week or ten days in time from the absence of 200 miles of road. Until we have good cross-roads in India, and metalled roads into the interior from every railway station, we shall never succeed in increasing the trade of India, nor in civilizing its inhabitants. The Grand Trunk road is, however, the best in the world, and is formed of soft white nodules, found in beds through North India, which when pounded and mixed with water is known as "kunkur," and makes a road hard, smooth, clean, and lasting, not unlike to that which asphalt gives.

At Umritsur, I first found myself in the true East—the East of myrtles, roses, and veiled figures with flashing eyes—the East of the "Arabian Nights" and "Lalla Rookh." The city itself is Persian, rather than Indian, in its character, and is overgrown with date-palms, pomegranates, and the roses from which the precious attar is distilled. Umritsur has the making of the attar for the world, and it is made from a rose which blossoms only once a year. Ten tons of petals of the ordinary country rose (*rosa centifolia*) are used annually in attar-making at Umritsur, and are worth from £20 to £30 a ton in the raw state. The petals are placed in the retort with a small quantity of water, and heat is applied until the water is distilled through a hollow bamboo into a second vessel, which contains sandal-wood oil. A small quantity of pure attar passes with the water into the receiver. The contents of the receiver are then poured out, and allowed to stand till the attar rises to the surface, in small globules, and is skimmed off. The pure attar sells for its weight in silver.

Umritsur is famous for another kind of merchandise more precious even than the attar. It is the seat of the Cashmere shawl trade, and three great French firms have their houses in the town, where, through the help of friends, shawls may be obtained at singularly low prices; but travellers in far-off regions are often in the financial position of the Texan hunter who was offered a million of acres for a pair of boots—they "have not got the boots."

It is only shawls of the second class that can be bought cheap at Umritsur; those of the finest quality vary in price from £40 to £250, £30 being the cost of the material. The shawl manufacture of the Punjaub is not confined to Umritsur; there are 900 shawl-making shops in Loodiana, I was told while there. There are more than sixty permanent dies in use at the Umritsur shawl-shops; cochineal, indigo, logwood, and saffron are the commonest and best. The shawls are made of the down which underlies the hair of the "shawl-goat" of the higher levels. The yak, the camel, and the dog of the Himalayas, all possess this down as well as their hair or wool; it serves them as a protection against the winter cold. *Chogas*—long cloaks used as dressing-gowns by Europeans—are also made in Umritsur, from the soft wool of the Bokhara camel, for Umritsur is now the head-quarters of the Central Asian trade with Hindostan.

The bazaar is the gayest and most bustling in India—the goods of all India and Central Asia are there. Dacca muslin—known as "woven air"—lies side by side with thick chogas of kinkob and embroidered Cashmere, Indian towels of coarse huckaback half cover Chinese watered silks, and the brilliant dies of the brocades of Central India are relieved by the modest grays of the soft *puttoo* caps. The buyers are as motley as the goods—Rajpoots in turbans of deep blue, ornamented with gold thread, Cashmere valley herdsmen in strange caps, nautch girls from the first three bridges of Srinuggur, some of the so-called "hill fanatics," whose only religion is to levy contributions on the people of the plains, and Sikh troopers, home on leave, stalking through the streets with a haughty swagger. Some of the Sikhs wear the pointed helmets of their ancestors, the ancient Sakæ; but, whether he be helmeted or not, the enormous white beard of the Sikh, the fierce curl of his moustache, the cock of the turban, and the amplitude of his sash, all suggest the fighting man. The strange closeness of the likeness of the Hungarians to the Sikhs would lead one to think that the races are identical. Not only are they alike in build, look, and warlike habits, but they brush their beards in the same fashion, and these little customs endure longer than manners—longer, often, than religion itself. One of the crowd was a ruddy-faced, red-bearded, Judas-haired fellow, that looked every inch a Fenian, and might have stepped here from the Kilkenny wilds; but the majority of the Sikhs had aquiline noses and fine features, so completely Jewish of the best and oldest type that I was reminded of Sir William Jones's fanciful derivation of the Afghan races from the lost Ten Tribes of Israel. It may be doubted whether the Sikhs, Afghans, Persians, ancient Assyrians, Jews, ancient Scythians, and Magyars were not all originally of one stock.

In India, dress still serves the purpose of denoting rank. The peasant is clothed in cotton, the prince in cloth of gold; and even religion, caste, and occupation are distinguished by their several well-known and unchanging marks. Indeed, the fixity of fashion is as singular in Hindostan as its infinite changeableness in New York or France. The patterns we see to-day in the Bombay bazaar are those which were popular in the days of Shah Jehan. This regulation of dress by custom is one of the many difficulties in the way of our English manufacturers in their Indian ventures. There has been an attempt made lately to bring about the commercial annexation of India to England : Lancashire is to manufacture the Longee, Dhotee, and Saree, we are told ; Nottingham or Paisley are to produce us shumlas ; Dacca is to give way to Norwich, and Coventry to supersede Jeypoor. It is strange that men of Indian knowledge and experience should be found who fail to point out the absurdity of our entertaining hopes of any great trade in this direction. The Indian women of the humbler castes are the only customers we can hope to have in India ; the high-caste people wear only ornamented fabrics, in the making of which native manufacturers have advantages which place them out of the reach of European competition : cheap labour ; workmen possessed of singular culture, and of a grace of expression which makes their commonest productions poems in silk and velvet; perfect knowledge of their customers' wants and tastes ; scrupulous regard to caste conservatism—all these are possessed by the Hindoo manufacturer, and absent in the case of the firms of Manchester and Rochdale. As a rule, all Indian dress is best made by hand ; only the coarsest and least ornamented fabrics can be largely manufactured at paying rates in England. As for the clothing of the poorer people, the men for the most part wear nothing, the women little, and that little washed often, and changed never. Even for the roughest goods we cannot hope to undersell the native manufacturers by much in the presidency towns. Up country, if we enter into the competition, it can scarcely fail to be a losing one. England is not more unlikely to be clothed from India than India from Great Britain. If European machinery is needed, it will be erected in Yokohama, or in Bombay, not in the West Riding.

It is hardly to be believed that Englishmen have for some years been attempting to induce the natives to adopt our flower patterns—peonies, butterflies, and all. Ornament in India is always subordinate to the purpose which the object has to serve. Hindoo art begins where English ends. The principles which centuries of study have given us as the maxims upon which the grammar of ornament is based are those which are instinctive in every native workman. Every costume, every vase, every temple and bazaar in India, gives eye-witness that there is truth in the saw that the finest taste is consistent with the deepest slavery of body, with the utmost slavishness of mind. A Hindoo of the lowest caste will spurn the gift of a turban or a loin-cloth the ornamentation of which consists not with his idea of symmetry and grace. Nothing could induce a Hindoo to clothe himself in such a gaudy, masquerading dress as maddens a Maori with delight and his friends with jealousy and mortification. In art as in deportment, the Hindoo loves harmony and quiet; and dress with the Oriental is an art: there is as much feeling—as deep poetry—

in the curves of the Hindoo Saree as in the outlines of the Taj.

Umritsur is the spiritual capital of the Sikhs, and the Durbar Temple in the centre of the town is the holiest of their shrines. It stands, with the sunbeams glancing from its gilded roof, in the middle of a very holy tank, filled with huge weird fish-monsters that look as though they fed on men, and glare at you through cruel eyes.

Leaving your shoes outside the very precincts of the tank, with the police guard that we have stationed there, you skirt one side of the water, and then leave the mosaic terrace for a still more gorgeous causeway, that, bordered on either side by rows of golden lamp-supporters, carries the path across towards the rich pavilion, the walls of which are as thickly spread with gems as are those of Akbar's palace. Here you are met by a bewildering din, for under the inner dome sit worshippers by the score, singing with vigour the grandest of barbaric airs to the accompaniment of lyre, harp, and tomtom, while in the centre, on a cushion, is a long-bearded grey old gooroo, or priest of the Sikh religion—a creed singularly pure, though little known. The effect of the scene is much enhanced by the beauty of the surrounding houses, whose oriel windows overhang the tank, that the Sikh princes may watch the evolutions of the lantern-bearing boats on nights when the temple is illuminated. When seen by moonlight, the tank is a very picture from the "Arabian Nights."

This is a time of ferment in the Sikh religion. A carpenter named Ram Singh—a man with all that combination of shrewdness and imagination, of enthusiasm and worldliness, by which the world is governed —another Mohamed or Brigham Young, perhaps—has preached his way through the Punjaub, infusing his own energy into others, and has drawn away from the Sikh Church some hundred thousand followers— reformers—who call themselves the Kookas. These modern Anabaptists—for many are disposed to look upon Ram Singh as another John of Leyden—bind themselves by some terrible and secret oath, and the Government fear that reformation of religion is to be accompanied by reformation of the State of a kind not advantageous to the English power. When Ram Singh lately proclaimed his intention of visiting the Durbar Temple, the gooroos incited the Sikh fanatics to attack his men with clubs, and the military police were forced to interfere. There is now, however, a Kooka temple at Lahore.

In spite of religious ferment, there is little in the bazaar or temples of Umritsur to remind one of the times—only some twenty years ago—when the Sikh army crossed the Sutlej, and its leaders threatened to sack Delhi and Calcutta, and drive the English out of India; it is impossible, however, to believe that there is no undercurrent in existence. Eighteen years cannot have sufficed to extinguish the Sikh nationality, and the men who beat us at Chillianwallah are not yet dead, or even old. When the Maharajah Dhuleep Singh returned from England in

1864 to bury his mother's body, the chiefs crowded round him as he entered Lahore, and besought him to resume his position at their head. His answer was a haughty "Jao!" ("Begone!") If the Sikhs are to rise once more, they will look elsewhere for their leader.

CHAPTER XI.

LAHORE.

CROSSING in a railway journey of an hour one of the most fertile districts of the Punjaub, I was struck with the resemblance of the country to South Australia: in each great sweeps of wheat-growing lands, with here and there an acacia or mimosa tree; in each a climate hot, but dry, and not unhealthy — singularly hot here for a tract in the latitude of Vicksburg, near which the Mississippi is sometimes frozen.

Through groves of a yellow-blossomed, sweet-scented, weeping acacia, much like laburnum, in which the fortified railway station seems out of place, I reached the tomb-surrounded garden that is called Lahore—a city of pomegranates, oleanders, hollyhocks, and roses. The date-groves of Lahore are beautiful beyond description; especially so the one that hides the Agra Bank.

Lahore matches Umritsur in the purity of its Orientalism, Agra in the strength and grandeur of its walls: but it has no Tank Temple and no Taj; the Great Mosque is commonplace, Runjeet Singh's tomb is tawdry, and the far-famed Shalimar Gardens inferior to those of Pinjore. The strangest sight of Lahore is its new railway station—a fortress of red brick, one of many which are rising all over India. The fortification of the railway stations is decidedly the next best step to that of having no forts at all.

The city of Lahore is surrounded by a suburb of great tombs, in which Europeans have in many cases taken up their residence by permission of the owner, the mausoleums being, from the thickness of their walls, as cool as cellars. Sometimes, however, a fanatical relative of the man buried in the tomb will warn the European tenant that he will die within a year—a prophecy which poison has once or twice brought to its fulfilment in the neighbourhood of Lahore and at Moultan.

Strolling in the direction of the Cabool Gate, I came on the Lieutenant-Governor of the Punjaub, driving in an open carriage drawn by camels; and passing out on to the plain, I met all the officers in garrison returning on Persian ponies from a game at the Afghan sport of "hockey upon horseback," while a little farther were some English ladies with hawks. Throughout the Northern Punjaub a certain settling down in comfort on the part of the English officials is to be remarked, and the adaptations of native habits to English uses, of which I had in one evening's walk the three examples which I have mentioned, is a sign of a tendency towards that making the best of things which in a newly-occupied country precedes the entrance upon a system of permanent abode. Lahore has been a British city for nineteen years, Bombay for two centuries and more; yet Lahore is far more English than Bombay.

Although there are as yet no signs of English settlement in the Punjaub, still the official community in many a Punjaub station is fast becoming colonial in its type, and Indian traditions are losing ground. English wives and sisters abound in Lahore, even the railway and canal officials having brought out their families; and during the cool weather race meetings, drag hunts, cricket matches, and croquet parties follow one another from day to day, and Lahore boasts a volunteer corps. When the hot season comes on, those who can escape to the hills, and the wives and children of those who cannot go run to Dalhousie, as Londoners do to Eastbourne.

The healthy English tone of the European communities of Umritsur and Lahore is reflected in the newspapers of the Punjaub, which are the best in India, although the blunders of the native printers render the "betting news" unintelligible, and the "cricket scores" obscure. The columns of the Lahore papers present as singular a mixture of incongruous articles as even the Government *Gazette* offers to its readers. An official notice that it will be impossible to allow more than 560 elephants to take part in the next Lucknow procession follows a report of the "ice meeting" of the community of Lahore, to arrange about the next supply; and side by side with this is an article on the Punjaub trade with Chinese Tartary, which recommends the Government of India to conquer Afghanistan, and to re-occupy the valley of Cashmere. A paragraph notices the presentation by the Punjaub Government to a native gentleman, who has built a serai at his own cost, of a valuable gift; another records a brush with the Wagheers. The only police case is the infliction on a sweeper of a fine of thirty rupees for letting his donkey run against a high-caste woman, whereby she was defiled; but a European magistrate reprimands a native pleader for appearing in court with his shoes on; and a notice from the Lieutenant-Governor gives a list of the holidays to be observed by the courts, in which the "Queen's Birthday" comes between "Bhudur Kalee" and "Oors data Gunjbuksh," while "Christmas" follows "Shubberat," and "Ash Wednesday" precedes "Holee." As one of the holidays lasts a fortnight, and many more than a week, the total number of *dies non* is considerable; but a postscript decrees that additional local holidays shall be granted for fairs and festivals, and for the solar and lunar eclipse, which brings the no-court days up to sixty or seventy, besides those in the Long Vacation. The Hindoos are in the happy position of having also six new-year's days in every twelvemonth; but the editor of one of the Lahore papers says that his Mohamedan compositors manifest a singular interest in Hindoo feasts, which shows a gratifying spread of toleration! An article on the "Queen's English in Hindostan," in the *Punjaub Times*, gives, as a specimen of the poetry of Young

Bengal, a serenade in which the skylark carols on the primrose bush. "Emerge my love," the poet cries:

> "The fragrant, dewy grove
> We'll wander through till gun-fire bids us part."

But the final stanza is the best:

> "Then, Leila, come! nor longer cogitate;
> Thy egress let no scruples dire retard;
> Contiguous to the portals of thy gate
> Suspensively I supplicate regard."

The advertisements range from books on the languages of Dardistan to Government contracts for elephant fodder, or price-lists of English beer; and an announcement of an Afghan history in the Urdu tongue is followed by a prospectus of Berkhampstead Grammar School. King Edward would rub his eyes were he to wake and find himself being advertised in Lahore.

The Punjaub Europeans, with their English newspapers and English ways, are strange governors for an empire conquered from the bravest of all Eastern races little more than eighteen years ago. One of them, taking up a town policeman's staff, said to me one day, "Who could have thought in 1850 that in 1867 we should be ruling the Sikhs with this?"

CHAPTER XII.

OUR INDIAN ARMY.

DURING my stay in Lahore, a force of Sikhs and Pathans was being raised for service at Hong Kong by an officer staying in the same hotel with myself, and a large number of men were being enlisted in the city by recruiting parties of the Bombay army. In all parts of India, we are now relying, so far as our native forces are concerned, upon the men who only a few years back were by much our most dangerous foes.

Throughout the East, subjects concern themselves but little in the quarrels of their princes, and the Sikhs are no exception to the rule. They fought splendidly in the Persian ranks at Marathon; under Shere Singh, they made their memorable stand at Chillianwallah; but, under Nicholson, they beat the bravest of the Bengal sepoys before Delhi. Whether they fight for us or against us is all one to them. They fight for those who pay them, and have no politics beyond their pockets. So far, they seem useful allies to us, who hold the purse of India. Unable to trust Hindoos with arms, we can at least rule them by the employment as soldiers of their fiercest enemies.

When we come to look carefully at our system, its morality is hardly clear. As we administer the revenues of India, nominally at least, for the benefit of the Indians, it might be argued that we may fairly keep on foot such troops as are best fitted to secure her against attack; but the argument breaks down when it is remembered that 70,000 British troops are maintained in India from the Indian revenues for that purpose, and that local order is secured by an ample force of military police. Even if the employment of Sikhs in times of emergency may be advisable, it cannot be denied that the day has gone by for permanently overawing a people by means of standing armies composed of their hereditary foes.

In discussing the question of the Indian armies, we have carefully to distinguish between the theory and the practice. The Indian official theory says that not only is the native army a valuable auxiliary to the English army in India, but that its moral effect on the people is of great benefit to us, inasmuch as it raises their self-respect, and offers a career to men who would otherwise be formidable enemies. The practice proclaims that the native troops are either dangerous or useless by arming them with weapons as antiquated as the bow and arrow, destroys the moral effect which might possibly be produced by a Hindoo force by filling the native ranks with Sikh and Goorkha aliens and heretics, and makes us enemies without number by denying to natives that promotion which the theory holds out to them. The existing system is officially defended by the most contradictory arguments, and on the most shifting of grounds. Those who ask why we should not trust the natives, at all events to the extent of allowing Bengal and Bombay men to serve, and to serve with arms that they can use, in bodies which profess to be the Bengal and Bombay armies, but which in fact are Sikh regiments which we are afraid to arm, are told that the native army has mutinied times without end, that it has never fought well except where, from the number of British present, it had no choice but to fight, and that it is dangerous and inefficient. Those who ask why this shadow of a native army should be retained are told that its records of distinguished service in old times are numerous and splendid. The huge British force maintained in India, and the still huger native army, are each of them made an excuse for the retention of the other at the existing standard. If you say that it is evident that 70,000 British troops cannot be needed in India, you are told that they are required to keep the 120,000 native troops in check. If you ask, Of what use, then, are the latter? you hear that in the case of a serious imperial war the English troops would be withdrawn, and the defence of India confided to these very natives who in time of peace require to be thus severely held in check. Such shallow arguments would be instantly exposed were not English statesmen bribed by the knowledge that their acceptance as good logic allows us to maintain at India's cost 70,000 British soldiers, who in time of danger would be available for our defence at home.

That the English force of 70,000 men maintained in India in time of peace can be needed there in peace or war is not to be supposed by those who remember that 10,000 men were all that were really needed to suppress the wide-spread mutiny of 1857, and that Russia—our only possible enemy from without—never succeeded during a two years' war in her own territory in placing a disposable army of 60,000 men in the Crimea. Another mutiny such as that of 1857 is, indeed, impossible, now that we retain both forts and artillery exclusively in British hands; and Russia having to bring her supplies and men across almost boundless deserts, or through hostile Afghanistan, would be met at the Khyber by our whole Indian army, concentrated from the most distant stations at a few days' notice, fighting in a well-known and friendly country, and supplied from the plains of all India by the railroads. Our English troops in India are sufficiently numerous, were it necessary, to fight both the Russians and our native army; but it is absurd that we should maintain in India, in a time of perfect peace, at a yearly cost to the people of that country of from fourteen to sixteen millions sterling, an army fit to cope with the most tremendous disasters that could overtake the country, and at the same time unspeakably ridiculous that we should in all our calculations be forced to set down the native army as a cause of weakness. The native rulers, moreover, whatever their unpopularity with their people, were always able to array powerful levies against enemies from without; and if our government of India is not a miserable failure, our influence over the lower classes of the people ought, at the least, to be little inferior to that exercised by the Mogul emperors or the Maratta chiefs.

As for local risings, concentration of our troops by means of the railroads that would be constructed in half-a-dozen years out of our military savings alone, and which American experience shows us cannot be effectually destroyed, would be amply sufficient to deal with them were the force reduced to 30,000 men; and a general rebellion of the people of India we have no reason to expect, and no right to resist should it by any combination of circumstances be brought about.

The taxation required to maintain the present Indian army presses severely upon what is in fact the poorest country in the world; the yearly drain of many thousand men weighs heavily upon us; and our system seems to proclaim to the world the humiliating fact, that under British government, and in times of peace, the most docile of all peoples need an army of 200,000 men, in addition to the military police, to watch them, or keep them down.

Whatever the decision come to with regard to the details of the changes to be made in the Indian army system, it is at least clear that it will be expedient in us to reduce the English army in India if we intend it for India's defence, and our duty to abolish it if we intend it for our own. It is also evident that, after allowing for mere police duties—which should in all cases be performed by men equipped as, and called by the name of, police—the native army should, whatever its size, be rendered as effective as possible, by instruction in the use of the best weapons of the age. If local insurrections have unfortunately to be quelled, they must be quelled by English troops; and against European invaders, native troops, to be of the slightest service, must be armed as Europeans. As the possibility of European invasion is remote, it would probably be advisable that the native army should be gradually reduced until brought to the point of merely supplying the body-guards and ceremonial-troops; at all events, the practice of overawing Sikhs with Hindoos, and Hindoos with Sikhs, should be abandoned as inconsistent with the nature of our government in India, and with the first principles of freedom.

There is, however, no reason why we should wholly deprive ourselves of the services of the Indian warrior tribes. If we are to continue to hold such outposts as Gibraltar, the duty of defending them against all comers might not improperly be entrusted wholly or partly to the Sikhs or fiery little Goorkhas, on the ground that, while almost as brave as European troops, they are somewhat cheaper. It is possible, indeed, that, just as we draw our Goorkhas from independent Nepaul, other European nations may draw Sikhs from us. We are not even now the only rulers who employ Sikhs in war; the Khan of Kokand is said to have many in his service: and, tightly ruled at home, the Punjaubees may not improbably become the Swiss of Asia.

Whatever the European force to be maintained in India, it is clear that it should be local. The Queen's army system has now had ten years' trial, and has failed in every point in which failure was prophesied.

The officers, hating India, and having no knowledge of native languages or customs, bring our Government into contempt among the people; recruits in England dread enlistment for service they know not where; and Indian taxpayers complain that they are forced to support an army over the disposition of which they have not the least control, and which in time of need would probably be withdrawn from India. Even the Dutch, they say, maintain a purely colonial force in Java, and the French have pledged themselves that, when they withdraw the Algerian local troops, they will replace them by regiments of the line. England and Spain alone maintain purely imperial troops at the expense of their dependencies.

Were the European army in India kept separate from the English service, it would be at once less costly and more efficient, while the officers would be acquainted with the habits of the natives and customs of the country, and not, as at present, mere birds of passage, careless of offending native prejudice, indifferent to the feelings of those among whom they have to live, and occupied each day of their idle life in heartily wishing themselves at home again. There are, indeed, to the existing system drawbacks more serious than have been mentioned. Sufficient stress has not hitherto been laid upon the demoralization of our army, and danger to our home freedom that must result from the keeping in India of half our regular force. It is hard to believe that men who have periodically to go through such scenes as those of 1857, or who are in daily contact with a cringing dark-skinned race, can in the long run continue to be firm friends to constitutional liberty at home ; and it should be remembered that the English troops in India, though under the orders of the Commander-in-Chief, are practically independent of the House of Commons.

It is not only constitutionally that Indian rotation service is bad. The system is destructive to the discipline of our troops, and a separate service is the only remedy.

CHAPTER XIII.

RUSSIA.

FOR fifty years or more, we have been warned that one day we must encounter Russia, and for fifty years Muscovite armies, conquering their way step by step, have been advancing southward, till we find England and Russia now all but face to face in Central Asia.

Steadily the Russians are advancing. Their circular of 1864, in which they declared that they had reached their wished-for frontier, has been altogether forgotten, and all Kokand, and portions of Bokhara, have been swallowed up, while our spies in St. Petersburg tell the Indian Council that Persia herself is doomed. Although, however, the distance of the Russian from the English frontiers has been greatly reduced of late, it is still far more considerable than is supposed. Instead of the Russian outposts being 100 miles from Peshawur, as one alarmist has said, they are still 400; and Samarcand, their nearest city, is 450 miles in a straight line over the summit of the Hindoo Koosh, and 750 by road from our frontier at the Khyber. At the same time, we must, in our calculations of the future, assume that a few years will see

Russia at the northern base of the Hindoo Koosh, and in a position to overrun Persia, and take Herat.

It has been proposed that we should declare to Russia our intention to preserve Afghanistan as neutral ground; but there arises this difficulty, that having agreed to this plan, Russia would immediately proceed to set about ruling Afghanistan through Persia. On the other hand, it is impossible, as we have already found, to treat with Afghanistan, as there is no Afghanistan with which to treat; nor can we enter into friendly relations with any Afghan chief, lest his neighbour and enemy should hold us responsible for his acts. If we are to have any dealings with the Afghans, we shall soon be forced to take a side, and necessarily to fight and conquer, but at a great cost in men and money. It might be possible to make friends of some of the frontier tribes by giving them lands within our borders on condition of their performing military service, and respecting the lives and property of our merchants; but the policy would be costly, and its results uncertain, while we should probably soon find ourselves embroiled in Afghan politics. Moreover, meddling in Afghanistan, long since proved to be a foolish and a dangerous course, can hardly be made a wise one by the fact of the Russians being at the gate.

Many would have us advance to Herat, on the ground that it is in Afghanistan, and not on the plains of India, that Russia must be met; but such is the fierceness of the Afghans, such the poverty of their country, that its occupation would be at once a source of weakness and a military trap to the invader. Were we to occupy Herat, we should have Persians and Afghans alike against us; were the Russians to annex Afghanistan, they could never descend into the plains of India without a little diplomacy, or a little money from us, bringing the Afghan fanatics upon their rear. When, indeed, we look carefully into the meaning of those Anglo-Indians who would have us repeat our attempt to thrash the Afghans into loving us, we find that the pith of their complaint seems to be that battles and conquests mean promotion, and that we have no one left in India upon whom we can wage war. Civilians look for new appointments, military men for employment, missionaries for fresh fields, and all see their opening in annexation, while the newspapers echo the cry of their readers, and call on the Viceroy to annex Afghanistan " at the cost of impeachment."

Were our frontier at Peshawur a good one for defence, there could be but little reason shown for an occupation of any part of Afghanistan; but as it is, the question of the desirability of an advance is complicated by the lamentable weakness of our present frontier. Were Russia to move down upon India, we should have to meet her either in Afghanistan or upon the Indus: to meet her at Peshawur, at the foot of the mountains and with the Indus behind us, would be a military suicide. Of the two courses that would be open to us, a retreat to the Indus would be a terrible blow to the confidence of our troops, and an advance to Cabool or Herat would be an advance out of reach of our railroad communications, and through a dangerous defile. To maintain our frontier force at Peshawur, as we now do, is to maintain in a pestilential valley a force which, if attacked, could not fight where it is stationed, but would be forced to advance into Afghanistan or retreat to the Indus. The best policy would probably be to withdraw the Europeans from Peshawur and Rawul Pindee, and place them upon the Indus in the hills near Attock, completing our railroad from Attock to Lahore and from Attock to the hill station, and to leave the native force to defend the Khyber and Peshawur against the mountain tribes. We should also encourage European settlement in the valley of Cashmere. On the other hand, we should push a short railroad from the Indus to the Bholan Pass, and there concentrate a second powerful European force, with a view to resisting invasion at that point, and of taking in flank and rear any invader who might advance upon the Khyber. The Bholan Pass is, moreover, on the road to Candahar and Herat; and, although it would be a mistake to occupy those cities except by the wish of the Afghans, still the advance of the Russians will probably one day force the Afghans to ally themselves to us, and solicit the occupation of their cities. The fact that the present ruler of Herat is a mere tool of the Persians or feudatory of the Czar will have no effect whatever on his country, for if he once threw himself openly into Russian hands, his people would immediately desert him. So much for the means of defence against the Russians, but there is some chance that we may have to defend India against another Mohamedan invasion, secretly countenanced, but not openly aided by Russia. While on my way to England, I had a conversation on this matter with a well-informed Syrian Pacha, but notorious Russian-hater. He had been telling me that Russian policy had not changed, but was now, as ever, a policy of gradual annexation; that she envied our position in India, and hated us because our gentle treatment of Asiatics is continually held up to her as an example. "Russia has attacked you twice in India, and will attack you there again," he said. Admitting her interference in the Afghan war, I denied that it was proved that she had any influence in Hindostan, or any hand in the rebellion of 1857. My friend made me no spoken answer, but took four caskets that stood upon the table, and, setting them in a row, with an interval between them, pushed the first so that it struck the second, the second the third, and the third the fourth. Then, looking up, he said, "There you have the manner of the Russian move on India. I push No. 1, but you see No. 4 moves. 1 influences 2, 2 influences 3, and 3 influences 4; but 1 doesn't influence 4. Oh, dear me, no! Very likely even 1 and 3 are enemies, and hate each other; and if 3 thought that she was doing 1's work, she would kick over the traces at once. Nevertheless, she *is* doing it. In 1857, Russia certainly struck at you through Egypt, and probably through Central Asia also. Lord Palmerston was afraid to send troops through Egypt, though, if that could have been largely done, the mutiny could have been put down in half the time, and with a quarter the cost; and Nana Sahib, in his proclamation, stated, not without reason, that Egypt was on his side. The way you are being now attacked is this:—Russia and Egypt are for the moment hand and glove, though their ultimate objects are conflicting. Egypt is playing for the leadership of all Islam, even of Moslems in Central Asia and India. Russia sees that this game is for the time her game, as through Egypt she can excite the Turcomans, Afghans, and other Moslems of Central Asia to invade India in the name of religion and the Prophet, but, in fact, in the hope of plunder, and can also at the same time raise your Mohamedan population in Hindostan—a population over which you admit you have absolutely no hold. Of course you will defeat these hordes whenever you meet them in the field; but their numbers are incalculable, and their bravery great. India has twice before been conquered from the north, from Central Asia, and you must remember that behind these hordes comes Russia herself. Mohamedanism is weak here, on the Mediterranean, I grant you; but it is very strong in Central Asia—as strong as it ever was. Can you trust your Sikhs, too? I doubt it."

When I asked the Pacha how Egypt was to put herself at the head of Islam, he answered:—"Thus. We Egyptians are already supporting the Turkish empire. Our tribute is a million (francs), but we pay five millions, of which four go into the Sultan's privy purse. We have all the leading men of Turkey in our pay : 30,000 of the best troops serving in Crete, and the whole of the fleet, are contributed by Egypt. Now, Egypt had no small share in getting up the Cretan insurrection, and yet, you see, she does, or pretends to do, her best to put it down. The Sultan, therefore, is at the Viceroy's mercy, if you don't interfere. No one else will if you do not. The Viceroy aims at being nominally, as he is really, 'the Grand Turk.' Once Sultan, with Crete and the other islands handed over to Greece or Russia, the present Viceroy commands the allegiance of every Moslem people— thirty millions of your Indian subjects included; that is, practically Russia commands that allegiance— Russia practically, though not nominally, at Constantinople wields the power of Islam, instead of being hated by every true believer, as she would be if she annexed Turkey in Europe. Her real game is a far grander one than that with which she is credited."

"Turkey is your vassal," the Pacha went on to say; "she owes her existence entirely to you. Why not use her, then? Why not put pressure on the Sultan to exert his influence over the Asian tribes—which is far greater than you believe—for your benefit? Why not insist on your Euphrates route? Why not insist on Egypt ceasing to intrigue against you, and annex the country if she continues in her present course? If you wish to bring matters to a crisis, make Abdul Aziz insist on Egypt being better governed, or on the slave-trade being put down. You have made your name a laughing-stock here. You let Egypt half bribe, half force Turkey into throwing such obstacles in the way of your Euphrates route that it is no nearer completion now than it ever was. You force Egypt to pass a law abolishing the slave-trade and slavery itself, and you have taken no notice of the fact that this law has never been enforced in so much as a single instance. You think that you are all right now that you have managed to force our Government into allowing your troops to pass to and fro through Egypt, thus making your road through the territory of your most dangerous enemy. Where would you be in case of a war with Russia?"

When I pleaded that, if we were refused passage, we should occupy the country, the Pacha replied: "Of course you would; but you need not imagine that you will ever be refused passage. What will happen will be that, just at the time of your greatest need, the floods will come down from the mountains, and wash away ten miles of the line, and all the engines will go out of repair. You will complain: we shall offer to lay the stick about the feet of all the *employés* of the line. What more would you have? Can we prevent the floods? When our Government wished to keep your Euphrates scheme from coming to anything, did they say: 'Do this thing, and we will raise Islam against you?' Oh no! they just bribed your surveyors to be attacked by the Bedouin, or they bribed a pacha to tell you that the water was alkaline and poisonous for the next hundred miles, and so on, till your company was ruined, and the plan at an end for some years.

Your Home Government does not understand us Easterns. Why don't you put your Eastern affairs into the hands of your Indian Government? You have two routes to India—Egypt and Euphrates valley, and both are practically in the hands of your only great enemy—Russia."

In all that my Syrian friend said of the danger of our relying too much upon our route across Egypt, and on the importance to us of the immediate construction of the Euphrates Valley Railway line, there is nothing but truth, but, in his fears of a fresh invasion of India by the Mohamedans, he forgot that for fighting purposes the Mohamedans are no longer one, but two peoples; for the Moslem races are divided into Sonnites and Shiites, or orthodox and dissenting Mohamedans, who hate each other far more fiercely than they hate us. Our Indian Moslems are orthodox, the Afghans and Persians are dissenters, the Turks are orthodox. If Egypt and Persia play Russia's game, we may count upon the support of the Turks of Syria, of the Euphrates valley, and of India. To unite Irish Catholics and Orangemen in a religious crusade against the English would be an easy task by the side of that of uniting Sonnite and Shiite against India. A merely Shiite invasion is always possible, but could probably be met with ease, by opposition at the Khyber, and resistance upon the Indus, followed by a rapid advance from the Bholan. Russia herself is not without her difficulties with the strictest and most fanatical Mohamedans. Now that she has conquered Bokhara, their most sacred land, they hate her as fiercely as they hate us. The crusade, if she provokes it, may be upon our side, and British commanders in green turbans may yet summon the Faithful to arms, and invoke the Prophet.

It is to be remarked that men who have lived long in India think that our policy in the East has overwhelming claims on the attention of our home authorities. Not only is Eastern business to be performed, and Eastern intrigues watched carefully; but, according to these Indian flies, who think that their Eastern cart-wheel is the world, Oriental policy is to guide home policy, to dictate our European friendships, to cause our wars.

No Englishman in England can sympathise with the ridiculous inability to comprehend our real position in India which leads many Anglo-Indians to cry out that we must go to war with Russia to "keep up our prestige;" and, on the other hand, it need hardly be shown that, apart from the extension of trade and the improvement of communication, we need not trouble ourselves with alliances to strengthen us in the East. Supported by the native population, we can maintain ourselves in India against the world; unsupported by them, our rule is morally indefensible, and therefore not long to be retained by force of arms.

The natives of India watch with great interest the advance of Russia; not that they believe that they would be any better off under her than under us, but that they would like, at all events, to see some one thrash us, even if in the end they lost by it; just as a boy likes to see a new bully thrash his former master, even though the later be also the severer tyrant. That the great body of the people of India watch with feverish excitement the advance of Russia is seen from the tone of the native press, which is also of service to us in demonstrating that the mass of the Hindoos are incapable of appreciating the benefits, and even of comprehending the character, of our rule. They can understand the strength which a steady purpose gives; they cannot grasp the principles which lie at the root of our half-mercantile, half-benevolent despotism.

No native believes that we shall permanently remain in India; no native really sympathised with us during the rebellion. To the people of India we English are a mystery. We profess to love them, and to be educating them for something they cannot comprehend, which we call freedom and self-government; in the meantime, while we do not plunder them, nor convert them forcibly, after the wont of the Mogul emperors, we kick and cuff them all round, and degrade the nobles by ameliorating the condition of humbler men.

No mere policy of disarmament or of oppression can be worth much as a system for securing lasting peace, for if our Irish constabulary cannot prevent the introduction of Fenian arms to Cork and Dublin, how doubly impossible must it be to guard a frontier of five or six thousand miles by means of a police force which itself cannot be trusted? That prolonged disarmament causes our subjects to forget the art of war is scarcely true; and if true would tell both ways. The question is not one of disarmament, and suppression of rebellion : it is that of whether we can raise up in India a people that will support our rule; and if this is to be done, there must be an end of cuffing.

Were the Hindoos as capable of appreciating the best points of our government as they are of pointing out the worst, we should have nothing to fear in comparison with Russia. Drunken, dirty, ignorant, and corrupt, the Russian people are no fit rulers for Hindostan. Were our rival that which she pretends to be,—a civilized European Power with " a mission" in the East ; were she even, indeed, an enlightened commercial Power, with sufficiently benevolent instincts but with no policy outside her pocket, such as England was till lately in the East, and is still in the Pacific,— we might find ourselves able to meet her with open arms, and to bring ourselves to believe that her advance into Southern Asia was a gain to mankind. As it is, the Russians form a barbarous horde, ruled by a German emperor and a German ministry, who, however, are as little able to suppress degrading drunkenness and shameless venality as they are themselves desirous of promoting true enlightenment and education. " Talk of Russian civilization of the East !" an Egyptian once said to me; " why, Russia is an organized barbarism ; why—the Russians are—why they are—why—nearly as bad as *we* are !" It should be remembered, too, that Russia, being herself an Asiatic power, can never introduce European civilization into Asia. All the cry of "Russia! Russia!" all this magnifying of the Russian power, only means that the English, being the strong men most hated by the weak men of Southern Asia, the name of the next strongest is used to terrify them. The offensive strength of Russia has been grossly exaggerated by alarmists, who forget that, if Russia is to be strong in Bokhara and Khiva, it will be Bokharan and Khivan strength. In all our arguments we assume that with three-fourths of her power in Asia, and with her armies composed of Asians, Russia will remain a European Power. Whatever the composition of her forces, it may be doubted whether India is not a stronger empire than her new neighbour. The military expenditure of India is equal to that of Russia; the homogeneousness of the Northern Power is at the best inferior to that of India; India has twice the population of Russia, five times her trade, and as large a revenue. To the miserable military administration of Russia, Afghanistan would prove a second Caucasus, and by their conduct we see that the Afghans themselves are not terrified by her advance. The people with whom an Asiatic prince seeks alliances are not those whom he most fears. That the Afghans are continually intriguing with Russia against us, merely means that they fear us more than they fear Russia.

Russia will one day find herself encountering the English or Americans in China, perhaps, but not upon the plains of Hindostan. Wherever and whenever the contest comes, it can have but one result. Whether upon India or on England falls the duty of defence,

Russia must be beaten. A country that was fifty years conquering the Caucasus, and that could never place a disposable force of 60,000 men in the Crimea, need give no fear to India, while her grandest offensive efforts would be ridiculed by America, or by the England of to-day. To meet Russia in the way that we are asked to meet her means to meet her by corruption, and a system of meddling Eastern diplomacy is proposed to us which is revolting to our English nature. Let us by all means go our own way, and let Russia go hers. If we try to meet the Russian Orientals with craft, we shall be defeated; let us meet them, therefore, with straightforwardness and friendship, but, if necessary, in arms.

It is not Russia that we need dread, but, by the destruction of the various nationalities in Hindostan by means of centralization and of railroads, we have created an India which we cannot fight. India herself, not Russia, is our danger, and our task is rather to conciliate than to conquer.

CHAPTER XIV.

NATIVE STATES.

QUITTING Lahore at night, I travelled to Moultan by a railway which has names for its stations such as India cannot match. Chunga-Munga, Wanrasharam, Cheechawutnee, and Chunnoo, follow one another in that order. During the night, when I looked out into the still moonlight, I saw only desert, and trains of laden camels pacing noiselessly over the waste sands; but in the morning I found that the whole country within eye-shot was a howling wilderness. Moultan, renowned in warlike history from Alexander's time to ours, stands upon the edge of the great sandy tract once known as the "Desert of the Indies." In every village, bagpipes were playing through the live-long night. There are many resemblances to the Gaelic races to be found in India; the Hindoo girl's saree is the plaid of the Galway peasantress, or of the Trongate fishwife; many of the hill tribes wear the kilt; but the Punjaubee pipes are like those of the Italian pfiferari rather than those of the Scotch Highlander.

The great sandy desert which lies between the Indus and Rajpootana has, perhaps, a future under

British rule. Wherever snowy mountains are met with in warm countries, yearly floods, the product of the thaws, sweep down the rivers that take their rise in the glaciers of the chain, and the Indus is no exception to the rule. Were the fall less great, the stream less swift, Scinde would have been another Cambodia, another Egypt. As it is, the fertilizing floods pour through the deep river bed instead of covering the land, and the silt is wasted on the Arabian Gulf. No native State with narrow boundaries can deal with the great works required for irrigation on the scale that can alone succeed; but, possessing as we do the country from the defiles whence the five rivers escape into the plains to the sandy bars at which they lose themselves in the Indian Seas, we might convert the Punjaub and Scinde into a garden which should support a happy population of a hundred millions, reared under our rule, and the best of bulwarks against invasion from the north and west.

At Umritsur, I had seen those great canals that are commencing to irrigate and fertilize the vast deserts that stretch to Scinde. At Jullundur, I had already seen their handiwork in the fields of cotton, tobacco, and wheat that blossom in the middle of a wilderness; and if the whole Punjaub and Indus valley can be made what Jullundur is, no outlay can be too costly a means to such an end. There can be no reason why, with irrigation, the Indus valley should not become as fertile as the valley of the Nile.

NATIVE STATES.

After admiring in Moultan, on the one hand, the grandeur of the citadel which still shows signs of the terrible bombardment which it suffered at our hands after the murder by the Sikhs of Mr. Van Agnew in 1848, and, on the other hand, the modesty of the sensitive mimosa which grows plentifully about the city, I set off by railway for Sher Shah, the point at which the railway comes to its end upon the banks of the united Jhelum and Chenab, two of the rivers of the Punjaub. The railway company once built a station on the river-bank at Sher Shah, but the same summer, when the floods came down, station and railway alike disappeared into the Indus. Embanking the river is impossible, from the cost of the works which would be needed; and building wing-dams has been tried, with the remarkable effect of sending off the river at right angles to the dam to devastate the country opposite.

The railway has now no station at Sher Shah, but the Indus-steamer captains pick out a good place to lie alongside the bank, and the rails are so laid as to bring the trains alongside the ships. After seeing nothing but flat plains from the time of leaving Umritsur, I caught sight from Sher Shah of the great Sooleiman chain of the Afghan mountains, rising in black masses through the fiery mist that fills the Indus valley.

I had so timed my arrival on board the river-boat that she sailed the next morning, and after a day's uneventful steaming, varied by much running aground, when we anchored in the evening we were in the native State of Bhawulpore.

While we were wandering about the river shore in the evening, I and my two or three European fellow-travellers, we met a native, with whom one of our number got into conversation. The Englishman had heard that Bhawulpore was to be annexed, so he asked the native whether he was a British subject, to which the answer was to the effect that he did not know. " To whom do you pay your taxes ? " " To the Government." " Which Government; the English Government or the Bhawulpore Government ? " His answer was that he did not care so long as he had to pay them to somebody, and that he certainly did not know.

Little as our Bhawulpore friend knew or cared about the colour of his rulers, he was nevertheless, according to our Indian Government theories, one of the people who ought to be most anxious for the advent of English rule. Such has been the insecurity of life in Bhawulpore, that, of the six last viziers, five have been murdered by order of the Khan, the last of all having been strangled in 1862 ; and no native State has been more notorious than Bhawulpore for the extravagance and gross licentiousness of the reigning princes. The rulers of Bhawulpore, although nominally controlled by us, have hitherto been absolute despots, and have frequently put to death their subjects out of mere whimsy. For years the country has been torn by ceaseless revolutions, to the ruin of the traders and the demoralization of the people ; the taxes have been excessive, peculation universal, and the army has lived at free quarters. The Khans were for many years in such dread of attempts upon their lives, that every dish for their table was tasted by the cooks; the army was mutinous, all appointments bought and sold, and the Khans being Mohamedans, no one need pay a debt to a Hindoo.

Bhawulpore is no exceptional case; everywhere we hear of similar deeds being common in native States. One of the native rulers lately shot a man for killing a tiger that the rajah had wounded; another flogged a subject for defending his wife; abduction, adultery, and sale of wives are common among them. Land is seized from its holders without compensation being so much as offered to them; extortion, torture, and denial of justice are common, open venality prevails in all ranks, and no native will take the pledged word of his king, while the revenues, largely made up of forced loans, are wasted on all that is most vile.

In a vast number of cases, the reigning families have degenerated to such an extent, that the sceptre has come into the hands of some mere driveller, whom, for the senselessness of his rule, it has at last been necessary to depose. Those who have made idiocy their study, know that in the majority of cases the infirmity is the last stage of the declension of a race worn out by hereditary perpetuation of luxury, vice, or disease the effect of vice. Every ruling family in the East, save such as slave marriages have re-invigorated, is one of these run-down and exhausted breeds. Not only unbounded tyranny and extortion, but incredible venality and corruption, prevail in the greater number of native States. The Rajah of Travancore, as it is said, lately requiring some small bungalow to be added to a palace, a builder contracted to build it for 10,000 rs. After a time, he came to apply to be let off, and on the Rajah asking him the reason, he said: " Your highness, of the 10,000 rs., your prime minister will get 5,000 rs., his secretary 1,000 rs., the baboos in his office another 2,000 rs., the ladies of the zenana 1,000 rs., and the commander of your forces 500 rs.; now, the bungalow itself will cost 500 rs., so where am I to make my profit?" Corruption, however, pervades in India all native institutions; it is not enough to show that native States are subject to it, unless we can prove that it is worse there than in our own dominions.

The question whether British or native rule be the least distasteful to the people of India is one upon which it is not easy to decide. It is not to be expected that our Government should be popular with the Rajpoot chiefs, or with the great nobles of Oude, but it may fairly be contended that the mass of the people live in more comfort, and, in spite of the Orissa case, are less likely to starve, in English, than in native territory. No nation has at any time ever governed an alien empire more wisely or justly than we the Punjaub. The men who cry out against our rule are the nobles and the schemers, who, under it, are left without a hope. Our levelling rule does not even, like other democracies, raise up a military chieftainship. Our native officers of the highest rank are paid and treated much as are European sergeants, though in native States they would of course be generals and princes.

Want of promotion for sepoys and educated native civilians, and the degrading treatment of the high-caste people by the English, were causes, among others, of the mutiny. The treatment of the natives cannot easily be reformed; if we punish or discourage such behaviour in our officers, we cannot easily reach the European planters and the railway officials, while punishment itself would only make men treat the natives with violence instead of mere disdain, when out of sight of their superiors. There is, however, reason to believe that in many districts the people are not only well off under our Government, but that they know it. During the native rule in Oude, the population was diminished by a continual outpour of fugitives. The British district of Mirzapore Chowhare, on the Oude frontiers, had a rural population of over 1,000 to each square mile—a density entirely owing to the emigration of the natives from their villages in Oude. Again, British Burmah is draining of her people Upper Burmah, which remains under the old rulers; and throughout India the eye can distinguish British territories from the native States by the look of prosperity which is borne by all our villages.

The native merchants and townsfolk generally are our friends. It is unfortunately the fact, however, that the cultivators of the soil, who form three-fourths of the population of India, believe themselves worse off under us than in the native States. They say that they care not who rules so long as their holdings are secured to them at a fixed rent, whereas under our system the zemindars pay us a fixed rent, but in many districts exact what they please from the competing peasants—a practice which, under the native system, was prevented by custom. In all our future land settlements, it is to be hoped that the agreement will be made, not with middlemen, but directly with the people.

It is not difficult to lay down certain rules for our future behaviour towards the native States. We already exercise over the whole of them a control sufficient to secure ourselves against attack in time of peace, but not sufficient to relieve us from all fear of hostile action in time of internal revolt or external war. It might be well that we should issue a proclamation declaring that, for the future, we should invariably recognise the practice of adoption of children by the native rulers, as we have done in the case of the Mysore succession; but that, on the other hand, we should require the gradual disbandment of all troops not needed for the preservation of internal peace. We might well commence our action in this matter by calling upon the native rulers to bind themselves by treaty no longer to keep on foot artillery. In the event of an invasion of Hindostan, a large portion of our European force would be needed to overawe the native princes, and prevent their marching upon our rear. It is impossible to believe that the native States would ever be of assistance to us except in cases where we could do without their help. During the mutiny, the Nepaulese delayed their promised march to join us until they were certain that we should beat the mutineers, and this although the Nepaulese are among our surest friends. After the mutiny, it came to light that Lucknow and Delhi—then native capitals—had been centres of intrigue, although we had "Residents" at each, and it is probable that Hyderabad and Cashmere city are little less dangerous to us now than was Delhi in 1857.

There is one native State, that of Cashmere and Jummoo, which stands upon a very different footing to the rest. Created by us as late as 1846,—when we sold this best of all the provinces conquered by us from the Maharajahs of Lahore to a Sikh traitor, Gholab Singh, an ex-farmer of taxes, for three-quarters of a million sterling, which he embezzled from the treasury of Lahore,—the State of Cashmere has been steadily misgoverned for twenty years. Although our tributary, the Maharajah of Cashmere forbids English travellers to enter his dominions without leave (which is granted only to a fixed number of persons every year), to employ more than a stated number of servants, to travel except by certain passes for fear of their meeting his wives, to buy provisions except of certain persons, or to remain in the country after the 1st November under any circumstances whatever. He imprisons all native Christians, prohibits the exportation of grain whenever there is a scarcity in our territory, and takes every opportunity that falls in his way of insulting our Government and its officials. Our Central Asian trade has been all but entirely destroyed by the duties levied by his officers, and Russia is the Maharajah's chosen friend. The unhappy people of the Cashmere valley, sold by us, without their consent or knowledge, to a family which has never ceased to oppress them, petition us continually for relief, and, by flocking into our Punjaub territory, give practical testimony to the wrongs they suffer.

In this case of Cashmere, there is ample ground for immediate repurchase or annexation, if annexation it can be called to remove or buy out a feudatory family which was unjustly raised to power by us twenty-two years ago, and which has broken every article of the agreement under which it was placed upon the tributary throne. The only reason which has ever been shown against the resumption by us of the government of the Cashmere Valley is the strange argument that, by placing it in the hands of a feudatory, we save the expense of defending the frontier against the dangerous hill-tribes; although the revenues of the province, even were taxation much reduced, would amply suffice to meet the cost of continual war, and although our experience in Central India has shown that many hill-tribes which will not submit to Hindoo rajahs become peaceable at once upon our annexation of their country. Were Cashmere independent and in the hands of its old rulers, there would be ample ground for its annexation in the prohibition of trade, the hindrance to the civilization of Central Asia, the gross oppression of the people, the existence of slavery, and the imprisonment of Christians; as it is, the non-annexation of the country almost amounts to a crime against mankind.

Although the necessity of consolidation of our empire and the progressive character of our rule are reasons for annexing the whole of the native States, there are other and stronger arguments in favour of leaving them as they are; our policy towards the Nizam must be regulated by the consideration that he is now the head of the Moslem power in India, and that his influence over the Indian Mohamedans may be made useful to us in our dealings with that dangerous portion of our people. Our military arrangements with the Nizam are, moreover, on the best of footings. Scindia is our friend, and no bad ruler, but some interference may be needed with the Guicodar of Baroda and with Holkar. Our policy towards Mysore is now declared, and consists in the respecting the native rule if the young prince proves himself capable of good government, and we might impose similar conditions upon the remaining princes, and also suppress forced labour in their States as we have all but suppressed suttee.

In dealing with the native princes, it is advisable that we should remember that we are no interlopers of to-day coming in to disturb families that have been for ages the rulers of the land. Many of the greatest of the native families were set up by ourselves; and of the remainder, few, if any, have been in possession of their countries so long as have the English of Madras or Bombay.

The Guicodars of Baroda and the family of Holkar are descended from cowherds, and that of Scindia from a peasant, and none of them date back much more than a hundred years. The family of the Nabobs of Arcot, founded by an adventurer, is not more ancient, neither is that of Nizam: the great Hyder Ali was the son of a police-constable, and was unable to read or write. While we should suspiciously adhere to the treaties that we have made, we are bound, in the interests of humanity, to intervene in all cases where it is certain that the mass of the people would prefer our rule, and where they are suffering under slavery or gross oppression.

Holka has permitted us to make a railway across his territory, but he levies such enormous duties upon goods in transit as to cramp the development of trade in a considerable portion of our dominions. Now, the fact that a happy combination of circumstances enabled the cowherd, his ancestor, to seize upon a certain piece of territory a hundred years ago can have given his descendants no prescriptive right to impede the civilization of India; all that we must aim at is to so improve our governmental system as to make the natives themselves see that our rule means the moral advancement of their country.

The best argument that can be made use of against our rule is that its strength and minuteness enfeeble the native character. When we annex a State, we put an end to promotion alike in war and learning; and under our rule, unless it change its character, enlightenment must decline in India, however much material prosperity may increase.

Under our present system of exclusion of natives from the Indian Civil Service, the more boys we educate, the more vicious and discontented men we have beneath our rule. Were we to throw it open to them, under a plan of competition which would admit to the service even a small number of natives, we should at least obtain a valuable body of friends in those admitted, and should make the excluded feel that their exclusion was in some measure their own fault. As it is, we not only exclude natives from our own service, but even to some extent from that of the native States, whose levies are often drilled by English officers. The Guicodar of Baroda's service is popular with Englishmen, as it has become a custom that when he has a review he presents each of his officers with a year's full pay.

Our plan of shutting out the natives from all share in the government not only makes our rule unpopular, but gives rise to the strongest of all the arguments in favour of the retention of the existing native States, which is, that they offer a career to shrewd and learned natives, who otherwise would spend their leisure in devising plots against us. One of the ablest men in India, Madhava Rao, now premier of Travancore, was born in our territory, and was senior scholar of his year in the Madras College. That such men as Madhava Rao and Salar Jung should be incapable of finding suitable employment in our service is one of the standing reproaches of our rule.

Could we but throw open our services to the natives, our Government might, with advantage to civilization, be extended over the whole of the native States; for whether we are ever to leave India or whether we are to remain there till the end of time, there can be no doubt but that the course best adopted to raise the moral condition of the natives is to mould Hindostan into a homogeneous empire sufficiently strong to stand by itself against all attacks from without, and internally governed by natives, under a gradually weakened control from at home. If, after careful trial, we find that we cannot educate the people to become active supporters of our power, then it will be time to make use of the native princes and grandees, but it is to be hoped that the people, as they become well-taught, will also become the mainstay of our democratic rule.

The present attitude of the mass of the people is one of indifference and neutrality, which in itself lends a kind of passive strength to our rule. During the mutiny of 1857, the people neither aided nor opposed us; and even had the whole of the landowners been against us, as were those of Oude, it is doubtful whether they could have raised their villagers and peasants. Were our policemen relatively equal to their officers and to the magistrates, we should never hear of native disaffection, but we cannot count upon the attachment of the people so long as it is possible for our constables to procure confessions by the bribery of villagers, or the application of pots full of wasps to their stomachs.

In the matter of the annexation of those native States which still cumber the earth, we are not altogether free agents. We swallow up States like Bhawulpore just as Russia consumes Bokhara. Everywhere indeed, in Asia, strong countries must inevitably swallow up their weaker neighbours. Failure of heirs, broken treaties, irregular frontiers—all these are reasons or assumed reasons for advance ; but the end is certain, and is exemplified in the march of England from Calcutta to Peshawur and of Russia from the Aral to Turkestan. Our experience in the case of the Punjaub shows that even honest discouragement of farther advances on the part of the rulers of the stronger power will not always suffice to prevent annexation.

CHAPTER XV.

SCINDE.

NEAR Mithun Kote, we steamed suddenly into the main stream of the Indus, the bed of which is here a mile and a quarter wide. Although the river at the time of my visit was rising fast, it was far from being at its greatest height. In January, it brings down but forty thousand cubic feet of water every second, but in August it pours down four hundred and fifty thousand. The river-bed is rarely covered with running water, but the stream cuts a channel for itself upon one shore, and flows in a current of eight or nine miles an hour, while the remainder of the bed is filled with half-liquid sand.

The navigation of the Indus is monotonous enough. Were it not for the climate, the view would resemble that on the Maas, near Rotterdam, though with alligators lining the banks instead of logs from the Upper Meuse; but climate affects colour, and every country has tints of its own. California is golden, New Zealand a black-green, Australia yellow, the Indus valley is of a blazing red. Although every evening the Beloochee mountains came in sight as the sun sank down behind them, and revealed their shapes in shadow, all through the day the landscape was one of endless flats. The river is a dirty flood, now swift, now sluggish, running through a country in which sand deserts alternate only with fields of stone. Villages upon the banks there are none, and from town to town is a day's journey at the least. The only life in the view is given by an occasional sail of gigantic size and curious shape, belonging to some native craft or other on her voyage from the Punjaub to Kurrachee. On our journey down the Indus, we passed hundreds of ships, but met not one. They are built of timber, which is plentiful in the Himalayas, upon the head waters of the river, and carry down to the sea the produce of the Punjaub. The stream is so strong, that the ships are broken up in Scinde, and the crews walk back 1,000 miles along the bank. In building his ships upon the Hydaspes, and sailing them down the Indus to its mouth, Alexander did but follow the custom of the country. The natives, however, break up their ships at Kotree, whereas the Macedonian entrusted his to Nearchus for the voyage to the Gulf of Persia, and a survey of the coast.

Geographically, the Indus valley is but a portion of the Great Sahara. Those who know the desert well, say that from Cape Blanco to Khartoom, from Khartoom to Muscat, from Muscat to Moultan, the desert is but one; the same in the absence of life, the same in such life as it does possess. The Valley of the Nile is but an oasis, the Gulfs of Persia and of Aden are but trifling breaks in its vast width. Rainless, swept by dry hot winds laden with prickly sand, traversed everywhere by low ranges of red and sunburnt rocks, strewn with jagged stones, and dotted here and there with a patch of dates gathered about some ancient well, such is the Sahara for a length of near six thousand miles. On the Indus banks, the sand is as salt as it is at Suez, and there are as many petrified trees between Sukkur and Kurrachee as there are in the neighbourhood of Cairo.

Our days on board were all passed upon one plan. Each morning we rose at dawn, which came about half-past four, and, watching the starting of the ship from the bank where she had been moored all night, we got a cool walk in our sleeping clothes before we bathed and dressed. The heat then suffocated us quietly till four, when we would reassert the majesty of man by bathing, and attempting to walk or talk till dinner, which was at five. At dark we anchored, and after watching the water-turtles at their play, or hunting for the monstrous water-lizards known as "gos,"—apparently the ichneumons called in Egypt "gots,"—or sometimes fishing for great mud-fish with wide mouths and powerful teeth, we would resume our sleeping clothes (in which, but for the dignity of the Briton in the eyes of the native crew, we should have dined and spent the day). At half-past seven or eight, we lay down on deck, and forgot our sorrows in sleep, or engaged in a frantic struggle with the cockroaches. In the latter conflict we—in our dreams at least—were not victorious, and once in an awful trance I believed myself carried off by one leg in the jaws of a gigantic cockroach, and pushed with his feelers down into his horrid hole.

Each hour passed on the Indus differs from the others only in the greater or less portion of it which is devoted to getting off the sand-banks. After steaming gallantly down a narrow but deep and swift piece of the river, we would come to a spot at which the flood would lose itself in crossing its bed from one bank to the other. Backing the engines, but being whirled along close to the steep bank by the remaining portion of the current, we soon felt a shock, the recoil from which upset us, chairs and all, it being noticeable that we always fell up stream, and not with our heads in the direction in which the ship was going. As soon as we were fairly stuck, the captain flew at the pilot, and kicked him round the deck—a process always borne with fortitude, although the pilot was changed every day. The only pilot never kicked was one who came on board near Bhawulpore, and who carried a jewelled tulwar, or Afghan scimitar, but even he was threatened. The kicking over, an entry of the time of grounding was made by the captain in the pilot's book, and the mate was ordered out in a boat to sound, while the native soldiers on board the flats we were towing began quietly to cook their dinner. The mate having found a sort of channel, though sometimes it had a ridge across it over which the steamer could not pass without touching, he returned for a kedge, which he fixed in the sand, and we were soon warped up to it by the use of the capstan, the native crew singing merrily the while. Every now and then, however, we would take the ground in the centre of the ship, and with deep water all round, and then, instead of getting off, we for hours together only pivoted round and round. One of the Indus boats, with a line regiment on board, was once aground for a month near Mithun Kote, to the entire destruction of all the wild boars in the neighbourhood.

The kicking of the unfortunate pilots was not a pleasant sight, but there were sometimes comic incidents attached to our periodic groundings. Once I noticed that the five men who were constantly sounding with coloured poles in different parts of the ship and flats, had got into a monotonous chorus of "pánché——ó pot" ("five feet")—we drawing only three, so that we went ahead confidently at full speed, when suddenly we ran aground with a violent shock. On the re-sounding of our course by the boat's crew, we found that our pole-men must, for some time past, have been guessing the soundings to save the trouble of looking. These fellows richly deserved a kicking, but the pilots are innocent of any fault but inability to keep pace with the rapid changes of the river-course.

Another curious scene took place one day when we were steaming down a reach in which the river made many sudden twists and turns. We had on board a merchant from the Persian Gulf, a devout Mohamedan. In the afternoon, he carried his praying-carpet on to the bridge between the paddle-boxes, and there, turning to the west, commenced to pray. The sun was on his left, but almost facing him; in an instant, round whirled the ship, making her course between two sand-bars, and Mecca and the sun into the bargain were right behind our worshipper. This was too much even for his devotion, so, glancing at the new course, he turned his carpet, and, looking in the fresh direction, recommenced his prayers. After a minute or two, back went the ship, and we began again to steer a southerly course. All this time the Persian kept his look of complete abstraction, and remained unshaken through all his difficulties. This seriousness in face of events which would force into shouts of laughter any European congregation is a characteristic of a native. It is strange that Englishmen are nowhere so easily provoked to loud laughter as in a church or college chapel, natives at no time so insusceptible of ridicule as when engaged upon the services of their religions.

The shallowness of the Indus, its impracticability for steamships during some months of the year, and the many windings of the stream—all these things make it improbable that the river will ever be largely available for purposes of trade; at the same time, the Indus valley must necessarily be the line taken by the commerce of the Punjaub, and eventually by that of some portions of Central Asia, and even of Southern China. Whether Kurrachee becomes our great Indian port, or whether our railway be made through Beloochistan, a safe and speedy road up the Indus valley for troops and trade is needed.

If we take into consideration the size of India, the amount of its revenues, and the length of time during which we have occupied that portion of its extent which we at present hold, it is impossible to avoid the conclusion that not even in Australia have railways been more completely neglected than they have been in India. We have opened but 4,000 miles, or one mile for every 45,000 people. Nothing has been touched as yet but the Grand Trunk and great military and postal routes, and even these are little more than half completed. Even the Bombay and Calcutta mail line and the Calcutta and Lahore lines are hardly finished; the Peshawur line and the Indus road not yet begun. While at home people believe that the Euphrates Valley Railway is under consideration, they will find, if they come out to India, that to reach Peshawur in 34° N. latitude, they must go to Bombay in 18°, if not to Galle in 6°. Even if they reach Kurrachee, they will find it a month's journey to Peshawur. While we are trying to tempt the wool and shawls of Central Asia down to Umritsur and Lahore, the goods with which we would buy these things are sent round by the Cape of Good Hope and Calcutta.

It is true that the Indus line will be no easy one to make. To bridge the river at Mithun Kote or even at Kotree would be difficult enough, and were it to be bridged at Sukkur, where there is rock, and a narrow pass upon the river, the line from Sukkur to Kurrachee would be exposed to depredation from the frontier tribes. The difficulties are great, but the need is greater, and the argument of the heavy cost of riverside railroads should not weigh with us in the case of lines required for the safety of the country. The Lahore and Peshawur, the Kotree and Moultan, the Kotree and Baroda, and the Baroda and Delhi lines, instead of being set one against the other for comparison, should be simultaneously completed as necessary for the defence of the empire, and as forming the trunk lines for innumerable branches into the cotton and wheat-growing districts.

One of the branches of the Indus line will have to be constructed from the Bholan Pass to Sukkur, where we lay some days embarking cotton. Sukkur lies on the Beloochistan side; Roree fort—known as the "Key of Scinde," the seizure of which by us provoked the great war with the Ameers—on an island in mid-stream; and Bukkur city on the eastern or left bank, and the river, here narrowed to a width of a quarter of a mile, runs with the violence of a mountain torrent.

Sukkur is one of the most ancient of Indian cities, and was mentioned as time-worn by the Greek geographers, while tradition says that its antiquities attracted Alexander; but towns grow old with great rapidity in India, and, once ancient in their look, never to the eye become in the slightest degree older.

In Sukkur I first saw the Scindee cap, which may be described as a tall hat with the brim atop, but the Scindees were not the only strangely-dressed traders in Sukkur and Roree: there were high-capped Persians, and lean Afghans with long gaunt faces and high cheek-bones, and furred merchants from Central Asia. It is even said that goods find their way overland from China to Sukkur, through Eastern Persia and Beloochistan, the traders preferring to come round four thousand miles than to cross the main chain of the Himalayas, or pass through the country of the Afghans.

In ancient times there was considerable intercourse between China and Hindostan; at the end of the seventh century, indeed, the Chinese invaded India through Nepaul, and captured five hundred cities. It is to be hoped that the next few years may see a railway built from Rangoon to Southern China, and from Calcutta to the Yang-tse-Kiang, a river upon which there are ample stores of coal, which would supply the manufacturing wants of India.

After viewing from a lofty tower the flat country in the direction of Shikapore, we spent one of our Sukkur evenings upon the island of Roree watching the natives fishing. Casting themselves into the river on the top of skins full of air, or more commonly on great earthenware pitchers, they floated at a rapid pace down with the whirling stream, pushing before them a sunken net which they could close and lift by the drawing of a string. About twice a minute they would strike a fish, and, lifting their head, would impale the captive on a stick slung behind their back, and at once lower again the net in readiness for further action.

Sukkur, like seven other places that I had visited within a year, has the reputation of being the hottest city in the world, and the joke on the boats of the

Bancroft Library

OVERLAND ROUTES.

Indus flotilla is that Moultan is too hot to bear, and Sukkur much hotter; but that Jacobabad, on the Beloochee frontier, near Sukkur, is so hot that the people come down thence to Sukkur for the hot season, and find its coolness as refreshing as ordinary mortals do that of Simla. Hot as is Sukkur, it is fairly beaten by a spot at the foot of the Ibex Hills, near Sehwan. I was sleeping on the bridge with an officer from Peshawur, when the crew were preparing to put off from the bank for the day's journey. We were awakened by the noise, but, as we sat up and rubbed our eyes, a blast of hot wind came down from the burnt-up hills, laden with fine sand, and of such a character that I got a lantern—for it was not fully light—and made my way to the deck thermometer. I found it standing at 104°, although the hour was 4·15 A.M. At breakfast time, it had fallen to 100°, from which it slowly rose, until at 1 P.M. it registered 116° in the shade. The next night, it never fell below 100°. This was the highest temperature I experienced in India during the hot weather, and it was, singularly enough, the same as the highest which I recorded in Australia. No part of the course of the Indus is within the tropics, but it is not in the tropics that the days are hottest, although the nights are generally unbearable on sea-level near the equator.

At Kootree, near Hydrabad, the capital of Scinde, where the tombs of the Ameers are imposing, if far from beautiful, we left the Indus for the railway, and, after a night's journey, found ourselves upon the sea-shore at Kurrachee.

CHAPTER XVI.

OVERLAND ROUTES.

Of all the towns in India, Kurrachee is the least Indian. With its strong south-westerly breeze, its open sea and dancing waves, it is to one coming from the Indus valley a pleasant place enough; and the climate is as good as that of Alexandria, though there is at Kurrachee all the dust of Cairo. For a stranger detained against his will to find Kurrachee bearable there must be something refreshing in its breezes: the town stands on a treeless plain, and of sights there are none, unless it be the sacred alligators at Muggur Peer, where the tame "man-eaters" spring at a goat for the visitor's amusement as freely as the Wolfsbrunnen trout jump at the gudgeon.

There is no reason given why the alligators' pool should be reputed holy, but in India places easily acquire sacred fame. About Peshawur there dwell many hill-fanatics, whose sole religion appears to consist in stalking British sentries. So many of them have been locked up in the Peshawur gaol that it has become a holy place, and men are said to steal and riot in the streets of the bazaar in order that they may be consigned to this sacred temple.

The nights were noisy in Kurrachee, for the great Mohamedan feast of the Mohurrum had commenced, and my bungalow was close to the lines of the police, who are mostly Belooch Mohamedans. Every evening at dusk, fires were lighted in the police-lines and the bazaar, and then the tomtom-ing gradually increased from the gentle drone of the daytime until a perfect storm of " tom-a-tom, tomtom, tom-a-tom, tomtom," burst from all quarters of the town, and continued the whole night long, relieved only by blasts from conch-shells and shouts of " Shah Hassan ! Shah Hoosein ! Wah Allah ! Wah Allah!" as the performers danced round the flames. I heartily wished myself in the State of Bhawulpore, where there is a licence-tax on the beating of drums at feasts. The first night of the festival I called up a native servant who " spoke English," to make him take me to the fires and explain the matter. His only explanation was a continual repetition of " Dat Mohurrum, Mohamedan Christmas-day." When each night, about dawn, the tomtom-ing died away once more, the chokedars — or night watchmen — woke up from their sound sleep, and began to shout " Ha ha ! " into every room to show that they were awake.

The chokedars are well-known characters in every Indian station : always either sleepy and useless, or else in league with the thieves, they are nevertheless a recognised class, and are everywhere employed. At Rawul-Pindee and Peshawur, the chokedars are armed with guns, and it is said that a newly-arrived English officer at the former place was lately returning from a dinner-party, when he was challenged by the chokedar of the first house he had to pass. Not knowing what reply to make, he took to his heels, when the chokedar fired at him as he ran. The shot woke all the chokedars of the parade, and the unfortunate officer received the fire of every man as he passed along to his house at the farther end of the lines, which he reached, however, in perfect safety. It has been suggested that, for the purpose of excluding all natives from the lines at night, there should be a shibboleth or standing parole of some word which no native can pronounce. The word suggested is "Shoeburyness."

Although chokedars were silent and tomtom-ing subdued during the daytime, there were plenty of other sounds. Lizards chirped from the walls of my room, and sparrows twittered from every beam and rafter of the roof. When I told a Kurrachee friend that my slippers, my brushes, and soldier's writing-case had all been thrown by me on to the chief beam during an unsuccessful attempt to dislodge the enemy, he replied that for his part he paraded his drawing-room every morning with a double-barrelled gun, and frequently fired into the rafters, to the horror of his wife.

In a small lateen-rigged yacht lent us by a fellow-traveller from Moultan, some of us visited the works which have long been in progress for the improvement of the harbour of Kurrachee, and which form the sole topic of conversation among the residents in the town. The works have for object the removal of the bar which obstructs the entrance to the harbour, with a view to permit the entry of larger ships than can at present find an anchorage at Kurrachee.

The most serious question under discussion is that of whether the bar is formed by the Indus silt or merely by local causes, as, if the former supposition is correct, the ultimate disposition of the ten thousand millions of cubic feet of mud which the Indus annually brings down is not likely to be affected by such works as those in progress at Kurrachee. When a thousand sealed bottles were lately thrown into the Indus for it to be seen whether they would reach the bar, the result of the "great bottle trick," as Kurrachee people called it, was that only one bottle reached and not one weathered a point six miles to the southward of the harbour. The bar is improving every year, and has now some twenty feet of water, so that ships of 1,000 tons can enter except in the monsoon, and the general belief of engineers is that the completion of the present works will materially increase the depth of water.

The question of this bar is not one of merely local interest: a single glance at the map is sufficient to show the importance of Kurrachee. Already rising at an unprecedented pace, having trebled her shipping and quadrupled her trade in ten years, she is destined to make still greater strides as soon as the Indus Railway is completed; and finally—when the Persian Gulf route becomes a fact—to be the greatest of the ports of India.

That a railway must one day be completed from Constantinople or from some port on the Mediterranean to Bussorah on the Persian Gulf is a point which scarcely admits of doubt. From Kurrachee or Bombay to London by the Euphrates valley and

Constantinople is all but a straight line, while from Bombay to London by Aden and Alexandria is a wasteful curve. The so-called "Overland Route" is half as long again as would be the direct line. The Red Sea and Isthmus route has neither the advantage of unbroken sea nor of unbroken land transit; the direct route with a bridge near Constantinople might be extended into a land road from India to Calais or Rotterdam. The Red Sea line passes along the shores of Arabia, where there is comparatively little local trade; the Persian Gulf route would develop the remarkable wealth of Persia, and would carry to Europe a local commerce already great. At the entrance of the Persian Gulf, near Cape Mussendoom or Ormuz, we should establish a free port on the plan of Singapore. In 1000 A.D., the spot now known as Ormuz was a barren rock, but a few years of permanent occupation of the spot as a free port changed the barren islet into one of the wealthiest cities in the world. The Red Sea route crosses Egypt, the direct route crosses Turkey; and it cannot be too strongly urged that in war time "Egypt" means Russia or France, while "Turkey" means Great Britain.

In any scheme of a Constantinople and Gulf railroad, Kurrachee would play a leading part. Not only the wheat and the cotton of the Punjaub and of the then irrigated Scinde, but the trade of Central Asia would flow down the Indus, and it is hardly too much to believe that the silks of China, the teas of Northern India, and the shawls of Cashmere will all of them one day find in Kurrachee their chief port. The earliest known overland route was that by the Persian Gulf. Chinese ships traded to Ormuz in the fifth and seventh centuries, bringing silk and iron, and it may be doubted whether any of the Russian routes will be able to compete with the more ancient Euphrates valley line of trade. Shorter, passing through countries well known and comparatively civilized, admitting at once of the use of land and water transport side by side, it is far superior in commercial and political advantages to any of the Russian desert roads. A route through Upper Persia has been proposed, but merchants of experience will tell you that greater facilities for trade are extended to Europeans in even the "closed" ports of China than upon the coasts of Persia, and the prospect of the freedom of trade upon a Persian railroad would be but a bad one, it may be feared.

The return of trade to the Gulf route will revive the glory of many fallen cities of the Middle Ages. Ormuz and Antioch, Cyprus and Rhodes, have a second history before them; Crete, Brindisi, and Venice will each obtain a renewal of their ancient fame. Alexander of Macedon was the first man who took a scientific view of the importance of the Gulf route, but we have hitherto drawn but little profit from the lesson contained in his commission to Nearchus to survey the coast from the Indus to the Euphrates. The advantage to be gained from the completion of the railway from Constantinople to the Persian Gulf will not fall only to the share of India and Great Britain. Holland and Belgium are, in proportion to their wealth, at the least as greatly interested in the Euphrates route as are we ourselves, and should join us in its construction. The Dutch trade with Java would be largely benefited, and Dutch ports would become the shipping-places for Eastern merchandise on its way to England and north-east America, while, to the cheap manufactures of Liège, India, China, and Central Asia would afford the best of markets. If the line were a double one, to the west and north of Aleppo, one branch running to Constantinople and the other to the Mediterranean at Scanderoon, the whole of Europe would benefit by the Persian trade, and, in gaining the Persian trade, would gain also the power of protecting Persia against Russia, and of thus preventing the dominance of a crushing despotism throughout the Eastern world. In a thousand ways, however, the advantages of the line to all Europe are so plainly manifest, that the only question worth discussing is the nature of the difficulties that hinder its completion.

The difficulties in the way of the Gulf route are political and financial, and both have been exaggerated without limit. The project for a railway from Constantinople to the Persian Gulf has been compared to that for the construction of a railroad from the Missouri to the Pacific. In 1858, the American line was looked on as a mere speculator's dream, while the Euphrates Railway was to be commenced at once : ten years have passed, and the Pacific Railway is a fact, while the Indian line has been forgotten.

It is not that the making of the Euphrates line is a

more difficult matter than that of crossing the Plains and Rocky Mountains. The distance from St. Louis to San Francisco is 1,600 miles, that from Constantinople to Bussorah is but 1,100 miles; or from Scanderoon to Bussorah only 700 miles. From London to the Persian Gulf is not so far as from New York to San Francisco. The American line had to cross two great snowy chains and a waterless tract of considerable width: the Indian route crosses no passes so lofty as those of the Rocky Mountains or so difficult as those of the Sierra Nevada, and is well watered in its whole length. On the American line there is little coal, if any, while the Euphrates route would be plentifully supplied with coal from the neighbourhood of Bagdad. When the American line was commenced, the proposed track lay across unknown wilds: the Constantinople and Persian Gulf route passes through venerable towns, the most ancient of all the cities of the world, and the route itself is the oldest known highway of trade. The chief of all the advantages possessed by the Indian line which is wanting in America is the presence of ample labour on all parts of the road. Steamers are already running from Bombay and Kurrachee to the Persian Gulf; others on the Tigris, and a portion of the Euphrates; there is a much used road from Bagdad to Aleppo; and a Turkish military road from Aleppo to Constantinople, to which city a direct railroad will soon be opened; and a telegraph line belonging to an English company already crosses Asian Turkey from end to end. Notwithstanding the facilities, the

Euphrates Railway is still a project, while the Atlantic and Pacific line will be opened in 1870.

Were the financial difficulties those which the supporters of the line have in reality to meet, it might be urged that there will be a great local traffic between Bussorah, Bagdad, and Aleppo, and from all these cities to the sea, and that the Government mail subsidies will be huge, and the Indian trade, even in the worst of years, considerable. Were the indifference of Belgium, Germany, and Holland such that they should refuse to contribute towards the cost of the line, its importance would amply warrant a moderate addition to the debt of India.

The real difficulties that have to be encountered are political rather than financial; the covert opposition of France and Egypt is not less powerful for evil than is the open hostility of Russia. Happily for India, however, the territories of our ally Turkey extend to the Persian Gulf, for it must be remembered that for railway purposes Turkish rule, if we so please, is equivalent to English rule. As it happens, no active measures are needed to advance our line, but, were it otherwise, such intervention as might be necessary to secure the safety of the great highway for Eastern trade with Europe would be defensible were it exerted towards a purely independent Government.

The pressure to be put upon the Ottoman Porte must be direct and governmental. For a private company to conduct a great enterprise to a successful conclusion in Eastern countries is always difficult; but when the matter is political in its nature, or, if commercial, at least hindered on political grounds, a private company is powerless. It is, moreover, the practice of Eastern Governments to grant concessions of important works which they cannot openly oppose, but which in truth they wish to hinder, to companies so formed as to be incapable of proceeding with the undertaking. When others apply, the Government answers them that nothing further can be done : "the concession is already granted."

Whatever steps are taken, a bold front is needed. It might even be advisable that we should declare that the Euphrates Valley Railway through the Turkish territory from Constantinople and Scanderoon through Aleppo to Bagdad and Bussorah, and sufficient military posts to ensure its security in time of war, are necessary to our tenure of India, and that we should call upon Turkey to grant us permission to commence our work, on pain of the withdrawal of our protection.

Our general principle of non-interference is always liable to be set aside on proof of the existence of a higher necessity for intervention than for adherence to our golden rule, and it may be contended that sufficient proof has been shown in the present instance. Whether public action is to be taken, or the matter to be left to private enterprise, it is hard to resist the conclusion that the Direct Route to India is one of the most pressing of the questions of the day.

When, in company with my fellow-passengers from Moultan, I left Kurrachee for Bombay, we had on board the then Commissioner of Scinde, who was on his way to take his seat as a member of Council at

Bombay. A number of the leading men of Scinde came on board to bid farewell to him before he sailed, and among them the royal brothers who, but for our annexation of the country, would be the reigning Ameers at this moment.

Nothing that I had seen in India, even at Umritsur, surpassed in glittering pomp the caps and baldricks of these Scindee chieftains; neither could anything be stranger than their dress. One had on a silk coat of pale green shot with yellow, satin trousers, and velvet slippers with curled peaks; another wore a jacket of dark amber with flowers in white lace. A third was clothed in a cloth of crimson striped with amber; and the Ameer himself was wearing a tunic of scarlet silk and gold, and a scarf of purple gauze. All wore the strange-shaped Scindian hat; all had jewelled dirks, with curiously-wrought scabbards to hold their swords, and gorgeously embroidered baldricks to support them. The sight, however, of no number of sapphires, turquoises, and gold clothes could have reconciled me to a longer detention in Kurrachee; so I rejoiced when our bespangled friends disappeared over the ship's side to the sound of the Lascars' anchor-tripping chorus, and left the deck to the "Proconsul" and ourselves.

CHAPTER XVII.

BOMBAY.

CROSSING the mouths of the Gulfs of Cutch and Cambay, we reached Bombay in little more than two days from Kurrachee; but as we rounded Colaba Point and entered the harbour, the setting sun was lighting up the distant ranges of the Western Ghauts, and by the time we had dropped anchor it was dark, so I slept on board.

I woke to find the day breaking over the peaked mountains of the Deccan, and revealing the wooded summits of the islands, while a light land breeze rippled the surface of the water, and the bay was alive with the bright lateen sails of the native cotton-boats. The many woods coming down in rich green masses into the sea itself lent a singular softness to the view, and the harbour echoed with the capstan songs of all nations, from the American to the Beloochee, from the Swedish to the Greek.

The vegetation that surrounds the harbour, though the even mass of green is broken here and there by the crimson cones of the "gold mohur" trees, resembles that of Ceylon, and the scene is rather tropical than Indian, but there is nothing tropical and little that is Eastern in the bustle of the bay. The lines of huge steamers, and forests of masts backed by the still more crowded field of roofs and towers, impress you with a sense of wealth and worldliness from which you gladly seek relief by turning towards the misty beauty of the mountain islands and the Western Ghauts. Were the harbour smaller, it would be lovely; as it is, the distances are over great.

Notwithstanding its vast trade, Bombay for purposes of defence is singularly weak. The absence of batteries from the entrance to so great a trading port strikes eyes that have seen San Francisco and New York, and the marks on the sea-wall of Bombay Castle of the cannon-balls of the African admirals of the Mogul should be a warning to the Bombay merchants to fortify their port against attacks by sea, but act as a reminder to the traveller that, from a military point of view, Kurrachee is a better harbour than Bombay, the approach to which can easily be cut off, and its people starved. One advantage, however, of the erection of batteries at the harbour's mouth would be, that the present fort might be pulled down, unless it were thought advisable to retain it for the protection of the Europeans against riots, and that in any case the broad space of cleared ground which now cuts the town in half might be partly built on.

The present remarkable prosperity of Bombay is the result of the late increase in the cotton trade, to the sudden decline of which, in 1865 and 1866, has also been attributed the ruin that fell upon the city in the last-named year. The panic, from which Bombay has now so far recovered that it can no longer be said that she has "not one merchant solvent," was chiefly a reaction from a speculation-madness, in which the shares in a land reclamation company which never commenced its operations once touched a thousand per cent., but was intensified by the passage of the English panic-wave of 1866 across India and round the world.

Not even in Mississippi is cotton more completely king than in Bombay. Cotton has collected the hundred steamers and the thousands of native boats that are anchored between the Apollo Bunder and Mazagon; cotton has built the great offices and stores of seven and eight stories high; cotton has furnished the villas on Malabar Hill, that resemble the New Yorkers' cottages on Staten Island.

The export of cotton from India rose from five millions worth in 1859 to thirty-eight millions worth in 1864, and the total exports of Bombay increased in the same proportion, while the population of the city rose from 400,000 to 1,000,000. We are accustomed to look at the East as standing still, but Chicago itself never took a grander leap than did Bombay between 1860 and 1864. The rebellion in America gave the impetus, but was not the sole cause of this prosperity; and the Indian cotton-trade, though checked by the peace, is not destroyed. Cotton and jute are not the only Indian raw products the export of which has increased suddenly of late. The export of wool increased twenty-fold, of tobacco, threefold, of coffee, sevenfold in the last six years; and the export of Indian tea increased in five years from nothing to three or four hundred thousand pounds. The old Indian exports, those which we associate with the term "Eastern trade," are standing still, while the raw produce trade is thus increasing:—spices, elephants' teeth, pearls, jewels, bandannas, shellac, dates, and gum, are all decreasing, although the total exports of the country have trebled in five years.

India needs but railroads to enable her to compete successfully with America in the growth of cotton, but the development of the one raw product will open out her hitherto unknown resources.

While staying at one of the great merchant-houses in the Fort, I was able to see that the commerce of Bombay has not grown up of itself. With some experience among hard workers in the English towns, I was, nevertheless, astonished at the work got through by senior clerks and junior partners at Bombay. Although at first led away by the idea that men who wear white linen suits all day, and smoke in rocking-chairs upon the balcony for an hour after breakfast, cannot be said to get through much work, I soon found that men in merchants' houses at Bombay work harder than they would be likely to do at home. Their day begins at 6 A.M., and, as a rule, they work from then till dinner at 8 or 9 P.M., taking an hour for breakfast, and two for tiffin. My stay at Bombay was during the hottest fortnight in the year, and twelve hours' work in the day, with the thermometer never under 90° all the night, is an exhausting life. Englishmen could not long survive the work, but the Bombay merchants are all Scotch. In British settlements, from Canada to Ceylon, from Dunedin to Bombay, for every Englishman that you meet who has worked himself up to wealth from small beginnings without external aid, you find ten Scotchmen. It is strange, indeed, that Scotland has not become the popular name for the United Kingdom.

Bombay life is not without its compensation. It is not always May or June, and from November to March the climate is all but perfect. Even in the hottest weather, the Byculla Club is cool, and Mahabaleswar is close at hand, for short excursions, whenever the time is found; while the Bombay mango is a fruit which may bear comparison with the peaches of Salt Lake City, or the melons of San Francisco. The Bombay merchants have not time, indeed, to enjoy the beauties of their city, any more than Londoners have to visit Westminster Abbey or explore the Tower; and as for "tropical indolence," or "Anglo-Indian luxury," the bull-dogs are the only members of the English community in India who can discover anything but half-concealed hardships in the life. Each dog has his servant to attend to all his wants, and, knowing this, the cunning brute always makes the boy carry him up the long flights of stairs that lead to the private rooms over the merchants' houses in the Fort.

Bombay bazaar is the gayest of gay scenes. Besides the ordinary crowd of any "native town," there are solemn Jains, copper-coloured Jews, white-coated Portuguese, Persians, Arabs, Catholic priests, bespangled nautch girls, and grinning Seedees. The Parsees are strongest of all the merchant peoples of Bombay in numbers, in intelligence, and in wealth. Among the shopkeepers of their race, there is an over-prominence of trade shrewdness in the expression of the face, and in the shape even of the head. The Louvre bust of Richelieu, in which we have the ideal of a wheedler, is a common type in the Parsee shops of the Bombay bazaar. The Parsee people, however, whatever their looks, are not only in complete possession of Bombay, but are the dark-skinned race to which we shall have to entrust the largest share in the regeneration of the East. Trading as they do in every city between Galle and Astrakan, but everywhere attached to the English rule, they bear to us the relative position that the Greeks occupy towards Russia.

Both in religion and in education, the Parsees are, as a community, far in advance of the Indian Mohamedans, and of the Hindoos. Their creed has become a pure deism, in which God's works are worshipped as the manifestations or visible representatives of God on earth, fire, the sun, and the sea taking the first places; although in the climate of Bombay prayers to the sun must be made up of more supplications than thanksgivings. The Parsee men are soundly taught, and there is not a pauper in the whole tribe. In the education and elevation of women, no Eastern race has as yet done much, but the Parsees have done the most and have paved the way for further progress.

In the matter of the seclusion of women, the

Parsee movement has had some effect even upon others than Parsees, and the Hindoos of Bombay city stand far before even those of Calcutta in the earnestness and success of their endeavours to promote the moral elevation of women. Nothing can be done towards the regeneration of India so long as the women of all classes remain in their present degradation; and although many native gentlemen in Bombay already recognise the fact, and act upon it, progress is slow, since there is no basis upon which to begin. The Hindoos will not send their wives to schools where there are European lady teachers, for fear of proselytism taking place; and native women teachers are not yet to be found; hence all teaching must needs be left to men. Nothing, moreover, can be done with female children in Western India, where girls are married at from five to twelve years old.

I had not been two days in Bombay when a placard caught my eye, announcing a performance at the theatre of "Romeo and Juliet, in the Maratta tongue;" but the play had no Friar Lawrence, no apothecary, and no nurse; it was nothing but a simple Maratta love tale, followed by some religious tableaux. In the first piece an Englishman was introduced, and represented as kicking every native that crossed his path with the exclamation of "Damned fool:" at each repetition of which the whole house laughed. It is to be feared that this portion of the play was "founded upon fact." On my way home through the native town at night, I came on a marriage procession better than any that I had seen. A band of fifers were screaming the most piercing of notes in front of an illuminated house, at which the horsemen and carriages were just arriving, both men and women clothed in jewelled robes, and silks of a hundred colours, that flashed and glittered in the blaze of the red torches. The procession, like the greater number of the most gorgeous ceremonials of Bombay, was conducted by Parsees to celebrate the marriage of one of their own people ; but it is a curious fact that night-marriages were forced upon the Parsees by the Hindoos, and one of the conditions upon which the Parsees were received into India was, that their marriage processions should take place at night.

The Caves of Elephanta have been many times described. The grandest sight of India, after the Taj, is the three-faced bust of the Hindoo Trinity, or God in his threefold character of Creator, Preserver, and Destroyer. No Grecian sculpture that I have seen so well conveys the idea of Godhead. The Greeks could idealize man, the Italians can paint the saint, but the builders of Elephanta had the power of executing the highest ideal of a pagan god. The repose which distinguishes the heads of the Creator and Preserver is not the meditation of the saint, but the calm of unbounded power; and the Destroyer's head portends not destruction, so much as annihilation, to the world. The central head is, in its mysterious solemnity, that which the Sphinx should be, and is not, but one attribute alone is common to the expression of all three faces,—the presence of the Inscrutable.

CHAPTER XVIII.

THE MOHURRUM.

ALTHOUGH Poonah is the ancient Maratta capital, and a thoroughly Hindoo city, it is famed throughout India for the splendour with which its people celebrate the Mohamedan Mohurrum, so I timed my visit in such a way as to reach the town upon the day of the "taboot procession."

The ascent from the Konkan, or flat country of Bombay, by the Western Ghauts to the table-land of the Deccan, known as the Bhore Ghaut incline, in which the railway rises from the plain 2,000 feet into the Deccan, by a series of steps sixteen miles in length, is far more striking as an engineering work than the passage of the Alleghanies on the Baltimore and Ohio track, and as much inferior to the Sierra Nevada railway works. The views from the carriage windows are singularly like those in the Kaduganava Pass between Columbo and Kandy; in fact, the Western Ghauts are of the same character as the mountains of Ceylon, the hills being almost invariably either flat-topped or else rent by volcanic action into great pinnacles and needle peaks.

The rainy season had not commenced, and the vegetation that gives the Ghauts their charm was wanting, although the "mango showers" were beginning, and spiders and other insects, unseen during the hot weather, were creeping into the houses to seek shelter from the rains. One of the early travellers to the Deccan told the good folks at home that after the rains the spiders' webs were so thickly laced across the jungle, that the natives of the country were in the habit of hiring elephants to walk before them and force a passage! At the time of my visit, neither webs nor jungle were to be seen, and the spiders were very harmless-looking fellows. One effect of the approaching monsoon was visible from the summit of the Ghaut, for the bases of the mountains were hid by the low clouds that foretell the coming rains. The inclines are held to be unsafe during the monsoon, but they are not so bad as the Kotree and Kurrachee line, which runs only "weather permitting," and is rendered useless by two hours' rain—a fall which, luckily for the shareholders, occurs only about once in every seven years. On the Bhore Ghaut, on the contrary, 220 inches in four months is not unusual, and "the rains" here take the place of the avalanche of colder ranges, and carry away bridges, lines, and trains themselves; but in the dry season there is a want of the visible presence of difficulties overcome, which detracts from the interest of the line.

At day-break at Poonah, the tomtom-ing, which had lasted without intermission through the ten days' fast, came to a sudden end, and the police and European magistrates began to marshal the procession of the taboots, or shrines, in the bazaar.

A proclamation in English and Maratta was posted on the walls, announcing the order of the procession and the rules to be enforced. The orders were, that the procession to the river was to commence at 7 A.M. and to end at 11 A.M., and that tomtom-ing, except during those hours, would not be allowed. The taboots of the light cavalry, of three regiments of native infantry, and of the followers of three English regiments of the line, and of the Sapper and Miners, were, however, to start at six o'clock: the order of precedence among the cantonment or regimental taboots was carefully laid down, and the carrying of arms forbidden.

When I reached the bazaar, I found the native police were working in vain in trying to force into line a vast throng of bannermen, drummers, and saints, who surrounded the various taboots or models of the house of Ali and Fatima where their sons Hassan and Hoosein were born. Some of the shrines were of the size and make of the dolls'-houses of our English children, others in their height and gorgeousness resembed the most successful of our burlesques upon Guy Fawkes : some were borne on litters by four men ; others mounted on light carts and drawn by bullocks, while the gigantic taboot of the Third Cavalry required six buffaloes for its transport to the river. Many privates of our native infantry regiments had joined the procession in uniform, and it was as strange to me to see privates in our service engaged in howling round a sort of Maypole, and accompanying their yells with the tomtom, as it must have been to the English in Lucknow in 1857 to hear the bands of the rebel regiments playing "Cheer, boys, cheer."

Some of the troops in Poonah were kept within their lines all day, to be ready to suppress disturbances caused by the Moslem fanatics, who, excited by the Mohurrum, often run a-muck among their Hindoo neighbours. In old times, quarrels between the Sonnites and Shiites, or orthodox and dissenting Mussulmen, used to be added to those between Mohamedans and Hindoos at the season of the Mohurrum, but except upon the Afghan border these feuds have all but died out now.

At the head of the procession marched a row of pipers, producing sounds of which no Highland regiment would have felt ashamed, followed by long-bearded, turban-wearing Marattas, on foot and horseback, surrounding an immense pagoda-shaped taboot placed on a cart, and drawn by bullocks; boys swinging incense walked before and followed, and I remarked a gigantic cross—a loan, no doubt from the Jesuit College for this Mohamedan festivity. After each taboot, there came a band of Hindoo "tigers"—men painted in thorough imitation of the jungle king, and wearing tiger ears and tails. Sometimes, instead of tigers, we had men painted in the colours worn by "sprites" in an English pantomime, and all—sprites and tigers—danced in the fashion of the mediæval mummers. Behind the tigers and buffoons there followed women, walking in their richest dress. The nautch girls of Poonah are reputed the best in all the East, but the monotonous Bombay nautch is not to be compared with the Cashmere nautch of Lahore.

Some taboots were guarded on either side by sheiks on horseback, wearing turbans of the honourable green which denotes direct descent from the Prophet, though the genealogy is sometimes doubtful, as in the case of the Angel Gabriel, who, according to Mohamedan writers, wears a green turban, as being an "honorary" descendant of Mohamed.

Thousands of men and women thronged the road down which the taboots were forced to pass, or sat in the shade of the peepul trees until the taboot of their family or street came up, and then followed it, dancing and tomtom-beating like the rest.

Poonah is famed for the grace of its women and the elegance of their gait. In the hot weather, the saree is the sole garment of the Hindoo women, and lends grace to the form without concealing the outlines of the trunk or the comely shapes of the well-turned limbs. The saree is eight yards long, but of such soft thin texture that it makes no show upon the person. It is a singular testimony to the strength of Hindoo habits, that at this Mohamedan festival the Mohamedan women should all be wearing the long seamless saree of the conquered Hindoos.

In the Mohurrum procession at Poonah there was nothing distinctively Mohamedan. Hindoos joined in the festivities, and "Portuguese," or descendants of the slaves, half-castes, and native Christians who at the time of the Portuguese occupation of Surat assumed high-sounding names and titles, and now form a large proportion of the inhabitants of towns in the Bombay Presidency. The temptation of a ten days' holiday is too great to be resisted by the prejudices of even the Christians or Hindoos.

The procession ended at the Ghauts on the riverside, where the taboots, one after the other, made their exit from ten days of glory into unfathomable slush; and such was the number of the "camp taboots," as those of the native soldiers in our service are styled, and the "bazaar taboots," or city contributions, that the immersion ceremonies were not completed when the illumination and fireworks commenced.

After dark, the bazaar was lit with coloured fires, and with the ghostly paper-lanterns that give no light; and the noise of tomtoms and fire-crackers recommenced in spite of proclamations and police-rules. Were there in Indian streets anything to burn, the Mohurrum would cause as many fires in Hindostan as Independence-day in the United States; but, although houses are burnt out daily in the bazaars, they are never burnt down, for nothing but water can damage mud. We could have played our way into Lucknow in 1857 with pumps and hoses at least as fast as we contrived to batter a road into it with shot and shell.

During the day I had been amused with the sayings of some British recruits, who were watching the immersion ceremonies, but in the evening one of them was in the bazaar, uproariously drunk, kicking every native against whom he stumbled, and shouting to an officer of another regiment, who did not like to interfere: "I'm a private soldier, I know, but I'm a gentleman; I know what the hatmosphere is, I do; and I knows a cloud when I sees it, damned if I don't." On the other hand, in some fifty thousand natives holiday-making that day, many of them Christians and low-caste men, with no prejudice against drink, a drunken man was not to be seen.

It is impossible to over-estimate the harm done to the English name in India by the conduct of drunken soldiers and "European loafers." The latter class consists chiefly of discharged railway guards and runaway sailors from Calcutta,—men who, travelling across India and living at free quarters on the trembling natives, become ruffianly beyond description from the effect upon their originally brutal natures of the possession of unusual power.

The popularity of Mohamedan festivals such as that of the Mohurrum has been one of the many causes which have led us to believe that the Mohamedans form a considerable proportion of the population of Hindostan, but the census in the North-West Provinces revealed the fact that they had there been popularly set down as three times as numerous as they are, and it is probable that the same is the case throughout all India. Not only are the Indian Mohamedans few, but their Mohamedanism sits lightly on them : they are Hindoos in caste distinctions, in ceremonies, in daily life, and all but Hindoos in their actual worship. On the other hand, this Mohurrum showed me that the Hindoos do not scruple to attend the commemoration of Hassan and Hoosein. At Benares there is a temple which is used in common by Mohamedans and Hindoos, and throughout India, among the low-caste people, there is now little distinction between the religions. The descendants of the Mohamedan conquerors, who form the leading families in several native States, and also in Oude itself, are among the most dangerous of our Indian subjects, but they appear to have but little hold upon the humble classes of their fellow-worshippers, and their attempts to stir up their people to active measures against the English have always failed. On the other hand, we have hitherto somewhat ignored the claims upon our consideration of the Indian Mohamedans and still more numerous hill-tribes, and permitted our Governments to act as though the Hindoos and the Sikhs were the only inhabitants of Hindostan.

CHAPTER XIX.

ENGLISH LEARNING.

THE English traveller who crosses India from Calcutta to Bombay is struck with the uncivilized condition of the land. He has heard in England of palaces and temples, of art treasures and of native poetry, of the grace of the Hindoo maidens, of Cashmere shawls, of the Taj, of the Pearl Mosque, of a civilization as perfect as the European, and as old as the Chinese. When he lands and surveys the people, he finds them naked barbarians, plunged in the densest ignorance and superstition, and safe only from extermination because the European cannot dwell permanently in the climate of their land. The stories we are told at home are in no sense false:—the Hindoos, of all classes, are graceful in their carriage; their tombs and mosques are of extraordinary beauty, their art patterns the despair of our best craftsman; the native poetry is at least equal to our own, and the Taj the noblest building in the world. Every word is true, but the whole forms but a singularly small portion of the truth. The religious legends, the art patterns, the perfect manner and the graceful eye and taste seem to have descended to the Hindoos of to-day from a generation whose general civilization they have forgotten. The poetry is confined to a few members of a high-caste race, and is mainly an importation from abroad; the architecture is that of the Moslem conquerors. Shah Jehan, a Mohamedan emperor and a foreigner, built the Taj; Akbar the Great, another Turk, was the designer of the Pearl Mosque; and the Hindoos can no more be credited with the architecture of their early conquerors than they can with the railways and bridges of their English rulers, or with the waterworks of Bombay city. The Sikhs are chiefly foreigners; but of the purely native races, the Rajpoots are only fine barbarians, the Bengalees mere savages, and the tribes of Central India but little better than the Australian aborigines or the brutes. Throughout India there are remains of an early civilization, but it has vanished as completely as it has in Egypt; and the Cave-temples stand as far from the daily life of Hindostan as the Pyramids do from that of Egypt.

It is to be feared that the decline has been extremely rapid since the day when we arrived in India. Just as it is almost impossible, by any exertion of the mind, to realize in Mexico the fact that the present degraded Aztecs are the same people whom the Spaniards found, only some three hundred years ago, dwelling in splendid palaces, and worshipping their unknown gods in golden temples through the medium of a sacred tongue, so now it is difficult to believe that the pauperized inhabitants of Orissa and the miserable peasantry of Oude are the sons of the chivalrous warriors who fought in the last century against Clive.

The truth is, that in surveying Oriental empires from a distance, we are dazzled by the splendour of the kings and priests; drawing near, we find an oppressed and miserable slave class, from whose hard earnings the wealth of the great is wrung; called on to govern the country, we extinguish the kings and priests in the fashion in which Captain Hodson, in 1857, shot the last sons of the Imperial family of India in a dry ditch, while we were transporting the last Mogul, along with our native thieves, in a convict ship to British Burmah. There remains the slave class, and little else. We may select a few of these to be our policemen and torturers-in-chief, we may pick another handful to wear red coats, and be our guards and the executioners of their countrymen; we may teach a few to chatter some words of English, and then, calling them great scoundrels, may set them in our railway stations and our offices; but virtually, in annexing any Eastern country, we destroy the ruling class, and reduce the government to a mere imperialism, where one man rules and the rest are slaves. No parallel can be drawn in Europe or North America to that state of things which exists wherever we carry our arms in the East: were the President and Congress in America, and all the wealthy merchants of the great towns, to be destroyed to-morrow, the next day would see the government proceeding quietly in the hands of another set every bit as intelligent, as wise, and good. In a lesser degree, the same would be the case in England or in France. The best example that could be given nearer home of that which occurs continually in the East would be one which should suppose that the Emperor and nobility in Russia were suddenly destroyed, and the country left in the hands of the British ambassador and the late serfs. Even this example would fail to convey a notion of the extent of the revolution which takes place on the conquest by Britain of an Eastern country; for in the East the nobles are better taught and the people more ignorant than they are in Russia, and the change causes a more complete destruction of poetry, of literature, and of art.

It being admitted, then, that we are in the position of having, in Hindostan, a numerous and ignorant, but democratic people to govern from without, there comes the question of what should be the general character of our government. The immediate questions of the day may be left to our subordinates in India; but the direction and the tendencies of legislation are matters for us at home. There can be nothing more ridiculous than the position of those of our civilians in India who, while they treat the natives with profound contempt, are continually crying out against government from at home, on the ground set forth in the shibboleth of "India for the Indians." If India is to be governed by the British race at all, it must be governed from Great Britain. The general conditions of our rule must be dictated at London by the English people, and nothing but the execution of our decrees, the collection of evidence, and the framing of mere rules, left to our subordinates in the East.

First among the reforms that must be introduced from London is the general instruction in the English language of the native population. Except upon a theory that will fairly admit of the forcing upon a not unwilling people of this first of all great means of civilization, our presence in India is wholly indefensible. Unless also that be done, our presence in India, or that of some nation stronger than us and not more scrupulous, must endure for ever, for it is plainly impossible that a native government capable of holding its own against Russia and America can otherwise be built up in Hindostan. Upon the contrary supposition,—namely, that we do not intend at any time to quit our hold on India,—the instruction of the people in our language becomes still more important. Upon the second theory, we must teach them English, the language of the British Government; upon the first, English, the language of the world. Upon either theory we must teach them English. Nothing can better show the trivial character of the much-talked-of reforms introduced into India in the last few years, since our Queen has assumed the imperial throne of Hindostan, than the fact that no progress whatever has been made in a matter of far more grave importance than are any number of miles of railway, canal, or Grand Trunk roads. Our civilians in India tell us that, if you teach the natives English, you expose them to the attacks of Christian missionaries, and us to revolt—an exposure which speaks not too highly of the Government which is forced to make it. Our military officers, naturally hating the country to which they now are exiled, instead of being sent as formerly of their own free will, tell you that every native who can speak English is a scoundrel, a liar, and a thief, which is, perhaps, if we except the Parsees, not far from true at present, when teaching is given only to a few lads, who thus acquire a monopoly of the offices in which money passes through native hands. Their opinion has no bearing whatever upon a general instruction of the people, under which we should evidently be able to pick our men, as we now pick them for all employments in which a knowledge of English is not required.

A mere handful of Spaniards succeeded in naturalizing their language in a country twice as large as Europe: in the whole of South America, the Central States, and Mexico. Not only there, but in the United States, the Utes and Comanches, wild as they are, speak Spanish, while their own language is forgotten. In the west of Mexico there is no trace of pure Spanish blood, there is even comparatively little mixture—yet Spanish, and that of the best, is spoken, to the exclusion of every other language in Manzanillo and Acapulco. This phenomenon is not confined to the Western world. In Bombay Presidency, five millions of so-called Portuguese—who, however, for the most part are pure Hindoos—speak a Latin tongue, and worship at the temples of the Christian God. French makes progress in Saigon, Dutch in Java. In Canada, we find the Huron Indians French in language and religion. English alone, it would seem, cannot be pressed upon any of the dark-skinned tribes. In New Zealand, the Maories know no English; in Natal, the Zulus; in India, the Hindoos. The Dutch, finally expelled from South Africa in 1815 and from Ceylon in 1802, have yet more hold by their tongue upon the natives of those lands than have the English —masters of them since the Dutch expulsion.

To the early abolition or total non-existence of slavery in the British colonies, we may, perhaps, trace our unfortunate failure to spread our mother tongue. Dutch, Portuguese, Spaniards, all practised a slavery of the widest kind; all had about them not native servants, frequently changing from the old master to the new, and passing unheeded to whatever service money could tempt them to engage in, but domestic slaves, bred up in the family, and destined, probably, to die within the house where they were reared, to whom the language of the master was taught, because your Spanish grandee, with power of life and death over his family slaves, was not the man to condescend to learn his servants' tongue in order that his commands should be more readily understood. Another reason may have caused the Portuguese and other dominant races of the later middle ages to have insisted that their slaves should learn the language of the master and the government; namely, that in learning the new, the servile families would speedily forget the older tongue, and thus become as incapable of mixing in the conspiracies and insurrections of their brother natives as Pyrenean shepherd dogs of consorting with their progenitors, the wolves. Whatever their reasons, however, the Spaniards succeeded where we have failed.

The greatest of our difficulties are the financial. No cheap system is workable by us, and our dear system we have not the means to work. The success of our rule immediately depends upon the purity and good feeling of the rulers, yet there are villages in British India where the people have never seen a white man, and off the main roads, and outside the district towns, the sight of a European official is extremely rare. To the inhabitants of the greater portion of rural India, the governor who symbolizes British rule is a cruel and corrupt Hindoo policeman : himself not improbably a Bengal mutineer in 1857, or drawn from the classes whom our most ignorant Sepoys themselves despised. It is not easy to see how this vital defect can be amended, except by the slow process of raising up a native population that we can trust and put in office, and this is impossible unless we encourage and reward the study of the English tongue. The most needed of all social reforms in India, an improvement in the present thoroughly servile condition of the native women, could itself in no way be more easily brought about than by the familiarization of the Hindoos with English literature ; and that greatest of all the curses of India, false-swearing in the courts, would undoubtedly be both directly and indirectly checked by the introduction of our language. The spread of the English tongue need be no check to that of the ancient classical languages of the East : the two studies would go hand in hand. It is already a disgrace to us that while we spend annually in India a large sum upon our chaplains and church schools, we toss only one hundredth part of the sum—a paltry few thousands of rupees—to the native colleges, where the most venerable of languages—Sanscrit, Arabic, and Persian—are taught by the men who alone can thoroughly understand them. At the moment when England, Germany, and America are struggling for the palm in the teaching of Oriental literature—when Oxford, Edinburgh, and London are contending with each other, and with Berlin, Yale, and Harvard, in translating and explaining Eastern books—our Government in India is refusing the customary help to the publication of Sanscrit works, and starving the teachers of the language.

So long as the natives remain ignorant of the English tongue, they remain ignorant of all the civilization of our time—ignorant alike of political and physical science, of philosophy and true learning. It is needless to say that, if French or German were taught them instead of English, they would be as well off in this respect; but English, as the tongue of the ruling race, has the vast advantage that its acquisition by the Hindoos will soon place the government of India in native hands, and thus, gradually relieving us of an almost intolerable burthen, will civilize and set free the people of Hindostan.

CHAPTER XX.

INDIA.

"ALL general observations upon India are necessarily absurd," said to me at Simla a distinguished officer of the Viceroy's government; but, although this is true enough of theories that bear upon the customs, social or religious, of the forty or fifty peoples which make up what in England we style the "Hindoo race," it has no bearing on the consideration of the policy which should guide our actual administration of the Empire.

England in the East is not the England that we know. Flousy Britannia, with her anchor and ship, becomes a mysterious Oriental despotism, ruling a sixth of the human race, nominally for the natives' own good, and certainly for no one else's, by laws and in a manner opposed to every tradition and every prejudice of the whole of the various tribes of which this vast population is composed—scheming, annexing, out-manœuvering Russia, and sometimes, it is to be feared, out-lying Persia herself.

In our island home, we plume ourselves upon our hatred of political extraditions: we would scorn to ask the surrender of a political criminal of our own, we would die in the last ditch sooner than surrender those of another crown. What a contrast we find to this when we look at our conduct in the East. During the mutiny of 1857, some of our rebel subjects escaped into the Portuguese territory at Goa. We demanded their extradition, which the Portuguese refused. We insisted. The offer we finally accepted was, that they should be transported to the Portuguese settlement at Timor, we supplying transports. An Indian transport conveying these men to their island grave, but carrying the British flag, touched at Batavia in 1858, to the astonishment of the honest Dutchmen, who knew England as a defender of national liberty in Europe.

Although despotic, our government of India is not bad; indeed, the hardest thing that can be said of it is that it is too good. We do our duty by the natives manfully, but they care little about that, and we are continually hurting their prejudices and offending them in small things, to which they attach more importance than they do to great. To conciliate the Hindoos, we should spend 10,000*l.* a year in support of native literature to please the learned, and 10,000*l.* on fireworks to delight the wealthy and the low-caste people. Instead of this, we worry them with municipal institutions and benevolent inventions that they cannot and will not understand. The attempt to introduce trial by jury into certain parts of India was laudable, but it has ended in one of those failures which discredit the Government in the eyes of its own subordinates.

If there is a European foreman of jury, the natives salaam to him, and ask: " What does the sahib say ?" If not, they look across the court to the native barristers, who hold up fingers, each of which means 100 rs., and thus bid against each other for the verdict; for, while natives as a rule are honest in their personal or individual dealings, yet in places of trust—railway clerkships, secretaryships of departments, and so on—they are almost invariably willing to take bribes.

Throughout India, such trials as are not before a jury are conducted with the aid of native assessors as members of the court. This works almost as badly as the jury does, the judge giving his decision without any reference to the opinion of the assessors. The story runs that the only use of assessors is, that in an appeal—where the judge and assessors had agreed—the advocate can say that the judge " has abdicated his functions, and yielded to the absurd opinion of a couple of ignorant and dishonest natives,"—or, if the judge had gone against his client in spite of the assessors being inclined the other way, that the judge " has decided in the teeth of all experienced and impartial native opinion, as declared by the voices of two honest and intelligent assessors."

Our introduction of juries is not an isolated instance of our somewhat blind love for " progress." If in the already-published portions of the civil code—for instance, the parts which relate to succession, testamentary and intestate—you read in the illustrations

York for Delhi, and Pimlico for Sultanpore, there is not a word to show that the code is meant for India, or for an Oriental race at all. It is true that the testamentary portion of the code applies at present only to European residents in India; but the advisability of extending it to natives is under consideration, and this extension is only a matter of time. The result of over-great rapidity of legislation, and of unyielding adherence to English or Roman models in the Indian codes, must be that our laws will never have the slightest hold upon the people, and that, if we are swept from India, our laws will vanish with us. The Western character of our codes, and their want of elasticity and of adaptability to Eastern conditions, is one among the many causes of our unpopularity.

The old school Hindoos fear that we aim at subverting all their dearest and most venerable institutions, and the free-thinkers of Calcutta and the educated natives hate us because, while we preach culture and progress, we give them no chance of any but a subordinate career. The discontent of the first-named class we can gradually allay, by showing them the groundlessness of their suspicions, but the shrewd Bengalee baboos are more difficult to deal with, and can be met only in one way—namely, by the employment of the natives in offices of high trust, under the security afforded by the infliction of the most degrading penalties on proof of the smallest corruption. One of the points in which the policy of Akbar surpassed our own was in the association of qualified Hindoos with his Mohamedan fellow-countrymen in high places in his government. The fact, moreover, that native governments are still preferred to British rule, is a strong argument in favour of the employment by us of natives; for, roughly speaking, their governmental system differs from ours only in the employment of native officers instead of English. There is not now existent a thoroughly native government; at some time or other, we have controlled in a greater or less degree the governments of all the native States. To study purely native rule, we should have to visit Caboul or Herat, and watch the Afghan princes putting out each other's eyes, while their people are engaged in never-ending wars, or in murdering strangers in the name of God.

Natives might more safely be employed to fill the higher than the lower offices. It is more easy to find honest and competent native governors or councilmen than honest and efficient native clerks and policemen. Moreover, natives have more temptations to be corrupt, and more facilities for being so with safety, in low positions than in high. A native policeman or telegraph official can take his bribe without fear of detection by his European chief: not so a native governor, with European subordinates about him.

The common Anglo-Indian objections to the employment of natives in our service are, when examined, found to apply only to the employment of incompetent natives. To say that the native lads of Bengal, educated in our Calcutta colleges, are half educated and grossly immoral, is to say that, under a proper system of selection of officers, they could never come to be employed. All that is necessary at the moment is that we should concede the principle by appointing, year by year, more natives to high posts, and that, by holding the civil service examinations in India as well as in England, and by establishing throughout India well-regulated schools, we should place the competent native youths upon an equal footing with the English.

That we shall ever come to be thoroughly popular in India is not to be expected. By the time the old ruling families have died out, or completely lost their power, the people whom we rescued from their oppression will have forgotten that the oppression ever existed, and as long as the old families last, they will hate us steadily. One of the documents published in the *Gazette of India*, while I was at Simla, was from the pen of Asudulla Muhamadi, one of the best known Mohamedans of the North-West Provinces. His grievances were the cessation of the practice of granting annuities to the "sheiks of noble families," the conferring of the "high offices of Mufti, Sudr'-Ameen, and Tahsildar," on persons not of "noble extraction," "the education of the children of the higher and lower classes on the same footing, without distinction," "the desire that women should be treated like men in every respect," and "the formation of English schools for the education of girls of the lower order." He ended his State paper by pointing out the ill effects of the practice of conferring on the poor "respectable berths, thereby enabling them to indulge in luxuries which their fathers never dreamt of, and to play the upstart;" and declared that to a time-honoured system of class government there had succeeded "a state of things which I cannot find words to express." It is not likely that our rule will ever have much hold on the class that Asudulla represents, for not only is our government in India a despotism, but its tendency is to become an imperialism, or despotism exercised over a democratic people, such as we see in France, and are commencing to see in Russia.

We are levelling all ranks in India; we are raising the humblest men, if they will pass certain examinations, to posts which we refuse to the most exalted of nobles unless they can pass higher. A clever son of a bheestie, or sweeper, if he will learn English, not only may, but must rise to be a railway baboo, or deputy-collector of customs; whereas for Hindoo rajahs or Mohamedan nobles of Delhi creation, there is no chance of anything but gradual decline of fortune. Even our Star of India is democratic in its working: we refuse it to men of the highest descent, to confer it on self-made viziers of native States, or others who were shrewd enough to take our side during the rebellion. All this is very modern, and full of "progress," no doubt; but it is progress towards imperialism, or equality of conditions under paternal despotism.

Not only does the democratic character of our rule set the old families against us, but it leads also to the failure of our attempt to call around us a middle class, an educated thinking body of natives with something to lose, who, seeing that we are ruling India for her own good, would support us heart and soul, and form the best of bucklers for our dominion. As it is, the attempt has long been made in name, but, as a matter of fact, we have humbled the upper class, and failed to raise a middle-class to take its place. We have crushed the prince without setting up the trader in his stead.

The wide-spread hatred of the English does not prove that they are bad rulers; it is merely the hatred that Easterns always bear their masters; yet masters the Hindoos will have. Even the enlightened natives do not look with longing towards a future of self-government, however distant. Most intelligent Hindoos would like to see the Russians drive us out of India, not that any of them think the Russians would be better rulers or kinder men, but merely for the pleasure of seeing their traditional oppressors beaten. What, then, are we to do? The only justification for our presence in India is the education for freedom of the Indian races; but at this moment they will not have freedom at a gift, and many Indian statesmen declare that no amount of education will ever fit them for it. For a score of centuries, the Hindoos have bribed and taken bribes, and corruption has eaten into the national character so deeply, that those who are the best of judges declare that it can never be washed out. The analogy of the rise of other races leads us to hope, however, that the lapse of time will be sufficient to raise the Hindoos as it has raised the Huns.

The ancients believed that the neighbourhood of

frost and snow was fatal to philosophy and to the arts; to the Carthaginians, Egyptians, and Phœnicians, the inhabitants of Gaul, of Germany, and of Britain, were rude barbarians of the frozen North, that no conceivable lapse of time could convert into anything much better than talking bears — a piece of empiricism which has a close resemblance to our view of India. It is idle to point to the tropics and say that free communities do not exist within those limits: the map of the world will show that freedom exists only in the homes of the English race. France, the authoress of modern liberty, has failed as yet to learn how to retain the boon for which she is ever ready to shed her blood; Switzerland, a so-called free State, is the home of the worst of bigotry and intolerance; the Spanish republics are notoriously despotisms under democratic titles; America, Australia, Britain, the homes of our race, are as yet the only dwelling-spots of freedom.

There is much exaggeration in the cry that self-government, personal independence, and true manliness can exist only where the snow will lie upon the ground, that cringing slavishness and imbecile submission follow the palm-belt round the world. If freedom be good in one country, it is good in all, for there is nothing in its essence which should limit it in time or place: the only question that is open for debate is whether freedom—an admitted good—is a benefit which, if once conferred upon the inhabitants of the tropics, will be maintained by them against invasion from abroad and rebellion from within; if it be given bit by bit, each step being taken only when public opinion is fully prepared for its acceptance, there can be no fear that freedom will ever be resigned without a struggle. We should know that Sikhs, Kandians, Scindians, Marattas, have fought bravely enough for national independence to make it plain that they will struggle to the death for liberty as soon as they can be made to see its worth. It will take years to efface the stain of a couple of hundred years of slavery in the negroes of America, and it may take scores of years to heal the deeper sores of Hindostan; but history teaches us to believe that the time will come when the Indians will be fit for freedom.

Whether the future advent of a better day for India be a fact or a dream, our presence in the country is justifiable. Were we to quit India, we must leave her to Russia or to herself. If to Russia, the political shrewdness and commercial blindness of the Northern Power would combine to make our pocket suffer by loss of money as much as would our dignity by so plain a confession of our impotence; while the unhappy Indians would discover that there exists a European nation capable of surpassing Eastern tyrants in corruption by as much as it already exceeds them in dull weight of leaden cruelty and oppression. If to herself, unextinguishable anarchy would involve our Eastern trade and India's happiness in a hideous and lasting ruin.

If we are to keep the country, we must consider gravely whether it be possible properly to administer its affairs upon the present system—whether, for instance, the best supreme government for an Eastern empire be a body composed of a chief invariably removed from office just as he begins to understand his duty, and a council of worn-out Indian officers, the whole being placed in the remotest corner of Western Europe, for the sake of removing the government from the "pernicious influence of local prejudice."

India is at this moment governed by the Indian Council at Westminster, who are responsible to nobody. The Secretary of State is responsible to Parliament for a policy which he cannot control, and the Viceroy is a head-clerk.

India can be governed in two ways; either in India or in London. Under the former plan, we should leave the bureaucracy in India independent, preserving merely some slight control at home—a control which should, of course, be purely parliamentary and English; under the other plan—which is that to which it is to be hoped the people of England will command their representatives to adhere—India would be governed from London by the English nation, in the interests of humanity and civilization. Under either system, the Indian Council in London would be valuable as an advising body; but it does not follow, because the Council can advise, that therefore they can govern, and to delegate executive power to such a board is on the face of it absurd.

Whatever the powers to be granted to the Indian Council, it is clear that the members should hold office for the space of only a few years. So rapid is the change that is now making a nation out of what was ten years ago but a continent inhabited by an agglomeration of distinct tribes, that no Anglo-Indian who has left India for ten years is competent even to advise the rulers, much less himself to share in the ruling, of Hindostan. The objection to the government of India by the Secretary of State is, that the tenant of the office changes frequently, and is generally ignorant of native feelings and of Indian affairs. The difficulty, however, which attends the introduction of a successful plan for the government of India from London is far from being irremovable, while the objection to the paternal government of India by a Viceroy is that it would be wholly opposed to our constitutional theories, unfitted to introduce into our Indian system those democratic principles which we have for ten years been striving to implant, and even in the long run dangerous to our liberties at home.

One reason why the Indian officials cry out against government from St. James's Park is, because they deprecate interference with the Viceroy; but were the Council abolished, except as a consultative body, and the Indian Secretaryship of State made a permanent appointment, it is probable that the Viceroy would be relieved from that continual and minute interference with his acts which at present degrades his office in native eyes. The Viceroy would be left considerable power, and certainly greater power than he has at present, by the Secretary of State;—that which is essential is merely, that the power of control, and responsible control, should lie in London. The Viceroy, would, in practice, exercise the executive functions, under the control of a Secretary of State, advised by an experienced Council and responsible to Parliament, and we should possess a system under which there would be that conjunction of personal responsibility and of skilled advice which is absolutely required for the good government of India.

To a scheme which involves the government of India from at home, it may be objected, that India cannot be so well understood in London as in Calcutta. So far from this being the case, there is but little doubt among those who best know the India of to-day, that while men in Calcutta understand the wants of the Bengalee, and men in Lahore the feelings of the Sikh, India, as a whole, is far better understood in England than in any presidency town.

It must be remembered, that with India within a day of England by telegraph, and within three weeks by steam, the old autocratic Governor-General has become impossible, and day by day the Secretary of State in London must become more and more the ruler of India. Were the Secretary of State appointed for a term of years, and made irremovable except by a direct vote of the House of Commons, no fault could be found with the results of the inevitable change : as it is, however, a council of advice will hardly be sufficient to prevent gross blundering while we allow India to be ruled by no less than four Secretaries of State in a single year.

The chief considerations to be kept in view in the framing of a system of government for India are briefly these :—a sufficient separation of the two countries to prevent the clashing of the democratic and paternal systems, but, at the same time, a control over the Indian administration by the English people active enough to ensure the progressive amelioration of the former; the minor points to be borne in mind are that in India we need less centralization, in London more permanence, and, in both, increased personal responsibility. All these requirements are satisfied by the plan proposed, if it be coupled with the separation of the English and Indian armies, the employment of natives in our service, and the creation of new governments for the Indus territories and Assam. Madras, Bombay, Bengal, Assam, the Central Provinces, Agra, the Indus, Oude, and Burmah, would form the nine presidencies, the Viceroy having the supreme control over our officers in the native States, and not only should the governors of the last seven be placed upon the same footing with those of Madras and Bombay, but all the local governors should be assisted by a council of ministers who should necessarily be consulted, but whose advice should not be binding on the governors. The objections that are raised against councils do not apply to councils that are confined to the giving of advice, and the ministers are needed, if for no other purpose, at least to divide the labour of the Governor, for all our Indian officials are at present overworked.

This is not the place for the suggestion of improvements in the details of Indian government. The statement that all general observations upon India are necessarily absurd is not more true of moral, social, educational, and religious affairs than of mere governmental matters : " regulation system" and " non-regulation system ;" "permanent settlement" and "thirty years' settlement ;" native participation in government, or exclusion of natives—each of these courses may be good in one part of India and bad in another. On the whole, however, it may be admitted, that our Indian government is the best example of a well-administered despotism, on a large scale, existing in the world. Its one great fault is over-centralization ; for, although our rule in India must needs be despotic, no reason can be shown why its despotism should be minute.

The greatest of the many changes in progress in the East is that India is being made—that a country is being created under that name where none has yet existed ; and it is our railroads, our annexations, and above all our centralising policy that are doing the work. There is reason to fear that this change will be hastened by the extension of our new codes to the former "non-regulation provinces," and by government from at home, where India is looked upon as one nation, instead of from Calcutta, where it is known to be still composed of fifty; but so rapid is the change, that already the Calcutta people are as mistaken in attempting to laugh down our phrase "the people of India," as we were during the mutiny when we believed that there was an "India" writhing in our clutches. Whether the India which is being thus rapidly built up by our own hands will be friendly to us, or the reverse, depends upon ourselves.

The two principles upon which our administration of the country might be based have long since been weighed against each other by the English people, who, rejecting the principle of a holding of India for the acquisition of prestige and trade, have decided that we are to govern India in the interest of the people of Hindostan. We are now called on to deliberate once more, but this time upon the method by which our principle is to be worked out. That our administration is already perfect can hardly be contended so long as no officer not very high in our Indian service dares to call a native "friend." The first of all our cares must be the social treatment of the people, for while by the Queen's proclamation the natives are our fellow-subjects, they are in practice not yet treated as our fellow-men.

CHAPTER XXI.

DEPENDENCIES.

WHEN, on my way home to England, I found myself off Mocha, with the Abyssinian highlands in sight, and still more when we were off Massowah, with the peaks of Talanta plainly visible, I began to recall the accounts which I had heard at Aden of the proposed British colony on the Abyssinian table-lands, out of which the Home Government has since been frightened. The question of the desirability or the reverse of such a colony raises points of interest on which it would be advisable that people at home should at once take up a line.

As it has never been assumed that Englishmen can dwell permanently even upon high hills under the equator, the proposition for European colonization or settlement of tropical Africa may be easily dismissed, but that for the annexation of tropical countries for trade purposes remains. It has hitherto been accepted as a general principle regulating our intercourse with Eastern nations, that we have a moral right to force the dark-skinned races to treat us in the same fashion as that in which we are treated by our European neighbours. In practice we even now go much further than this, and inflict the blessings of Free Trade upon the reluctant Chinese and Japanese at the cannon's mouth. It is hard to find any law but that of might whereby to justify our dealings with Burmah, China, and Japan. We are apt to wrap ourselves up in our new-found national morality, and, throwing upon our fathers all the blame of the ill which has been done in India, to take to ourselves credit for the good; but it is obvious to any one who watches the conduct of our admirals, consuls, and traders in the China seas, that it is inevitable that China should fall to us as India fell, unless there should be a singular change in opinion at home, or unless, indeed, the Americans should be beforehand with us in the matter. To say this, is not to settle the disputed question of whether in the present improved state of feeling, and with the present control exercised over our Eastern officials by a disinterested press at home, and an interested but vigilant press in India and the Eastern ports, government of China by Britain might not be for the advantage of the Chinese and the world, but it is at least open to serious doubt whether it would be to the advantage of Great Britain. Our ruling classes are already at least sufficiently exposed to the corrupting influences of power for us to hesitate before we decide that the widening of the national mind consequent upon the acquisition of the government of China would outweigh the danger of a spread at home of love of absolute authority, and indifference to human happiness and life. The Americans, also, it is to be hoped, will pause before they expose republicanism to the shock that would be caused by the annexation of despotically-governed States. In defending the Japanese against our assaults, and those of the active but unsuccessful French, they may unhappily find, as we have often found, that protection and annexation are two words for the same thing.

Although the disadvantages are more evident than the advantages of the annexation for commercial purposes of such countries as Abyssinia, China, and Japan, the benefits are neither few nor hard to find. The abstract injustice of annexation cannot be said to exist in the cases of Afghanistan and Abyssinia, as the sentiment of nationality clearly has no existence there, and as the worst possible form of British government is better for the mass of the people than the best conceivable rule of an Abyssinian chief. The dangers of annexation in the weakening and corrupting of ourselves may not unfairly be set off against the blessings of annexation to the people, and the most serious question for consideration is that of whether dependencies can be said "to pay." Social progress is necessary to trade, and we give to mankind the powerful security of self-interest that we will raise the condition of the people, and, by means of improved communications, open the door to civilization.

It may be objected to this statement that our exaggerated conscientiousness is the very reason why our dependencies commercially are failures, and why it is useless for us to be totaling up our loss and profits while we wilfully throw away the advantages that our energy has placed in our hands. If India paid as well as Java, it may be shown, we should be receiving from the East 60 millions sterling a year for the support of our European officials in Hindostan, and the total revenue of India would be 200 or 250 millions, of which 80 millions would be clear profit for our use in England; in other words, Indian profits would relieve us from all taxation in England, and leave us a considerable and increasing margin towards the abolition of the debt. The Dutch, too, tell us that their system is more agreeable to the natives than our own clumsy though well-meant efforts for the improvement of their condition, which, although not true, is far too near the truth to allow us to rest in our complacency.

The Dutch system having been well weighed at home, and deliberately rejected by the English people as tending to the degradation of the natives, the question remains how far dependencies from which no profits are exacted may be advantageously retained for mere trade purposes. At this moment, our most flourishing dependencies do not bear so much as their fair share of the expenses of the empire:—Ceylon herself pays only the nominal and not the real cost of her defence, and Mauritius costs nominally 150,000*l.* a year, and above half a million really in military expenses, of which the colony is ordered to pay 45,000*l.* and grumbles much at paying it. India herself, although charged with a share of the non-effective expenses of our army, escapes scot free in war-time, and it is to be remarked that the throwing upon her of a small portion of the cost of the Abyssinian war was defended upon every ground except the true one—namely, that as an integral part of the empire she ought to bear her share in imperial wars. It is true that, to make the constitutional doctrine hold, she also ought to be consulted, and that we have no possible machinery for consulting her—a consideration which of itself shows our Indian government in its true light.

Whether, indeed, dependencies pay or do not pay their actual cost, their retention stands on a wholly different footing to that of colonies. Were we to leave Australia or the Cape, we should continue to be the chief customers of those countries: were we to leave India or Ceylon, they would have no customers at all; for falling into anarchy, they would cease at once to export their goods to us and to consume our manufactures. When a British Governor of New Zealand wrote that of every Maori who fell in war with us it might be said that, "from his ignorance, a man had been destroyed whom a few months' enlightenment would have rendered a valuable consumer of British manufactured goods," he only set forth with grotesque simplicity considerations which weigh with us all; but while the advance of trade may continue to be our chief excuse, it need not be our sole excuse for our Eastern dealings—even for use towards ourselves. Without repeating that which I have said with respect to India, we may especially bear in mind that, although the theory has suffered from exaggeration, our dependencies still form a nursery of statesmen and of warriors, and that we should irresistibly fall into national sluggishness of thought, were it not for the world-wide interests given us by the necessity of governing and educating the inhabitants of so vast an empire as our own.

One of the last of our annexations was close upon our bow as we passed on our way from Aden up the Red Sea. The French are always angry when we seize on places in the East; but it is hardly wonderful that they should have been perplexed about Perim. This island stands in the narrowest place in the sea, in the middle of the deep water, and the Suez Canal being a French work, and Egypt under French influence, our possession of Perim becomes especially unpleasant to our neighbours. Not only this, but the French had determined themselves to seize it, and their fleet, bound to Perim, put in to Aden to coal. The Governor had his suspicions, and, having asked the French admiral to dinner, gave him unexceptionable champagne. The old gentleman soon began to talk, and directly he mentioned Perim, the governor sent a pencil-note to the harbour-master to delay the coaling of the ships, and one to the commander of a gunboat to embark as many artillerymen and guns as he could get on board in two hours, and sail for Perim. When the French reached the anchorage next day, they found the British flag flying, and a great show of guns in position. Whether they put into Aden on their way back to France history does not say.

Perim is not the only island that lies directly in the

shortest course for ships, nor are the rocks the only dangers of the Red Sea. One night about nine o'clock, when we were off the port of Mecca, I was sitting on the fo'castle, right forward, almost on the sprit, to catch what breeze we made, when I saw two country boats about 150 yards on the starboard bow. Our three lights were so bright that I thought we must be seen, but as the boats came on across our bows, I gave a shout, which was instantly followed by "hard a-port!" from the Chinaman on the bridge, and by a hundred yells from the suddenly awakened boatmen. Our helm luckily enough had no time to act upon the ship. I threw myself down under a stancheon, and the sail and yard of the leading boat fell on our deck close to my head, and the boats shot past us amid shouts of "fire," caused by the ringing of the alarm bell. When we had stopped the ship, the question came —had we sunk the boat? We at once piped away the gig, with a Malay crew, and sent it off to look for the poor wretches—but after half-an-hour, we found them ourselves, and found them safe except for their loss of canvas, and their terrible fright. Our pilot questioned them in Arabic, and discovered that each boat had on board 100 pilgrims; but they excused themselves for not having a watch or light by saying that they had not seen us! Between rocks and pilgrim-boats, Red Sea navigation is hard enough for steamers, and it is easy to see which way its difficulties will cause the scale to turn when the question lies between Euphrates Railway and Suez Canal.

CHAPTER XXII.

FRANCE IN THE EAST.

It is no longer possible to see the Pyramids or even Heliopolis in the solitary and solemn fashion in which they should be approached. English "going out" and "coming home" are there at all days and hours, and the hundreds of Arabs selling German coins and mummies of English manufacture are terribly out of place upon the desert. I went alone to see the Sphinx, and, sitting down on the sand, tried my best to read the riddle of the face, and to look through the rude carving into the inner mystery; but it would not do, and I came away bitterly disappointed. In this modern democratic railway-girt world of ours, the ancient has no place; the huge Pyramids may remain for ever, but we can no longer read them. A few months may see a *café chantant* at their base.

Cairo itself is no pleasant sight. An air of dirt and degradation hangs over the whole town, and clings to its people, from the donkey-boys and comfit-sellers to the pipe-smoking soldiers and the money-changers who squat behind their trays. The wretched fellaheen, or Egyptian peasantry, are apparently the most miserable of human beings, and their slouching shamble is a sad sight after the superb gait of the Hindoos. The slave-market of Cairo has done its work; indeed, it is astonishing that the English should content themselves with a treaty in which the abolition of slavery in Egypt is decreed, and not take a single step to secure its execution, while the slave-market in Cairo continues to be all but open to the passer. That the Egyptian Government could put down slavery if it had the will, cannot be doubted by those who have witnessed the rapidity with which its officers act in visiting doubtful crimes upon the wrong men. During my week's stay in Alexandria, two such cases came to my notice :—in the first, one of my fellow passengers unwittingly insulted two of the Albanian police, and was shot at by one of them with a long pistol. A number of Englishmen, gathering from the public gaming-houses on the great square, rescued him, and beat off the cavasses; and the next morning, marched down to their consulate and demanded justice. Our acting consul went straight to the head of the police, laid the case before him, and procured the condemnation of the man who shot to the galleys for ten years, while the policeman who had looked on was immediately bastinadoed in the presence of the passenger. The other case was one of robbery at a desert village, from the tent of an English traveller. When he complained to the sheik, the order was given to bastinado the head men, and hold them responsible for the amount. The head men in turn gave the stick to the householders, and claimed the sum from them; while these bastinadoed the vagrants, and actually obtained from them the money.

Every male inhabitant having thus received the stick, it is probable that the actual culprit was reached, if, indeed, he lived within the village. " Stick-backsheesh " is a great institution in Egypt, but the Turks are not far behind. When the British Consulate at Bussorah was attacked by thieves some years ago, our Consul telegraphed the fact to the Pacha of Bagdad. The answer came at once :—" Bastinado forty men"—and bastinadoed they were, as soon as they had been selected at random from the population.

Coming to Egypt from India, the Englishman is inclined to believe that, while our Indian Government is an averagely successful despotism, Egypt is misgoverned in an extraordinary degree. As a matter of fact, however, it is not fair to the King of Egypt that we should compare his rule with ours in India, and it is probable that his government is not on the whole worse than Eastern despotisms always are. Setting up as a "civilized ruler," the King of Egypt performs the duties of his position by buying guns which he uses in putting down insurrections which he has fomented, and yachts for which he has no use; and he appears to think that he has done all that Peter of Russia himself could have accomplished, when he sends a young Egyptian to Manchester to learn the cotton trade, or to London to acquire the principles of foreign commerce, and, on his return to Alexandria, sets him to manage the soap-works, or to conduct the viceregal band. The aping of the forms of " Western civilization," which in Egypt means French vice, makes the Court of Alexandria look worse than it is :—we expect the slave-market and the harem in the East, but the King of Egypt superadds the Trianon, and a bad imitation of Mabile.

The Court influence shows itself in the actions of the people, or rather the influence at work upon the Court is pressing also upon the people. For knavery, no place can touch the modern Alexandria. One word, however, is far from describing all the infamies of the city. It surpasses Cologne for smells, Benares for pests, Saratoga for gaming, Paris itself for vice. There is a layer of French "civilization" of the worst kind over the semi-barbarism of Cairo; but still the town is chiefly Oriental. Alexandria, on the other hand, is completely Europeanized, and has a white population of seventy or eighty thousand. The Arabs are kept in a huge village outside the fortifications, and French is the only language spoken in the shops and hotels. Alexandria is a French town.

It is evident enough that the Suez Canal scheme has been from the beginning a blind for the occupation of Egypt by France, and that, however interesting to the shareholders may be the question of its physical or commercial success, the probabilities of failure have had but little weight with the French Government. The foundation of the Messagerie Company with national capital, to carry imaginary mails, secured the preponderance of French influence in the towns of Egypt, and it is not certain that we should not look upon the occupation of Saigon itself as a mere blind.

Of the temporary success of the French policy

there can be no doubt: the English railway-guards have lately been dismissed from the Government railway line, and a huge tricolour floats from the entrance to the new docks at Suez, while a still more gigantic one waves over the hotel; the King of Egypt, glad to find a third Power which he can play off, when necessary, against both England and Russia, takes shares in the canal. It is when we ask, "What is the end that the French have in view?" that we find it strangely small by the side of the means. The French of the present day appear to have no foreign policy, unless it is a sort of desire to extend the empire of their language, their dance-tunes, and their fashions; and the natural wish of their ruler to engage in no enterprise that will outlast his life prevents their having any such permanent policy as that of Russia or the United States. An Egyptian Pacha hardly put the truth too strongly when he said, "There is nothing permanent about France except Mabile." Bancroft Library

The Suez Canal is being pushed with vigour, although the labour of the hundreds of Greek and Italian navvies is very different to that of the tens of thousands of impressed fellaheen. The withdrawal from the Company of the forced labour of the peasants has demonstrated that the King is at heart not well-disposed towards the scheme, for the remonstrances of England have never prevented the employment of slave labour upon works out of which there was money to be made for the viceregal purse. The difficulty of clearing and keeping clear the channel at Port Said, at the Mediterranean end, is well known to the Pacha and his engineers:—it is not difficult, indeed, to cut through the bar, nor impossible to keep the cutting open, but the effect of the great piers will merely be to push the Nile silt farther seawards, and again and again new bars will form in front of the canal. That the canal is physically possible no one doubts, but it is hard to believe that it can pay. Even if we suppose, moreover, that the canal will prove a complete success, the French Government will only find that it has spent millions upon digging a canal for England's use.

The neutralization of Egypt has lately been proposed by writers of the Comtist school, but to what end is far from clear. "The interests of civilization" are the pretext, but when summoned by a Comtist, "civilization" and "humanity" generally appear in a French shape. Were we to be attacked in India by the French or Russians, no neutralization would prevent our sending our troops to India by the shortest road, and fighting wherever we thought best. If we were not so attacked, neutralization, as far as we are concerned, would be a useless ceremony. If France goes beyond her customary meddlesomeness and settles down in Egypt, we shall evidently have to dislodge her, but to neutralize the country would be to settle her there ourselves. It would be idle to·deny that the position of France in the East is connected with the claim put forth by her to the moral leadership of the world. The "chief power of Europe" and "leader of Christendom" must needs be impatient of the dominance of America in the Pacific and of Britain in the East, and seeks by successes on the side of India to bury the memories of Mexico. One of the hundred "missions of France," one of the thousand "Imperial ideas," is the "regeneration of the East." Treacherous England is to be confined to her single island, and barbarous Russia to be shut up in the Siberian snows. England may be left to answer for herself, but before we surrender even Russia to the Comtist priests, we should remember that, just as the Russian despotism is dangerous to the world from the stupidity of its barbarism, so the French democracy is dangerous through its feverish sympathies, blundering "humanity," and unlimited ambition.

The present reaction against exaggerated nationalism is in itself a sign that our national mind is in a healthy state; but, while we distrust nationalism because it is illogical and narrow, we must remember that "cosmopolitanism" has been made the excuse for childish absurdities, and a cloak for desperate schemes. Love of race, among the English, rests upon a firmer base than either love of mankind or love of Britain, for it reposes upon a subsoil of things known: the ascertained virtues and powers of the English people. For nations such as France and Spain, with few cares outside their European territories, national fields for action are, perhaps, too narrow, and the interests of even the vast territories inhabited by the English race may, in a less degree, be too small for English thought; but there is India,—and the responsibility of the absolute government of a quarter of the human race is no small thing. If we strive to advance ourselves in the love of truth, to act justly towards Ireland, and to govern India aright, we shall have enough of work to occupy us for many years to come, and shall leave a greater name in history than if we concerned ourselves with settling the affairs of Poland. If we need a wider range for our sympathies than that which even India will supply, we may find it in our friendships with the other sections of the race; and if, unhappily, one result of the present awakening of England to free life should be a return of the desire to meddle in the affairs of other folk, we shall find a better outlet for our energy in aiding our Teutonic brethren in their struggle for unity than in assisting Imperial France to spread Benôitonisme through the world.

We cannot, if we would, be indifferent spectators of the extravagances of France: if she is at present weak in the East, she is strong at home. At this moment, we are spending ten or fifteen millions a year in order that we may be equal with her in military force, and we hang upon the words of her ruler to know whether we are to have peace or war. Although it may not be wise for us to declare that this humiliating spectacle shall shortly have an end, it is at least advisable that we should refrain from aiding the French in their professed endeavours to obtain for other peoples liberties which they are incapable of preserving for themselves.

If the English race has a "mission" in the world, it is the making it impossible that the peace of mankind on earth should depend upon the will of a single man.

CHAPTER XXIII.

THE ENGLISH.

In America we have seen the struggle of the dear races against the cheap—the endeavours of the English to hold their own against the Irish and Chinese. In New Zealand, we found the stronger and more energetic race pushing from the earth the shrewd and laborious descendants of the Asian Malays; in Australia, the English triumphant, and the cheaper races excluded from the soil not by distance merely, but by arbitrary legislation; in India, we saw the solution of the problem of the officering of the cheaper by the dearer race. Everywhere we have found that the difficulties which impede the progress to universal dominion of the English people lie in the conflict with the cheaper races. The result of our survey is such as to give us reason for the belief that race distinctions will long continue, that miscegenation will go but little way towards blending races; that the dearer are, on the whole, likely to destroy the cheaper peoples, and that Saxondom will rise triumphant from the doubtful struggle.

The countries ruled by a race whose very scum and outcasts have founded empires in every portion of the globe, even now consist of 9½ millions of square miles, and contain a population of 300 millions of people. Their surface is five times as great as that of the empire of Darius, and four and a half times as large as the Roman Empire at its greatest extent. It is no exaggeration to say that in power the English countries would be more than a match for the remaining nations of the world, whom in the intelligence of their people and the extent and wealth of their dominions they already considerably surpass. Russia gains ground steadily, we are told, but so do we. If we take maps of the English-governed countries and of the Russian countries of fifty years ago, and compare them with the English and Russian countries of to-day, we find that the Saxon has outstripped the Muscovite in conquest and in colonization. The extensions of the United States alone are equal to all those of Russia. Chili, La Plata, and Peru must eventually become English: the Red Indian race that now occupies those countries cannot stand against our colonists; and the future of the table lands of Africa and that of Japan and of China is as clear. Even in the tropical plains, the negroes alone seem able to withstand us. No possible series of events can prevent the English race itself in 1970 numbering 300 millions of beings —of one national character and one tongue. Italy, Spain, France, Russia become pigmies by the side of such a people.

Many who are well aware of the power of the English nations are nevertheless disposed to believe that our own is morally, as well as physically, the least powerful of the sections of the race, or, in other words, that we are overshadowed by America and Australia. The rise to power of our southern colonies is, however, distant, and an alliance between ourselves and America is still one to be made on equal terms. Although we are forced to contemplate the speedy loss of our manufacturing supremacy as coal becomes cheaper in America and dearer in Old England, we have nevertheless as much to bestow on America as she has to confer on us. The possession of India offers to ourselves that element of vastness of dominion which, in this age, is needed to secure width of thought and nobility of purpose; but to the English race our possession of India, of the coasts of Africa, and of the ports of China offers the possibility of planting free institutions among the darkskinned races of the world.

The ultimate future of any one section of our race, however, is of little moment by the side of its triumph as a whole, but the power of English laws and English principles of government is not merely an English question—its continuance is essential to the freedom of mankind.

Steaming up from Alexandria along the coasts of Crete and Arcadia, and through the Ionian Archipelago, I reached Brindisi, and thence passed on through Milan towards home. This is the route that our Indian mails should take until the Euphrates road is made.

INDEX.

INDEX.

ABORIGINES, American treatment of, contrasted with English, i. 125, 126; extirpation of, in Tasmania, ii. 95; hostility of English military to, 96; contempt of the settlers for, *ib.*
Acapulco (*see* Mexico).
Adelaide, ii. 111; climate of, *ib.*; curious fact relating to wheat trade, 112; "the farinaceous village, so-called by Victorians," 113; character of the buildings, dress, and people, *ib.*; the bay of, at early morning, 123.
Agra (*see* India :—Mohamedan Cities).
Alabama claims, feeling of Americans respecting, i. 301; their opinion of England's refusal to arbitrate on the entire question, 301—303.
Albany (*see* Convict).
Alexandria, a French town, ii. 400 (*see also* French in Egypt).
Allahabad (*see* India :—Mohamedan Cities).
Alleghanies, eastern and western slopes of, i. 107.
America, wear and tear of life in, i. 55; indoor life of children, *ib.*; unhealthiness of tilling virgin soil, &c., *ib.*; politics discarded by the most intellectual men in the slave-ruling days, 58, 59; new map of the States, 73; splendid appropriations for educational purposes, 93; (*see* Pacific Railroad) railways preceding population, 100; North America, conformation of, as compared with other continents, 106; American scenery, 223, 224; difficulty of forming an idea of America, 308; apparent Latinization of, *ib.*; power of, now predominant in the Pacific, 402; democracy of, different from that of Australia, ii. 49; social difference, *ib.*
American Desert, the, i. 139; alkali dust, 139, 189, 207; highwaymen, 207.
——— Union, not likely to fall to pieces, 274; tendency of the time to great powers, not small ones, 274; interest of all the States in union, 274, 275; real danger from the seizure of the Atlantic coast cities by the Irish, 275; shape of North America, rendering almost impossible the existence of distinctive peoples within it, 311.
American Opinion of Great Britain, France, and Russia, i. 278; of the Fenians and Irish complaints, 300; the *Alabama* claims, 301—304.
——— Parties, Republican and Democratic, 283—285; Radical watchfulness needed to guard the country against great dangers, 285; great issue involved in the struggle between the parties, 287; possibility of the future abolition of the Presidency, 288.
——— Sensitiveness to English opinion, i. 305; an instance of the injustice done to Americans during the war, *ib.*; their firmness while the *Trent* affair was pending, 306.
Ann Arbor Institute, men sent by it to the war, i. 92; officers returned to complete their studies, *ib.*
Artemus Ward, joke of, to Elder Stenhouse, i. 158; in Virginia city, 202.
Atlantic States of America (*see* Western States).
Attar of roses (*see* India :—Umritsur).
Auckland, effect on, of the Banana-tree, i. 27 (*see also* Australia *and* Rival Colonies).
Aurora, in California, i. 209.
Austin, the pleasures and immunities of a Western tour, i. 194, 195; Chinese quarter of, 195, 196; a farewell "swop," 196.
Australasia, misuse of the term in England, ii. 4 (*see also* Rival Colonies); youth of Australia and their future, 9; climate of, *ib.*; eager democracy of, 10; different from the republicanism of the United States, *ib.* (*see* Coal); poetic native names, 35, 36;

social differences between Australia and America, 49; prospects of, 140; progress and extent of, 140, 141; obstacles to the peopling of the whole of, 141; want of railroads, 142; small amount of agricultural land as compared with extent of territory, 143; moral and intellectual health of, *ib.*; love of mirth, and absence of the American downrightness, &c. in pursuit of truth, *ib.*; waste of food, *ib.*; manners, &c. *ib.*; dress, 144; imitation of home customs, *ib.*; the University of Sydney, *ib.*; its Conservatism as distinguished from the Radicalism of the Western Universities, 147.

Australia, rivalry of the colonies of, i. 102.

—— West (*see* Convicts).

—— South, probability of becoming the granary of the Pacific colonies, ii. 113; production of wheat, 116; the land system, 116, 117 (*see* Women, 117, 120); Scotch and German immigrants, 121; political life of the colony, *ib.*; expedition to fix a new capital for the northern territory, 122; possibility that the north may be found a land of gold, 123; from South to West Australia, 124.

B.

BALLARAT (*see* Victorian Ports).
Ballot (*see* Tasmania).
Banana-tree, injurious effect of, in affording food without labour in the Southern States of America, Panama, Ceylon, Mexico, Auckland, &c. i. 27; a devil's agent, *ib.*; its danger to Florida and Louisiana, 28.
Benares (*see* India).
Bendigo (*see* Sandhurst).
Benita, Cape, i. 245.
Bentham, his philosophy in Utah, i. 148.
Bhawulpore (*see* India:—Native States).
Black Mountains (*see* Rocky Mountains), i. 137.
Bombay (*see* India:—Bombay).
Boston, its Elizabethan English and old English names, i. 60; its readiness during the war, 62.
Brannan, the chief mover in repressing disorders by lynch law in California, i. 229; his speech to his fellow-citizens, 231.
Brigham Young, Elder Evans, the "Shaker's," opinion of, i. 146 a conversation of three hours with, 147; his blessing at parting, *ib.*; "Is Brigham sincere?" 148; his position as a Prophet, while in fact a Utilitarian deist, *ib.*; his practical revelations, 149, and manner of announcing them, 150; his definition of the highest inspiration, *ib.*; his position among his people, 151; his immense personal influence, 152; his sons sent out each to work his own way in the world, 179.

Brisbane (*see* Queensland).
Broadbrim, the, mark of the Southern Guerilla, i. 5.
Buffalo herds on the plains, i. 113; skeletons of, 114.
Buffalo town, gloom of, i. 83.
Buller, the (*see* Hokitika).

C.

CAIRO, dirt and degradation of, ii. 397; slave market, 398; punishment by selection, 398, 399; misgovernment of the country, 399, 400 (*see also* French in Egypt).
Calcutta (*see* India).
California and Nevada, rectification of frontiers of, i. 209.
California, the terms Golden State and El Dorado well applied to, i. 214; scenery, *ib.*; names given to places by diggers, 217; luxury, &c. 219 (*see* Lynch Law); Episcopalianism flourishing in, 254; its prospects in the Pacific, *ib.*; nitro-glycerine, the nightmare of, 256; the valley of, 258; position of, on the overland route to the Pacific, 269; extent of, *ib.*; climate, 270.
Californian celebrities, portraits of, i. 200.
Cambridge, Mass. (*see* Harvard).
Canada, i. 66 (*see* Quebec); religion and politics, 71; disunion of French and Irish Catholics, *ib.*; French support of the Confederation scheme, 72; Fenians in, *ib.*; need of British Columbia to the Confederation, *ib.*; difficulties in the way of real confederation, 74, 75; emigration to, 75, 76; emigration from, to the United States, 77; jealousy of the Canadian States, *ib.*; their dislike to America, 78; difficulty of defending, *ib.*; protective duties, *ib.*; advantages of independence, 79; narrowness of English views respecting, 80; belief of the Canadians that they pos-

INDEX   413

sessed the only possible road to China for the trade of the future, 94 (see Pacific Railroad).
Canterbury, New Zealand, Episcopalian colony, i. 343; province of, divided both politically and geographically, ib.; antagonism between the Christchurch people and the diggers, ib.; dignified Episcopalian character of Christchurch, 346; its importation of rooks from England to caw in the elm-trees of the cathedral close, while Hokitika imports men, ib.
Capital, future, of the United States, i. 107.
Carolina, North, crackers, i. 7.
Cartier, early explorer, i. 94.
Cashmere (see India:—Colonization and Native States).
Caste, assailed by railways and telegraph, ii. 195; difficulty of discovering the opinion of a Hindoo, 206; idea of good manners, ib.; the secret history of the great rebellion, 207; British ignorance of the real feeling of the people, ib.; census as viewed by the Hindoos, 208; its revelations with respect to caste and "callings," 209, 210; beggars, 210; superstition, 211; a play at demonology, ib.; the praying wheel, 212; a saint's privileges in the days of the Emperor Akbar, ib.; strength of caste, 214; missionaries and Hindoo reformers, 214, 215; Hindoo deists, 217; Christians, 217, 218; different position of native Catholics and Protestants, 218; fewness of native Christians, 219; infanticide, 219, 220; remarkable changes in the last few years, 220; progress of the spirit of Christianity, ib.
Catholicism not "fashionable" in America, i. 254.
Caucus, King, i. 292; Americans, on the derivation of the term, 293.
Cawnpore (see India:—Mohamedan Cities).
Cemeteries, Hollywood, Richmond, i. 17; Lone Mountain Cemetery in California, the most beautiful in America, 247; other American cemeteries, ib.
Census, curious results of, in India, ii. 207—210.
Centre, government from the, i. 103; ancient and modern views of, 103, 104; centre of United States, 107.
Ceylon (see Kandy).
Ceylon, Maritime, ii. 161; the streets of Point du Galle, 163; women and men of, ib.; mixture of races, 164; American missionaries, quaint humour of, ib.; beggars, ib.; gem and jewel sellers, trade in precious stones, ib.; British soldiers in white, 166; heat at night, ib.; the morning gun, 167; character of the Cinghalese, 168; translucent water, and brilliance of colour at the bottom, 168, 169; a Cinghalese dinner, 169; a stage-coach ride to Colombo, ib.; aspect o f the fine road, crowded with all rank s of the people, 169, 170; one continu - ous village, 171; dense populatio n and food of the people on the coas t, ib.; Colombo, ib.; trees and foliag e, 171, 172; a garden scene, ib.; Fo rt, or "European town" of, 172; t he most graceful street in the world, i b.; the peak where Adam mourned his son a hundred years, ib.; Ceylon Coffee Company's Establishme nt, 173; steam factory, ib.; Fre nch Catholic priests, ib.; their succ ess, 174; the old Dutch quarter, 174, 175; rapid changes from heat to cold, 175.
Chaudière Falls (Ottawa), i. 81.
Chicago (see San Francisco and Chicago, &c).
Chickahominy, the, scene of M'Clellan's defeat, i. 12.
China, coolies from, in the Southern States of America, i. 26; "one man and a Chinaman," 259; a Chinese theatre, 260; peculiarity of its drama, ib.; the second month and third act of the play, 261; a Chinese restaurant, 262; saucer and chopsticks for the Author, ib.; gaming-houses, 263; Chinese industry and cleanliness, 264; similarity of faces common to all coloured races, ib.; benevolent societies, 265; wealth of merchants, ib.; prejudice against, on the part of the Americans, as also on that of the Australians, 265, 266; Chinese expostulations against the prejudice, 266; cowardice of, ib.; practical slavery in California, ib.; the Irish of Asia, 267; capability for work, ib.; the serious side of the Chinese problem, 268.
Chinese, first arrival among, i. 196; in California, 215; a tiny Chinese theatre, 216; as taxpayers, ib. (see China); at Melbourne, ii. 19; at Sandhurst, 29; anti-Chinese mobs,

29; unjust treatment of, 29, 30; hunted with blood-hounds, 30; marriage between, and Irish women, *ib.*; character of, as citizens in Australia, 31; restaurants of, *ib.*; in the Australian labour market, 77—80.

Churches, in America, Catholic and Episcopalian, i. 254, 314; Spiritualists and Unitarians, 314; Shakers and Communists, 315; Mormons, *ib.*; Radical Unitarians, *ib.*; tenets and claims of the Spiritualists, 316; the *Spiritual Clarion, ib.*; rumoured number of Spiritualists in America, 317; the Germans mostly pure Materialists, *ib.* (*see also* Canterbury, Otago, *and* New Zealand); Catholics, in Australia, ii. 47; "godless education," *ib.*; Churches in Victoria nearly all of the well-known English names, 55; absence of the American names, *ib.*; dignity of character arising from the American religious feeling, 56; Australian Churches, 146; Hindoo churches, English and native, 214; Church of Hindoo Deists, 205—220; a Sikh revival, 284; Parsee religion, 354, 355.

Cincinnati, smoke of, i. 83.

Civilization, limits of Westward, i. 109; "civilization means whisky," *ib.*

Coal (*see* Pacific), in New South Wales, ii. 17; its importance to Australia, *ib.*; value to Sydney, 18.

Coalville, the Mormon Newcastle, i. 144.

Cocoas, Island of, kingdom of John Ross, ii. 161.

Colonial Government (*see* Squatter *and* Democracy).

Colonies, taxation of England in aid of wealthy, ii. 148, 149; of Canada, 149; exclusion of English productions from, *ib.*; cost to England, 150; refusal of the, to contribute towards the cost of Imperial wars, *ib.*; readiness of the old American colonists to do so, *ib.*; position of Imperial soldiers in the colonies, 151; absurdity of supposing that the Australians would be in danger if separated from England, 152; our defence of, necessarily of least value when most needed, *ib.*; and really a source of weakness to the colonies, 153; separation no loss to England, *ib.*; trade with Canada and with the United States of America, 153, 154; with Egypt, 154; question of the outlet for population, 154; strength of great and small states, 155; the question of colonies preventing the insularity of mind that might belong to a nation of a limited area, *ib.*; separation not to be desired if union can be continued on fair terms to the mother land, and with advantage to the colonies, 156, 157; if not so, separation not dangerous to either, 157.

Coloradan farm, i. 116; a Coloradan boast, 121; Coloradan "boys" a fine handsome race, 135; strange insects, *ib.*

Colorado, rival Governors of, i. 117; great idea of Gilpin the Pioneer, 118; extent and beauty of country, 131—134; Upper Colorado, or Green River, lost for a thousand miles in undiscovered wilds, 140.

Columbo (*see* Ceylon, Maritime).

Conservative, Colonial, what is a, ii. 39 (*see* Squatters).

Convicts (*see* Tasmania), settlement of South Australia, ii. 125; petition to be made a penal settlement, *ib.*; convicts or emancipists in the colony, *ib.*; population of West Australia, *ib.*; convict escapes, 126; punishment, *ib.*; "bolters for a change," 127; murder to escape convict labour, *ib.*; transportation, past and present, 127, 128; entire colonies formed of convicts, 128; "society" at Botany Bay, 129; all professions, &c. filled by convicts, *ib.*; petition against transportation from Tasmania, *ib.*; fearful demoralization of the colony, 130, 131; free female labourers sent out, 131; the assignment system, 132; crime in the colony, 133; bushrangers, *ib.*; end of the system, 134; demoralization of the convict voyage, *ib.*; horrid conversation, 135; the hope that Tasmania may be purified by the gold-find and free selection, *ib.*; the transportation system, *ib.*; its cost, *ib.*; its severity to the least guilty, *ib.*; the future of convict treatment, 136–138.

Co-operative labour, negro (*see* Davis).

Costa Rica, i. 307.

Cumberland and *Merrimac*, wrecks of, i. 4.

D.

DANITES, i. 150; Porter Rockwell, chief of, 184; strange stories of, *ib.*; bands

organized to defend the first Presidency of the Mormons, 185 ; their reported deeds, *ib.*
Davidson, Mount, Nevada, i. 204 ; its silver mines, 204, 205.
Davis, Joseph (brother of Jefferson Davis), scheme of, for negro co-operative labour, i. 31.
Deseret (the Mormon country), "Land of the Bee," i. 170.
Devil's Gate, Nevada, i. 206.
Diego Mendoza's discovery of California, i. 213.
Dirt storm, a, i. 115.
Dixon, Mr. Hepworth, meeting with, at St. Louis, i. 102 ; name in Nebraska, 137 ; parting from the Author, 183.
Democracy (*see* Squatters), colonial, ii. 46 ; payment of members, *ib.*; reasons for, *ib.*; the Catholic party in power, 47 ; driven from office on the question of appointing only Irishmen to the police, *ib.* ; the O'Shaughnessey Government, *ib.* ; Victorians mending the constitution, 48 ; democracy of Victoria not American but English in tone, 49 ; difference between the democracy of Victoria and New South Wales, 52 ; earnestness of colonial democracy in the cause of education, *ib.* ; danger of the crushing influence of democracy upon individuality, 55 ; no great party in the colonies at all like the great Republican party of America, 56 ; the future of Australian Democracy, 57 ; tendency of the women to cling to the old "colonial court" society, *ib.* ; democratic principles in Australia, 57, 58.
Denver, letter from, i. 109 ; vigilance committees in, 243.
Dependencies, English, ii. 390 ; Abyssinian war, *ib.*; free trade forced on China and Japan, 390, 391 ; future policy of England and America with respect to China, 391, 392 ; profit and loss of our dependencies, 392, 393 ; the Dutch system, 393 ; deliberately rejected by the English people, *ib.* ; cost of several dependencies, *ib.*; India's part in the Abyssinian war, 393, 394 ; the retention of dependencies and colonies on different grounds, 394 ; India as a nursery of warriors and statesmen, *ib.*; the advantage to a nation of having world-wide interests to govern, 395 ; seizure of Perim, *ib.*; amusing incident of, *ib.*

Drama, Chinese, peculiarity of, i. 260.
Dutch element of population gone from New York, i. 40.
Dutch Gap, i. 10.

E.

EAST, the, first view of, ii. 138.
Education, "godless," in Australia, ii. 47, 48 ; earnestness of the colonial democracy in the cause of, 52, 53 ; the Australian as compared with the English view of the real use of, 53 ; illiterate men in the colonies striving to educate their children, 53, 54.
El Dorado, i. 213—215.
Emerson, his opinion of the vitality of Mormonism, i. 181.
Emigrants, classes of, that do not succeed, and that do, ii. 13 ; tendency to hang about great towns in America and Australia, 19.
English, old, names in the Southern States of America, i. 15, 16 ; and families, 16 ; in Boston, 60 ; flowers at the New Zealand diggings, 332 ; officers at the New Zealand diggings, 339.
English race, pushing on towards the setting sun, i. 273 (*see* Race in America); in the struggle of races, ii. 405 ; extent of districts ruled by the English race, 406 ; the Saxon has outstripped the Muscovite, *ib.* ; alliance on equal terms with America, 407 ; prospects of the race as a whole, *ib.*
Episcopalian Church in America, flourishing, 254.

F.

FENIAN Brothers, the, i. 296 ; meetings of, in New York, Chicago, and Canada, *ib.*; Irish support of, 297 ; nature of Irish antipathy to Great Britain, *ib.* ; its probable effect, *ib.* ; the Irish at home not Fenians in the American sense, *ib.*; land laws in Ireland, 298 ; unsatisfactory position of Irishmen in America, *ib.* ; Fenian agreement to drop the word "English" as applied to language, and to use only the term "American," 299 ; opinion of Americans respecting Fenianism, 300 ; the raid into Canada and the St. Alban's raid, *ib.*; Fenian power owing to the anti-English feeling of the Democratic party and the *Alabama* claims, 301.

Flies, the two, i. 390; probable cause of English natural productions supplanting the Maori ones in New Zealand, 390, 391; the English fly beats down and will exterminate the Maori fly, 391; suitability of the New Zealand soil and climate for English productions—men, seeds, and insect-germs, 392; the Maori differs from other aboriginal races—he farms, owns villages and ships, is a good rider, mechanic, soldier, sailor, and trader, yet he is passing away like the native fly, 393; the descendants of Captain Cook's pigs, 394; conduct of the British Government towards the Maories, 394, 395 (*see* Thompson, William); half-breeds, 396; a chance for the Maories surviving by miscegenation, *ib.*; unchastity of the Maori unmarried women, "Christian as well as heathen," 396, 397 (*see also* Pacific).

Florida, banana in, i. 28.

Florida privateer, under water, i. 8.

Forged notes, novel agreement of Colorado and Nevada people respecting, i. 203.

Freedom and slavery, their contrary effects, i. 13.

Free labour and slave labour, i. 22, 23.

Freemasonry of travel, i. 193.

Fremont, the Pathfinder, his report of Utah, i. 145; his conquest in the West, 246.

French, attempt of, to precede us in New Zealand and Australia, ii. 106; possessions in India, 190, 191; the island of Perim, 395; France in the East, 397; state of Egypt, 398, 399; preponderance of French influence there, 400; the Suez Canal, *ib.*; its commercial success not of first importance to the French Government, *ib.*; French power played off by the King of Egypt against England and Russia, 401; prospects of the canal, 402; and use to England, *ib.*; proposed neutralization of Egypt, *ib.*; French aims in Egypt, 402, 403; Comtist theories, 403; nationalism and cosmopolitanism, *ib.*; the work of England as distinguished from that of France, 404.

G.

GALLE (*see* Point de Galle).

Geelong (*see* Victorian Ports).

Germans, justice-loving, their descendants in Western America, i. 238; their influence on the religious thought of America, 317.

Gold and silver diggers, contempt of the former for the latter, i. 206.

Gold, discovery of, in any part of the world, certain to be followed by English government there, i. 273.

Golden City, i. 245; seeing the "lions" there, *ib.*; subterranean forces, 248; "What Cheer House," 249; mint juleps, *ib.*; domestic servants, their enviable position, *ib.*; hotel life, 249, 250; excellency of climate, 252; gaiety of the people, *ib.*; mixed population, 253, 254.

Golden Gate, the gap in the Contra Costa range of mountains by which the Pacific breeze rushes on San Francisco, i. 251; beneficial effects of the breeze, 252; curious facts connected with it, 252, 253.

Gilpin, Governor, i. 137, 269.

Grand Plateau, overtaken on, by a company of "overlanders," i. 189; compliments in the desert, *ib.*

Grant, General, i. 9; the secret of his success, 13.

Great Salt Lake City, i. 187; the lake gradually sinking, *ib.*; its extent, 209.

Greeley, Horace, i. 188, 210.

Guatemala, 307.

H.

HANGTOWN, where lynch law was inaugurated, i. 217.

Hank Monk's "piece," i. 210; a reckless drive, 211.

Harvard College (Cambridge, Mass.), foundation of, i. 51; the Harvard family, *ib.*; defects of the college, 52; its need of a ten days' revolution, *ib.*; hope of reform, 53; new constitution, *ib.*; outdoor sports, 54, 56; "Alumni celebration," 57; New England love for, *ib.*; old students, 58; past reform, *ib.*; its noble bands of volunteers for the war, 59; classic repose of the town, 60.

Heights, the, among the "Nameless Alps" of Western America, supper on, at 8 A.M., i. 188.

Himalayan yâk, its suitability for the desert, i. 139.

Hobarton (*see* Tasmania).

Hodson, Captain, his shooting down the sons of the last Mogul Emperor, ii. 231.

Hokitika and the Buller—new gold fields of the colony, i. 329; nature of the voyage from Melbourne to Hokitika, 330; a fine sunrise, *ib.*; the bar, 331; a "toss" for a newspaper, 332; *the* hotel, *ib.*; English flowers among the diggers, *ib.*; the diggings, 333; soil and climate of, *ib.*; political economy on board the steamer, 334; rapid rise of Hokitika, *ib.*; its excellent roads, 335; the product of convict labour,*ib.*; the term "convict" made to include persons committed for the smallest offences, 335, 336; bushrangers, 337; New Zealand Thugs, *ib.*; a favourite amusement at the diggings, 340; the new road from Hokitika, *ib.*; rivalry between the town and the religious settlements, 346.

Homestead Act (United States), frauds on, i. 241.

Hotel life in America, its effect on women and children, i. 249, 250; profligacy and assurance of Young America, *ib.*

Hudson Bay Company, the blight of its monopoly, i. 71, 74; impossibility of the Company resisting American immigration, 74.

Hunting party, a, lost, i. 110.

Hydrabad (*see* India:—Scinde).

I.

INDIA, spelling of native names, ii. 160.

——— Benares, early morning in, ii. 197; the Hindoo as a babbler, *ib.*; Temple of Sacred Monkeys, *ib.*; Queen's College for native students, 198; observatory of Jai Singh, and the Golden Temple, *ib.*; streets of Benares, 198, 199; banks of the Ganges, 199; scenery, *ib.*; ornamentation of pavilions, 200; taste in painting, *ib.*; people taken to the banks of the Ganges to die, 201; similar customs among the Cinghalese and Maories, 202; immorality of the holy city, *ib.*; conservatism of the Oriental mind, 203; fewness of Europeans in India, *ib.*; a hot white fog, *ib.*; demoralization of English soldiers, 204; brandy-and-soda-water, *ib.*; Benares a type of India, 205; position of missionaries in, *ib.*

——— Bombay, 349; vegetation, *ib.*; harbour of, 350; weak defences of, *ib.*; rapid rise of, owing to the cotton trade, 350, 352; hard work in the mercantile houses, 352; Scotchmen in Bombay, 353; compensations of Bombay life, *ib.*; the bazaar, *ib.*; the Parsees, 354; their religion and culture, 354, 355; the stage as a means of satirising English foibles, 355; a Parsee marriage, *ib.*; Caves of Elephanta, 356; bust of the Hindoo Trinity, *ib.*; its grandeur, *ib.*

India, Calcutta to Benares, &c. ii. 190; Chandernagore, *ib.*; French possessions, *ib.*; railway in Oriental dress, 191; Monghyr Hills, 192; the Ganges, first view of, *ib.*; scenery, *ib.*; over the plains, 193; Patna, Oriental independence of railway time-tables, *ib.*; taking tickets in good time, *ib.*; working of the railways, 194; effect of railways on the state of the country, *ib.*; on caste, 195; destruction of forests, *ib.*; Mogul Serai, the junction for Benares, *ib.* (*see* Benares).

——— Colonization of, i. 252; attempts at, made in six districts, 252, 253; Cashmere the best for European settlers, 253; civilians and rulers of India jealous of settlers, 253, 254; dread of "low caste" Englishmen, 254; holding of landed estates by Englishmen in India, 255; English planters would assist to give a healthy tone to the social system, *ib.*; indigo plantations in Bengal, 256; two securities against the further degradation of India, 257, 258.

——— English learning in, ii. 365; ignorance of the people, *ib.*; their high art a relic of a bygone age, 365, 366; apparent rapid decline since the English arrived in India, 366; humiliation of the ruling classes of the country, 367; what should be the character of the government of such a people, 368; "India for the Indians," the meaning of the cry, *ib.*; necessary radical reforms, 369; trivial character of those introduced a few years ago, *ib.*; importance of naturalizing the English language in India, *ib.*; naturalization of the Spanish language in America, 370; England's want of success in that particular, 371; early abolition of slavery probably one cause of it, *ib.*; our system of government a dear one, 372; servile condition of native women, *ib.*;

false swearing, 372; small amount of money spent in encouraging learning, 373.

India, England in the East different from the England at home, 374–376; trial by jury and law courts, 375, 376; the old school Hindoos and the free-thinkers both opposed to us, 377; superiority of Akbar's policy, 377, 378; employment of natives in higher offices, 378, 379; a Mohamedan protest against our policy, 379; levelling tendency of our competitive examinations, 380; hatred to English rule, the hatred that Easterns always have to their masters, 381; not a wish for self-government, *ib.*; the Anglo-Saxon race in possession of the only homes of freedom known at the present time, 382; freedom not understood by the Hindoos, *ib.*; consequences of our leaving India, 383; prospects of our government there, 384; Anglo-Indian opposition to government from London, 385, 386; the creation of new governments, 387; fundamental question whether we wish to hold India for our prestige merely, or in the interest of the people of Hindostan, 388, 389.

——— *Gazette*, ii. 260; value and variety of contents of, 260—264; evidence with respect to "ghautmurder," 264, 265; evidence as to polyandry and polygyny, in India, 266—271.

——— Lahore, ii. 286; appearance of, *ib.*; suburb of tombs, 287; Cabool Gate, *ib.*; English characteristics of Lahore, 288; newspapers of, *ib.*; the rulers of Lahore, 290.

——— Madras to Calcutta, ii. 185; the Massullah boat, *ib.*; sighting the Temple of Juggernauth, 186; the Hoogly, *ib.*; scenery on, *ib.*; palace of the ex-King of Oude, 187; extravagance and debauchery of the ex-King, *ib.*; apprehension of one of his wives for assisting in, *ib.*; general immorality of wealthy natives in Calcutta, *ib.*; character of the Indian Government, and its influence on the popular life, 188; Government House, and Calcutta buildings, *ib.*; hospitality of great mercantile houses, 188, 189; mixed population of Calcutta, 189.

——— Mohamedan cities of, ii. 221; Allahabad, 221; Cawnpore, *ib.*; Lucknow, *ib.*; beauty of Lucknow, 221, 222; stories of the mutiny, 222, 223; ill-treatment of natives by the English, 223; a notice in hotels, 224; Anglo-Indian jokes, *ib.*; looting, 225; contempt for native lives, *ib.*; officers and natives, 226; English cruelties in Oude, 227; a war, not a rebellion in Oude, *ib.*; the Residency at Lucknow, *ib.*; rapid repair of the wrecks of the rebellion, 227, 228; Agra, 228; the Taj Mahal and Pearl of Mosques, 228—230; Akbar's draught-board and pieces, 229; great works of the Mogul conquerors, 230, 231; contrast of Mohamedan great cities and those of the three Presidencies, 231; changes in Delhi, 232.

India, Mohamedan Mohurrum, celebrated at Poonah, ii. 357; the ascent to Poonah, 357, 358; the procession, 359–361; elegance and grace of the females of Poonah, 361; the procession joined in by the Hindoos and Christians as well as Mohamedans, 362; drunken British soldiers, 363; Indian Mohamedans, their small number and Hindoo feelings, 364.

——— Native States, ii. 313; resemblance of the people of, to Gaelic races, *ib.*; need of irrigation in country, 313, 314; Moultan, 315; rail and river, *ib.*; State of Bhawulpore, 316; talk of annexation of, *ib.*; demoralization, 317; degeneracy of ruling families, *ib.*; British or native rule, 318; reasons for believing that the people know they are well off under British rule, 319; merchants and townspeople our friends, 320; danger of interfering with native customs, *ib.*; the Nepaulese during the mutiny, 321; the State of Cashmere, *ib.*; its creation as a State, *ib.*; grounds for repurchase or annexation, 321, 322; the Nizam, Scindia, the Guicodar of Baroda, and Holkar, 323; origin of present ruling families, 324; effect of shutting out the natives from the higher branches of the English service, 325; present attitude of the natives one of indifference and neutrality, 326; the question of future annexation, 327.

——— Our Army, ii. 291; the Sikhs, *ib.*; questionable morality of the present system of, 292, 293; Russia our only possible enemy from without, 294; her weakness as against India, *ib.*; taxation of the poorest country in the world for so large an army, 295; our duty to reduce the army, *ib.*; employment of Sikhs out of India, 296; British officers, 297; danger to English liberties from so large an army in India, 297, 298.

India, Overland routes, ii. 338; Kurrachee, character of, 338, 339; chokedars, 339; a shibboleth for excluding natives from the lines, 340; the harbour of Kurrachee, 340, 341; Kurrachee the direct route from Bombay, by the Euphrates valley and Constantinople to London, 341, 342; the earliest known overland route, 342, 343; interest of a return of trade to the Gulf route, 343; difficulties in the way of, 344—347; Scinde chieftains, 348.

―――― Russian approach to, ii. 299; at Bokhara, *ib.*; advice from different quarters as to the best means for dealing with, 300—302; opinion of a Syrian Pacha as to England's proper course and interest in opposition to Russia, 303—305; his view of our relation to Turkey and Egypt, 303—307; differences of Moslem races, 307, 308; opinion of old Indians that Indian policy should rule the policy of the nation, 308; advance of Russia watched by the natives, 308, 309; advantages to India of English government, if we can raise up a people that will support our rule, 310—312.

―――― Simla, ii. 234; a night ride up the hills to, 234, 235; languages of India, 235, 236; dawk travelling, 237; villages on the way, 238; aristocracy of colour, *ib.*; English haughtiness, *ib.*; Indian plains, 239; ruins, *ib.*; wheat harvest, 240; female reapers, *ib.*; jampan riding, *ib.*; servants, unpleasant number of, 240, 241; thirty-five required for one small family in Simla, 242; cheapness of labour, 243, 244; English soldiers, the possibility of keeping all at hill stations, 245; story-telling in the East, 245, 246; entry to Simla, 247; the Viceroy's children, *ib.*; climate, *ib.*; suitability of Simla as a refuge of the Indian Government from Calcutta heat, 248, 249; the question of new "Governorships," 249; Calcutta, disadvantages of, as capital, 249, 250; future capital of India, 250, 251; a sunrise scene from Simla, 251; a fair at Simla, 258, 259.

India, Scinde, ii. 328; the Indus valley a part of the great Sahara, 329; sailing on the Indus, 330—332; a Persian's prayer on shipboard, 333; shallowness of the river, *ib.*; necessity of a safe and speedy road up the valley, *ib.*; neglect of railways in India, 334; need and value of them, 334, 335; early trade between China and Hindostan, 336; Sukkur, *ib.*; native fishing, *ib.*; Hydrabad, 337; Kurrachee, *ib.* (*see* Overland Routes).

―――― Umritsur, ii. 272; Hindoo sacred fair, or camp meeting, *ib.*; Sikh pilgrims on the way from, *ib.*; cholera stricken, 273; a fearful march, *ib.*; nature of the great gathering, 273, 274; a dust storm, 275; Anglo-Indian engineering, 276; neglect of roads, 277; the Grand Trunk Railway, *ib.*; Umritsur, beauty of, *ib.*; fruits, foliage, &c. 278; its famous roses, *ib.*; the attar of roses, *ib.*; Cashmere shawl manufacture, *ib.*; cost of, *ib.*; material, 279; the bazaar, *ib.*; the Sikhs, Magyar appearance of, 280; Indian and English manufactures, 281, 282; ornament, Hindoo taste with respect to, 282; the spiritual capital of the Sikhs, 283; a Sikh revival, 284; its possible consequences, *ib.*

―――― East, trunk railway of, i. 100.

Indian customs (*see* Caste).

―――― Seas, the, ii. 161—163.

Indians of the American Plains, i. 111; stations robbed by, *ib.*; a formal Indian warning to the white men, 111, 112; a half-breed interpreter, 112; treaties with the, 112, 113; opposition of, to the Pacific Railway, 113; the chief, "Spotted Dog," *ib.*; treatment of squaws, 119; and general unseemliness, *ib.*; coming to town to be painted, 122; inferiority to the Indians of the Eastern States, 123; customs similar to those of the Maories, 123; degradation of the Indian, 124; rapid extermination of, 125; tendency when apparently civilized to return to barbarism, 126; rough and ready attempts by the English to civilize, 127; conservative character of the Indian, 128; American treaty with, 129; the Indian receding before the English race, but victorious over the Spaniards, 130; open

attempts to exterminate, by the Coloradan Government, 130 ; gangs of Indians working by proxy on the railway, 214 ; Digger Indians, 215 ; Red Indian supremacy in Mexico, 279, 280.
Irish in America, competition with the negro, i. 22 ; in New York, displacing the New Englanders, 41—43; danger to America, 44 ; corruption of, in New York, 45 ; possibility of their retaining their hold of the Atlantic cities, 275 (*see* Fenian Brothers) ; Irishmen not well off in America, 298 ; Belfast names in higher esteem than Cork ones, 299 ; the Irish remaining in towns, and losing their attachment to the soil, *ib.* ; number of, sent to gaol in America, 300 ; an Irish opinion of the thermometer, ii. 37 ; Irish party in office in Victoria, 47 ; appointment of Irishmen to all police offices, *ib.* ; checks on Irish immigration to the colonies, 73—77 ; workhouse girls sent to the colonies, 118—120.

J.

JAFFA, colony founded there by New Englanders, i. 64.
Jamaica, homilies on the condition of, by Southern planters, i. 25.
Japan, its probable great future, i. 401, 402.
Jenny Lind, the hall where she sang on first landing in America, i. 41.
Jockey Club, Sydney, meeting of (*see* Sydney).
Johnson, President, absurdity of his policy, i. 37.

K.

KANDY (Ceylon), the highland kingdom, and one of the holiest of Buddhist towns, ii. 176 ; dress and appearance of the people, 177 ; the Upper Town one great garden, *ib.*; tooth of Buddha, *ib.* ; the coffee district, *ib.* ; Government Botanical Gardens—medicinal plants, 178 ; importance of the coffee-trade to Ceylon, *ib.* ; want of capital in, *ib.*; Dutch system of labour, 179 ; in Java, *ib.* ; Dutch Government jobbery, *ib.*; immorality of, 180, 181 ; Ceylon petitions for self-government, 182 ; the meaning of the term, *ib.* ; small number of whites in the country, 182, 183 ; mountain scenery, 183 ; trees and foliage, 183, 184.
Kansas, emancipation of women in, &c. i. 84, 91 ; parallel lines of railway in, 101 ; Nebraska opinion of Kansas, *ib.* ; female suffrage in, the opposite pole to Utah polygamy, 156 ; evasion of the Homestead Act in, 241.
Kimball, Heber, Mormon, i. 158.
King George's Sound (*see* Convicts).
Kit Carson, i. 207, 208.
Kurrachee (*see* India:—Overland Route).

L.

LABOUR in Australia, ii. 71 ; great power of working men in Australia as compared with, in the United States, *ib.*; the real grievance of the working-classes throughout the world, *ib.*; laws by workmen in the colonies, and in those parts of America where they have power, to meet the want, 71, 72 ; opposition of the Sydney workmen to both immigration and transportation, 72 ; defence of the labour laws, 73—75 ; English Factory Act, a step which diminished the powers of production, 75 ; Know-nothingism in America a protest against the exaggerations of free trade, 76 ; proposals to introduce cheap labour, 77 ; the fundamental basis of the labour question, 77, 78 ; our recent ridicule of the Chinese exclusiveness, 78 ; our present opposition to Chinese immigration, 79 ; the Chinese pushing to the front whenever they have an opportunity, 79, 80 ; the colonial labour laws not unlike those of a trade union, 80 ; the old relation between master and servant dying out, 81 ; new aspect of labour in accordance with democratic principles, *ib.* ; co-operative labour supplanting the middle-age system, *ib.* ; industrial partnerships a return to the earliest and noblest forms of labour, 82.
Lahore (*see* India:—Lahore).
Land tenure in Australia (*see* Squatters *and* Democracy).
Latin Church, the, in America, i. 43.
——— Empire in America, i. 278 ; its virtual downfall, *ib.*
Latinization, the apparent, of the English in America, i. 308.
Launceston (*see* Tasmania).
Lawrence, St. the, i. 66 ; Lawrentian range of mountains, 67.

INDEX. 421

Louisiana, banana in, i. 28.
Lucknow (*see* India:—Mohamedan Cities).
Lynch Law, where inaugurated, i. 217; vigilance committees, 226; great need for, in California, in 1848, *ib.*; influx of English convicts and desperadoes from all parts, 227, 228; first attempted action on the part of the people for their own protection, 228; united attempt, 229; trial by lynch law, 229, 230; vigilance committee formed, *ib.*; its regular organization and prompt action, 231; police show of resistance to, *ib.*; but warned away, *ib.*; the trial, *ib.* and execution, 232; full public account of the circumstances, 233; trial and execution endorsed by the citizens in public meeting, *ib.*; struggle with authority—the committee victorious, 233, 234; sending the convicts back to Australia, 234; a fearful year (1855), *ib.*; resolute action of the people, 234—236; end of the work, 236; necessity for the action, 237; somewhat different action in Melbourne for the same purpose, *ib.*; public spirit of the people, 238; descendants of the justice-loving Germans, *ib.*; two memorable Lynch-law trees, 242; vigilance committees in Denver, Leavenworth, &c. 243, 244.

M.

MAINE LIQUOR LAW, likelihood of being the first cause of the reaction against the now triumphant Radicals, i. 290.
Malthusianism rejected in America, i. 131.
Maori (*see* Race):—Question of Maories being natives of the New Zealand soil, i. 347; legend of their flight to New Zealand, 348; Polynesian names in their language, *ib.*; traditional account of the cradle of race, 349; resemblance between, and the Red Indians of America, 350, 351; similarity of religious rites and social customs of, 352; the Malay race in the Pacific, 353; the most widely scattered of all the nations of the world before the English, *ib.*; the Maories, Malays, 354; Malay breach of a law of nature in going to New Zealand, *ib.*; paying the penalty in extinction, *ib.*; Parewanui Pah, 355;

a Maori song, 355; meeting of the tribes to discuss with the white man a great question of the right to territory, 356; curious idea of the Maories as to the title of land, 357; a summons to the council, 358; vigorous speeches of the chiefs, 358—360; the representative of the Queen (Dr. Featherston) communicating with the chiefs, 361; adjournment for luncheon, *ib.*; the Maori *belles*, 362; views of the chiefs with respect to Dr. Featherston's decision, 363; business of the Council resumed, 364; oratorical abuse, *ib.*; breaking-up of the Council, 365; its singular resemblance to the Greek Council as described by Homer, 365, 366; alarming news of guns being sent for, 366; another general meeting of the tribes, 367; Maori names, *ib.*; the Queen's flag pulled down, 368; Dr. Featherston's refusal to attend any debate till the flag is re-hoisted, *ib.*; an interesting voyage in an English ship for cannibal purposes, *ib.*; the captain's compensation for the use of his ship, *ib.*; Maori dance song, 368, 369; sketching the Maories, 369; native tombs, 370; apology for the pulling-down of the flag, 371; the deed of land sale, *ib.*; "eternal friendship between" the tribes, 372; the money sent for by Dr. Featherston, *ib.*; misgivings and grief of the Maories, *ib.*; their song of lamentation, *ib.*; the money paid, 373; grand celebration, 373—376; effect of a war-dance on Lord Durham's settlers (in 1837), 376; specimens of native oratory—noble speech of the chief Hunia, 376—378; a long ramble in New Zealand, 379, 380; Maori Christianity, its hollowness, 380; baptized *out* of the Church, *ib.*; their Church of Englandism a failure, *ib.*; in spite of the earnestness and devotion of missionaries, 381; the great outbreak, *ib.*; deserting the mission-station for the bush, *ib.*; a question—Pork, beef, or man for food, 382; the Maori reply, *ib.*; rapid spread of Christianity among, when first presented, *ib.*; the native religion a vague Polytheism, 383; no caste among the Maories, *ib.*; reverence for high-born women, 384; influence of women, *ib.*; delicacy of the men towards, *ib.*; making it possible for an honest Englishman to respect or love an honest Maori, 385; Maori superiority to other native races in savage lands, 385, 386; noble Maori trait of "proclaiming" a war district, and never touching an enemy, however defenceless, when found elsewhere, 386; royal ideas of money, *ib.* (*see* Thompson, William, the Maori King-maker); Maori ability in war, 387, 388; their fondness for horses and skill as riders, *ib.*; their love for the sea, and possession of vessels on it, *ib.*; good deep-sea fishermen, *ib.*; and draught-players, 389; shrewd and thrifty, devoted friends and brave men, *ib.*; a Maori feast and bill-of-fare, Appendix to vol. i.; their saying, "We are gone like the moa" (*see* Flies, the two); customs of, ii. 202.

Massachusetts, progress of, i. 61.

Maximilian, received in Mexico by white men, and conquered by half-breeds, i. 279.

Mayflower, and the Pilgrim Fathers, i. 34, 41.

Mayhew, Hon. Ira, work on Education, i. 91.

Mean whites, i. 7; controlling power of the South, 33.

Melbourne (*see* Victoria), learned and distinguished men at, ii. 50; the Attorney-General, Mr. Higginbotham, *ib.*; a Government clerk's horror of the low pedigree of three ministers of state, *ib.*; a Colonial Parliament on its dignity, committal of a reporter, 51; his triumph, 52; early competition of Melbourne and Geelong, 88; voyage from Melbourne to Hokitika, 330; the great gold mania in 1848, *ib.*

Mexican saddle, peculiarity of, i. 256, 257.

Mexico, coasting to, i. 276; Cape St. Lucas, *ib.*; turtle and crocodile, 277; French army of occupation, *ib.*; Acapulco, 278; anniversary of Marshal Bazaine's order directing the execution of all Mexicans found with arms, *ib.*; Spanish Mexico becoming Red Indian, 280; resolution of the United States that Mexico shall not become a monarchy, *ib.*; the large Catholic population it would give in case of annexation to the American Union, 281; beauty of the Mexican Pacific coast, 282.

Michigan (*see* Massachusetts), University of, i. 83; Michigan men and maize, 84; democracy of the University, 85; Government of, 86; progress of the Michigan teaching system, *ib.*; supported by the taxpayers of the State, 87; jocose reports of superintendents of schools, 88; loyalty, 89; students sent to the war, *ib.*; dislike to competitive honours, 90; practical character of, 91; exclusion of women from the medical schools, *ib.*; the coasts of Michigan great lakes, 99.

"Mint Juleps" in San Francisco—the old name of the town, Yerba Buena, meaning mint, i. 249.

Miscegenation, French adoption of, English dislike to, i. 125.

Mission Dolores, near San Francisco, once a Jesuit Mission-house, now partly a blanket factory and partly a church, i. 245, 246.

Missouri, law for the punishment of drunkards, &c. i. 336.

Mohamedans (*see* India:—Mohamedan Mohurrum, *and* India:—Mohamedan Cities).

Mohurrum (*see* India).

Monitors, American, i. 9.

Monroe Doctrine, dignified action of America thereon, i. 282.

Monroe, Fort, i. 3; negroes at, 4; their tomb at, 18.

Montreal (*see* Canada), i. 72.

Mormons, i. 140; a camp on the way to Utah, 143; Coalville, the Mormon Newcastle, 144; first sight of the Promised Land, *ib.*; Jordan river, *ib.*; one great field of corn and wheat, 145 (*see* Brigham Young); a lady reading to her daughters in defence of polygamy, 146; first night in Utah, 147; arms at hand, *ib.*; interest of the Church paramount, 150; the Mormon constitution, 151; penalty for adultery, *ib.*; kind treatment by the Mormons, 153; the representative of Utah in Congress a Monogamist, 154; anecdote of, *ib.*; a Mormon theatre, *ib.*; the women, 154, 155; unconscious melancholy of, 155; their perfect freedom, and opportunity of escaping if they wished to do so, *ib.*; defence of polygamy, 156; Utah polygamy and Kansas female suffrage the opposite poles to each other, 156 (*see* Western Editors, Newspapers, Stenhouse, *and* Danites); misrepresentation of, 158; theatre and church clothes, 159; industry, 161–163, 170, 171; natural

INDEX.   423

poorness of the country, 171; Mormon faith, 173; their belief in approaching danger from United States interference, 174; detested by New England and defended by the South, *ib.*; evade the law, 176; democratic character of Mormonism, 179 (*see* Utah); vitality of Mormonism, 181; danger to it from the probable discovery of gold in Utah, 182; impossibility of its surviving a great immigration, *ib.*; they would in that case again make their way to new territory, *ib.* (*see* Nauvoo).
Moultan (*see* India :— Native States).

N.

NAUVOO, the city of Joe Smith, i. 313; first settlers of, forgotten there, *ib.*
Nebraska, i. 101.
Negroes, gallantry of, i. 14, 15; burial-place of 5,000 killed in battle, *ib.*; our English notions of, near the truth, 19; love of dress, *ib.*; planters' view of freedom of, *ib.*; reported negro view of monogamy, 20; need of soap, *ib.*; importance of the "negro question," *ib.*; fallacious evidence against negroes, 21; driving the Irish from hotel service, 22; asking for land, *ib.*; their position as slaves, 23; and as free men, *ib.*; testimony of General Grant to their excellency as soldiers, 24; a negro school, *ib.*; negro ability, *ib.*; superstition, *ib.*; alternative of ruling them by their own votes or by force, 29; reading and writing bases of suffrage absurd, *ib.*; co-operative labour (*see* Davis); the ballot for, 35.
Nepaulese, the (*see* India:—Native States).
Nevada, its silver mines, i. 204.
New Englanders, going westward, i. 41; in North or West the real Americans, 49; their affection for Harvard College, 57; earnest God-fearing principles, 62; influence of, on the nation, *ib.*; their lovable character, 65; dislike to Mormonism, 174; determination to put down rowdyism wherever they go, 242; wide-spread belief of, that the taint of alcoholic poison is hereditary, 290.
New England States, their superiority to the States of the South, i. 12 (*see* Southern States, Western States, *and* Mayflower); colleges of, 46; population of, 61; debt of the Union to

New England, 62; heroism of New England, 63; poverty of the soil, *ib.*; enterprise, &c. 64.
New South Wales, convict blood in, ii. 10 (*see* Rival Colonies); terrible depression of trade in, at present, 12; causes of, 13; reptiles in, 20 (*see* Tasmania).
New York, climate of, i. 39; strength of the Narrows, *ib.*; un-English character, *ib.*; sea spirit and busy life, *ib.*; race, Southern, 40; nothing of the Dutch foundation remaining, *ib.*; intensely Irish, 42, 43; low tone of local legislature, 45; denationalization of, *ib.*; neglect of native colleges and preference for foreign ones, 46; gigantic fortunes in, *ib.*; profligacy, petroleum, shoddy, and unrest, 47; equality and affected dislike of democracy, 48; scenery of, 49; democracy of, 295.
New Zealand (*see* Wellington, Hokitika, *and* Maori) :—University graduates and officers of the British army at the diggings, i. 333, 334; beauty and peculiarity of New Zealand scenery, 340; the Taramakoo, 341; the Snowy Range, *ib.*; Mount Rolleston, *ib.*; Lake Misery, *ib.*; plant peculiar to the banks of, 342; the Waimmokiriri Valley, *ib.*; New Zealand provinces, *ib.*; rivalry of, 343 (*see* Otago *and* Canterbury); cost of the Provincial system and Maori wars, 344; consequences of the division into two islands, *ib.*; rivalry of the great towns, 345; Karaka trees, the New Zealand sacred trees, 355 (*see* Race *and* Maories); New Zealand scenery, 379, 380 (*see* Flies, the two); its chance of being the future England of the Pacific, 401 (*see also* Rival Colonies).
Newspapers :—*New Orleans Tribune* (negro paper), i. 31; *British Columbian*, 73; the Salt Lake *Telegraph*, 151; the *Union Vedette* (Utah), 157; contents of the *Vedette*, 159, 160; the great superiority of, to the Mormon papers, the *Telegraph* and *Deseret News*, 161–165; the *Denver Gazette*, &c. 165-168; the *California Alta*, and journalism under difficulties, 169, 202; *Nevada Union Gazette*, 201; the *Francisco Bulletin*, 235; the *Spiritual Clarion*, 316; *Sydney Morning Herald*, agents of, intercepting the mail boat, ii. 7; the *Melbourne Argus*, 27; the *River-*

ina Herald, 34; advertisements, paragraphs, &c. of, 34—36; committal of an editor of the *Melbourne Argus*, 51; newspapers in India, 213; native satire of the English in, *ib.*; the Umritsur *Commercial Advertiser*, 214 (see India *Gazette*"); the *Dacca Prokash*, 265; Indian newspapers, 288, 289; the *Punjaub Gazette*, 289.

Niagara and Chaudière, i. 81, 82.

Nitro-glycerine, dread of, in California, i. 254, 255.

Norfolk, second city in Virginia, i. 4.

North (America), superiority of its arms during the war, i. 33.

North and South in America, the unvarying success of the former in any trial of strength, i. 98, 99.

Norwegian population in Wisconsin, i. 312; Milwaukee a Norwegian town, *ib.*; Canadian plan for a Norwegian colony on Lake Huron, *ib.*

O.

Ohio, beauty of scenery and wealth of soil, i, 83.

Otago (New Zealand), Presbyterian settlement, i. 343, 344.

Ottawa, capital of the New Dominion, i. 80; its Parliament house, 81; the Chaudière Falls, *ib.*

P.

Pacific, the, voyage across, from Panama to New Zealand, i. 323 (see Pitcairn Island); from Pitcairn Island, 327; climate of, 398, 399; unfavourable to the progress of New Zealand, *ib.*; effect of like causes elsewhere, 400; coal in the, *ib.*; Japan, Vancouver Island, and New Zealand, likely to rise to manufacturing greatness, *ib.*; Christmas-day on, ii. 3.

Pacific Railroad, growing at the rate of two miles a day at one end and one mile at the other, i. 94; probable completion of it in 1870, *ib.*; inducements to proceed quickly with the work, 96; rapid and steady progress westward, *ib.*; armed construction trains, 97; the great objects of the undertaking, *ib.*; Indian opposition to the, 113.

Panama, character of, i. 321; animals and birds of, *ib.*; scene at a railway station, 322; prospects of Panama, 322, 323; departure from, for Wellington, New Zealand, 323.

Paper money in the Western States of America, i. 202—204.

Parewanui Pah (see Maori).

Parsees (see India:—Bombay).

Party organization, despotism of, in America, i. 291; secret of party power, 292.

Pawnees, i. 118.

Petersburg, America, as left by the war, i. 11; defences of, 13.

Pioneer, a great, i. 117.

Pioneering in America, i. 102; on the Plains, 111.

Pitcairn Island, the banana-tree there, i. 37; arrival at, 324; visited by the people, *ib.*; "How do you do, captain? How's Victoria?" *ib.*; descendants of the *Bounty* mutineers, *ib.*; wish to submit to the captain a case for arbitration, *ib.*; the case stated for "advice," 325; its curious legal bearing, *ib.*; a temporary commercial treaty with the islanders, 326; inquiry for English periodicals, *ib.*; brandy as medicine, *ib.*; the Islanders strict teetotallers, *ib.*; standing out from the bay, 327.

Pittsburg, dirt of, i. 83.

Placerville, in California, 215—222, 224.

Plains, the, out on, i. 110; a "squar' meal," *ib.*; weird scene, 111; great distance of forts from each other, 112; sitting revolver in hand, 113; a million companions in the loneliness, 115; beauty of, 131; resemblance to the Tartar Plains, 132; vast extent, 132, 133; two curses on the land—want of water, 133, 134, and locusts, 134, 135; feeding ground for large flocks, 136.

Planter view of negro freedom, i. 19, 20; effect of slavery on both master and slave, 25; planters leaving the South, 36.

Plutocracy in Australia, ii. 39, 40 (see Squatter).

Point de Galle (see Maritime Ceylon).

Polygamy in India, ii. 266, 267; polyandry, 267; polygyny, 268—271.

Polynesians, Malay origin of, i. 347—354 (see Race *and* Maori); rapid spread of Christianity among, 382; the Maori religion common to all Polynesians, 383; a vague Polytheism in the songs, seeming to approach Pantheism, *ib.*; difference between the Maories and other Polynesians, *ib.*

INDEX. 425

Poonah(*see* the Mohamedan Mohurrum).
Potomac, i. 38.
Prairie dogs, for food, i. 112 ; on the Plains, 114.
Prairie flowers, i. 120.
Protection to native industry in the colonies, ii. 59'; the squatters alone in favour of free trade, 59, 60 ; defence of protection by the diggers, 61 ; its self-denying character, *ib.* ; defended on different grounds in Australia and America, 61—63 ; grandeur of the willingness to sacrifice private interest that a nation may be built up, 63 ; protection to a great degree a revolt against steam, 64 ; American defence of, as a necessity to a young nation, 65 ; and as a security against the pauper labour of Europe, 65, 66 ; "No America without protection," 67; eagerness for, in Victoria, 68, 69 ; American admission of the economical argument, but assertion that political objections overweigh it, 69 ; protection not the doctrine of a clique but a nation, 70.
Pyramids, the, ii. 397.

Q.

QUEBEC, terrace at, i. 66 ; change of scene from the States, *ib.* ; strength of the French population, 67, 68 ; customs and feelings of old France, *ib.* ; the only true French colony in the world, guarded by English troops against the inroads of the English race, 69 ; contrast with English energy, 70 ; climate of Quebec, *ib.* ; Northern Lights, 71; the oppressive monopoly of the Hudson Bay Company, *ib.*
Queensland (*see* Rival Colonies *and* Squatters) ; question of the cultivation of a tropical country not yet settled, ii. 15; little hope of the coloured races being received on equal terms of citizenship, 17 ; physical condition of the colonists on the Downs and in Brisbane, 23; population of (from 1860 to 1866), 77.

R.

RACE, war of, in America, i. 308, 309 ; in New Zealand, *ib.* ; in Mexico, 310 ; disappearance of physical type, 310, 311 (*see* Saxon *and* Latin Races) ; gradual destruction of races, the bearing of, on religion, 313 (*see* English Race); probable opposition of the Victorians to the Queensland colonists availing themselves of the labour of the dark-skinned races, ii. 15 ; unfairness of the planters to the dark-skins, 17 ; danger of peonage, *ib.*
Rail and river, i. 100; railways in America preceding population, *ib.* ; converging lines and parallel lines, 100, 101, 104, 105.
Ranchmen, cooks, and ostlers, i. 191 ; their roughness, 192 ; dislike to "biled shirts," *ib.*
Red Indians (*see* Indians).
Representation in the Northern and Southern States, i. 30.
Reptiles, in New South Wales, ii. 20; Tasmania, 104 ; a snake story, *ib.*
Republican party in the United States, complete organization and great power of, 294.
Rhode Island, smallness of territory and population, i. 61.
Richmond, i. 11 ; defences of, 13, 14 ; future prospects of, 17 ; Washington's statue in, *ib.* ; Hollywood Cemetery, *ib.*
Riley, Fort, the centre of the United States, i. 107.
Rival colonies and towns—Australia and New Zealand, ii. 4; New Zealand hitherto mainly aristocratic, New South Wales and Victoria democratic, 4, 5 ; separation of New Zealand and Australia by a wide ocean, 5; New Zealand presenting to Australia a rugged coast, while her ports and bays are turned towards America and Polynesia, 6 ; difference of climate, *ib.* ; energy of the Australians as compared with the supineness of the New Zealanders, 7; different appearance of the people in the two colonies, 9; New South Wales, Queensland, Victoria, 12 ; probable wide political differences in the future, 13 (*see* Squatters) ; Sydney and Melbourne, 23; rivalry of, 24; seasons in New Zealand and Australia, 36, 37; climate, 37, 38; the question of confederation of the Pacific colonies, 108 ; willingness of the colonies for free-trade with each other, 107; postal and customs union, *ib.*; difficulties in the way of confederation, *ib.*; choice of future capital, 108; desirability of selecting some obscure village and not a great town, *ib.* ; the bear-

VOL. II.　　　　　　　　　　　　　　　　　　　　　　F F

ing of confederation on imperial interests, 108; and on colonial ones, 109; our duty in case it should lead to independence, 110.

Riverina, the (*see* Victoria *and* Newspapers).

Rockwell, Porter, i. 184; death of Captain Gunnison, of the Federal Engineers, near Rockwell's house, 188, 189.

Rocky Mountains, i. 95; sublime view of, from Denver, 120, 121; Black Mountains, 138; the Wind River Chain, &c. *ib.*; dreaded alkali dust of the desert, 138, 139; a fine scene, 141; the Elk Mountains, *ib.*; game, &c. *ib.*; Rocky Mountain plateau, 142; solitude of, 143; sudden arrival by night at a Mormon camp, *ib.*; a Mormon welcome, *ib.*; Echo Canyon, 144.

Rowdyism in the West, put down by the God-fearing New Englanders, i. 248.

Russia (*see* India:—Russian approach to).

S.

SACRAMENTO, i. 225; the Sacramento river, *ib.*

San Francisco and Chicago, the cosmopolitanism of, compared, i. 314.

San Francisco, its future connexion with Europe by means of the Pacific Railway, i. 98 (*see* Golden City); its claim to be one of the chief stations of the Anglo-Saxon highway round the world, 269; remarks on its probable future, 270—273.

San José, the Garden City, i. 256.

Sandhurst, ii. 27, 28; aspect and character of the town, *ib.*; the "Government Reserve," 29; Chinese clerks and diggers, *ib.*; unjust treatment of, 29—31.

Sandridge (*see* Victorian Ports).

Saxon and Latin races in America (*see* Western States), sharp conflict between, i. 246.

Saxon, the, the only extirpating race on earth, i. 308.

Scinde (*see* India).

Scotch, the (*see* India, Bombay).

Servants, in India, ii. 240—242.

Sierra Nevada, i. 208; its grim aspect, *ib.*; and obstacles to travelling westward, 208, 210, 212.

Sikhs (*see* India:—Umritsur).

Simla (*see* India).

Slavery, effects of, i. 25; a slaver, 64.

South Australia, ii. 116, 117.

Southern States, planters of, formerly rulers of America, i. 8; disunion of society, during the war, 32; hatred to the New England States, 34—36.

South America, society of, disorganized, i. 21; injurious effect on, of the banana tree growing wild, and offering food without labour, 26, 27.

Sphinx, the, ii. 397.

Spiritualism (*see* Churches in America).

Squatters, the, tenants of the Crown land in Queensland, ii. 14; struggle in Victoria between, and the agricultural democracy, *ib.*; the monopolization of land discouraged by the democracy, 24; the Squatter Aristocracy, 40; meaning of the term, *ib.*; the squatter the nabob of Sydney and Melbourne, 41; squatter complaints, *ib.*; what the townsmen think of, *ib.*; evils of the squatter system, 42; almost entire appropriation of the lands in Victoria, *ib.*; colonial Democracy, perception by, of the dangers of the land monopoly, *ib.*; popular movement for the nationalization of land, 43; Radical legislation against land monopoly, *ib.*; the squatter denunciation of, 44; his right to impound cattle, *ib.*; interest of Victoria in putting down the monopoly, 44, 45.

Stenhouse, Elder, the Mormon, i. 147; his answer to the question, "Has Brigham's election ever been opposed?" 149; postmaster, 158; denounced by the *Vedette* newspaper, *ib.*; editor of the *Telegraph*, *ib.*; dislike to jokes, *ib.*; Artemus Ward's joke to, *ib.*; Stenhouse's opinion of Mormon and Welsh coal, 171; his rebuke of the Author, 173.

Suffrage, negro, reading and writing basis for, i. 29.

Sukkur (*see* India:—Scinde).

Sydney, ii. 3; arrival off the "Heads," 7; Sydney Cove, 8; appearance of the town, *ib.*; the Midsummer Meeting of the Sydney Jockey Club on New Year's Day, *ib.*; appearance of the ladies on the Grand Stand, 9; the young people, *ib.*; no trace of convict blood in the faces on the race-course, 10; the last of the bushrangers, *ib.*; English fruits, foliage, &c., *ib.*; heat, succeeded by a gale, 11; wealth in coal, 17, 18; the City of Pleasure, 19; tendency of the colonists to rush to towns to spend their money, 19, 20 (*see* Rival Colonies); opposition of the operative classes of, to immigration and transportation, 72, 73; University of, 144, 145.

T.

TAJ MAHAL (*see* India:—Mohamedan Cities—Agra).
Tasmania, pleasant climate of, ii. 93; English scenery, *ib.*; and homes, &c. *ib.*; *Maria* Van Diemen's Land, *ib.*; the Tamar river, *ib.*; Launceston, 94; southward to Hobarton, *ib.*; deserted and disheartening state of the country, *ib.*; bountifulness of nature, *ib.*; great number of naturalized fruits, &c. *ib.*; the Ireland of the South, 95; the almost abandoned harbour of Hobarton, *ib.*; blight of the convict settlement, *ib.*; total extirpation of the aborigines, *ib.*; slight increase of population in the colony, 97; iron and coal abundant, but seldom worked, *ib.*; consumption of spirits in, *ib.*; lotus-eating, *ib.*; the land not yet free from traces of convict blood, *ib.*; fearful character of convict punishment, 98; testimony of a Catholic bishop respecting, *ib.*; deeds of the Pierce-Greenhill party, 99; Mr. Frost at Port Arthur, *ib.*; the convict system as viewed in the colony, *ib.*; "Tasmanian bolters," 99, 100; objections to convicts entering the free colonies, 100; advantages reaped by the colonists from convict labour, *ib.*; the Australian colonies planted as convict settlements, 101; threats of the Victorians (and in old times the Virginians), to retaliate for the shipment to them of convicts, *ib.*; Tasmanian society, 102; and government, *ib.*; working of the ballot, *ib.*; a ride to see the naturalized salmon, 103; the salmon madness, *ib.*; causing the destruction of all indigenous birds, 104; and has introduced the British wasp in the ova, *ib.*; reptiles, *ib.*; moonlight in Tasmania, 105.
Thompson, William, the Maori king-maker, i. 387; his dress and high character, 395; true patriotism, *ib.*; insulted whenever he entered an English town, 395, 396; his death, 396.
Thugs, New Zealand, i. 337, 338, 341.
Teetotallers (*see* Pitcairn Island).
Telegraph, the, in the American desert, i. 139.
Territories, the, their capabilities, i. 150.
Toronto (*see* Canada).
Transportation (*see* Convicts).

U.

UMRITSUR (*see* India).
"Uncle Sam's money," opinions of how it goes, i. 289.
University, English, men at the New Zealand diggings, i. 338, 339.
Utah, i. 173; first occupation of, 176; annexed to the Union, *ib.*; theories of annexation, 177; approach of the Pacific Railway, *ib.*—intended to put down Mormonism, 178; the Mormons will not defend their country, but retreat and pioneer the way for further English settlements, *ib.*; the justice or injustice of interference, 180, 181.

V.

VAN DIEMEN's Land (*see* Tasmania).
Vancouver Island (*see* Pacific).
Victoria (*see* Rival Colonies), the smallest of our Southern colonies except Tasmania, ii. 21; and the wealthiest, *ib.*; settlement (in 1835) on the site where Melbourne now stands, *ib.*; population of Melbourne, *ib.*; buildings, railroad, income, and debt of Victoria, *ib.*; talent and energy brought in by the rush for gold, 22; public spirit of the people, 22, 23; more English, not more American, than the people of New South Wales, 23; effect of the gold discoveries, 24; discouragement, by the Democrats, of the monopolization of land, *ib.*; population of, now stationary, 25; admirable system of statistics, *ib.*; statistical history of, 26; three staples of, *ib.*; from Melbourne to Kyneton, *ib.*; harvest work in Victoria, *ib.*; the "Thistle Prevention Act," 27; agricultural villages, *ib.*; the towns of Castlemaine and Sandhurst, 27, 28 (*see* Sandhurst); a prairie fire, 31, 32; the Murray river, 33; its insignificance as a river, *ib.*; but importance to commerce, *ib.*; the "Riverina," 34; territory included in it, *ib.*; productious as shown by the newspapers, 34—36; seasons and climate, 36—38; plutocracy in, 39 (*see* Squatter); Upper House of, going into committee on its own constitution, 48; probability of its disappearance, *ib.*; class animosity in, 50, 51; education in, 52—54; protection to industry in, 59—68.

Victorian Ports—Williamstown, Sandridge, and Geelong, ii. 88; early prospects and present ruinous state of Geelong, *ib.*; ridicule of, at Melbourne, *ib.*; fine country round Geelong, 89; wheat and vines of, 90; Ballarat, *ib.*; mining district around, *ib.*; names of places at the mines, a chronological guide to date of settlement, 90, 91; climatic changes, 91.

Vigilance committees in Western America (*see* Lynch Law); San Francisco and the Sandwich Islands, i. 244.

Virginia City, arrival at, i. 197; an unsatisfactory governor, 198; dancing-rooms, 200; substitution for ladies, *ib.*; peculiarities of climate, *ib.*; whiskey shops, 202; Artemus Ward's opinion of, *ib.*

Virginia, approach to, i. 3; opinions in, respecting the war, 5, 6; rivers and mineral wealth of, 12; in production inferior to poorer states, *ib.*; competition of white and black labour in, 28.

Virginian twilight and scenery, i. 8.

W.

WASHINGTON, first view of, i. 38.
Washoe, in Nevada, its reputation, i. 199.
Wellington, i. 328; fruit and flowers of, *ib.*; cattle branding with an old college friend, 329.
West Honduras, i. 307.
West (America), future capital of, i. 101; empire setting towards the, 105—107; plains of the, 107; men and women of, their dignity, &c., 190; power of sheriff in, 239; qualifications for a sheriff, *ib.*
Western States (of America) growing more English, while the Atlantic cities are falling into the hands of the Irish, 42, 43; Western perception of the dangers from Irish preponderance on the Atlantic seaboard, 44; wideness of Western thought, 105; advantages of the Western over the Eastern States, 106; Western objection to greenbacks, 202; agreement to accept forged notes if well done, *ib.*; fancy for classical names, 217, 218; honesty, 253.
Western editors, i. 157; Connor, a Fenian, editor of the *Union Vedette*, *ib.*; his denunciation of Mormonism, *ib.*; an editor's room in Denver, 169; influence of Connor, 169, 170; "wasp-like" pertinacity of the *Vedette*, 172; injury done by it to liberty of thought throughout the world, *ib.*; editors in America as a rule foreigners, and mostly Irishmen, 201; editorial inquiry for "Tennyson and Thomas T. Carlyle," *ib.*; murder of James King, 235; an editor's story, 240.
Williamstown (*see* Victorian Ports).
Winthrop, Governor, founder of Plymouth, Mass. i. 3.
Wisconsin (*see* Norwegian).
Wolf, a white, i. 116.
Woman, in Victoria, ii. 83; female suffrage, *ib.*; social position of, bad both in England and Australia, 84; superiority of, in Western States of America, *ib.*; a Kansas argument for woman's rights, *ib.*; disproportion of the sexes in the Australian colonies, 85; the American Sewing Clubs during the war, *ib.*; woman's place among the British section of the Teutonic race, 86, 87; want of, in young countries, 117, 118; Irish workhouse girls sent to the colonies, 118—120; their bad character and influence, *ib.*

Y.

YORKTOWN, ancient memories of, i. 3.

THE END.

R. CLAY, SONS, AND TAYLOR, PRINTERS, BREAD STREET HILL.

www.ingramcontent.com/pod-product-compliance
Lightning Source LLC
Chambersburg PA
CBHW032137010526
44111CB00035B/602